TO RUN ACROSS THE SEA

Norman Lewis was born in London. He has written thirteen novels and eight non-fiction works. *A Dragon Apparent* and *Golden Earth* are considered classics of travel, and *Naples '44* has been described as one of the ten outstanding books about the Second World War. He relaxes by his travels to off-beat parts of the world, which he prefers to be as remote as possible; otherwise he lives with his family in introspective, almost monastic, calm, in the depths of Essex.

Norman Lewis

To Run Across
the Sea

V

VINTAGE

VINTAGE

20 Vauxhall Bridge Road, London SW1V 2SA

London Melbourne Sydney Auckland Johannesburg
and agencies throughout the world

First published by Jonathan Cape Ltd, 1989
Vintage edition 1991

Some of the essays in this collection have previously
appeared in the following publications: the *Sunday
Times* Magazine; the *Independent* Magazine; the *Observer*
Magazine; *Granta*; *Departures*; *Time Out*; *Marie Claire*;
Harpers & Queen; *Traveler*

Printed and bound in Great Britain by
Cox & Wyman Ltd, Reading

ISBN 0 09 977570 0

CONTENTS

FOREWORD

ONCE AGAIN IN recalling the seductions of travel I am reminded of Evelyn Waugh's glance backward at the days when, for him, 'the going was good'. My own journeyings, launched in a slightly later period, were overshadowed by premonitions of what was to come. In 1950, with the Far East on the brink of irreversible change, it was clear that if I ever hoped to go there, not a moment was to be lost. Instinct served me well, for no one in these days, or henceforward, making the journey to Vietnam, to Cambodia, Laos or Burma will ever experience a tenth of the enchantment these countries then possessed.

When the going was good . . . The process of the world's impoverishment in the things that really matter to most of us rushes forward at an ever-increasing tempo, although the full extent of post-war disasters has yet to be appreciated. The greatest catastrophe has been the burning of the trees. When I went to Brazil in 1979, three million hectares of forest had gone in the previous year. One car-manufacturing firm, wishing to diversify into cattle, had started a fire, photographed by satellite, that spread through an area as large as Luxembourg. Round Manaus where I stayed, forest-clearing had become a cottage industry. Truckloads of old tyres were supplied, and with these the peasantry got the fires going. In the event the areas cleared were too small to be economically viable so they were left to become pigmy deserts. Something of the kind was happening to forests everywhere in the world.

Whether the trees were taken out by loggers, or burned down, the wildlife they contained went with them. In a single decade the number of species to become extinct exceeded that known to have been lost in the whole of the preceding century. The loss was compounded by the trade in ivory, and the growth of the market for trophies such as gorillas' heads. Even worse was the spread of the sport of big-game hunting to all those who could buy a gun in developing or Third World countries. Kenya has become the graveyard of the last of the great elephant herds. 'Enjoy them while you can,' said the guide at the sight of a herd. 'You'll never see them again.'

You can shoot a blue sheep in Mongolia by license of the USSR government for an all-in cost of about £5,000, and several other countries issue price-lists for the elimination of similar rarities. Nevertheless, it is the protected species that attract the attention of the adventurous sportsman. To shoot a jaguar somewhere in the Amazon will run to at least £10,000. Although protected, brown bears, of which some forty to fifty survive in the mountains of northern Spain, come relatively cheap at about £4,000. The protocol of slaughter demands that the cornered animal should be tied down by stalkers, for despatch by the hunter using a spear. An inordinate fee would be demanded for the opportunity to assassinate a rhinoceros – in part reclaimable by the sale of the horn (for aphrodisiac purposes), at about £2,000.

Twenty thousand or so different tribal peoples made their homes until recently in the wild places of the earth, and they are to go with the trees. Their fate, whether they like it or not, is to constitute a harvest of souls for missionary sects from the American Bible belt, carried now by the thousand in their short take-off and landing planes into every corner of the earth. They are believers in the inevitability of Armageddon, to be followed by the fiery destruction of the world from which only they and their converts will be saved. Nothing, therefore, must be allowed to stand in the way of the fundamentalist salvation, which is to be imposed at all costs, whether the recipients like it or not. The evangelists equate pleasure with sin, and will therefore have none of it. Converts must turn their backs on fun, on traditional ceremonies of any kind, on dancing, on song. They will work and pray, but laughter is to be extinguished.

If you are an amateur of primitive scenes and festivals, hunt them down and enjoy them while you can. Because they, too, like the elephant herds of Kenya, are about to vanish from the earth.

Norman Lewis, 1989

ANOTHER
SPAIN

'THEY CHANGE THEIR sky, not their soul,' as Horace said, 'who run across the sea.' The sad old Roman truth is not to be refuted. Escape is never more than partial. Nevertheless, at a minor geographical level small, reviving evasions can be planned. This one was to Spain, an unlikely bolthole, it might be supposed, in the era of the package deal; yet far from the Costas in the deep interior rich lodes of undisturbed *hispanidad* remain to be discovered.

In preparing such an evasion simple rules are to be followed. Bring or hire a car, avoid great cities, travel by second- or third-class roads, make for the remoter parts of the south and west which are too far from anywhere to have made it worthwhile setting up industries. Here, where there has been no money to spend on development, the old Spain stubbornly survives. Rare and extraordinary flowers flourish in hedgerows that have never been reached by sprays. Towns built with the proceeds of the plunder of Moorish kingdoms, or of the Indies, remain intact. The best of them offer no accommodation for the traveller except occasionally a government *parador*. By way of a bonus, some of the latter are housed in grand buildings: castles, old convents, Renaissance palaces. It is normal, too, for them to be sited in areas of outstanding historic interest.

Carmona comes under this heading. It is a two days' drive by the slow roads from Valencia, Alicante or Madrid. When Seville is *en fête* – as this alluring and anachronistic town is during most of the spring and summer – and there is not a bed to be had, Carmona supplies a small-scale and concentrated alternative. It is full of tremendous churches, the scent of incense, and scuttling nuns. Its window grilles, coming right down to the pavement, symbolise the Andalusian exclusion of the world from private affairs, and within the house – since shutters remain closed – the gloom Alexander Dumas noted as characteristic of these southern interiors, persists until lamps are lit or switched on at night.

Apart from palaces and churches, Carmona possesses no fewer than three Moorish fortresses, whose red walls spread a russet light through the streets like the glow beneath chestnuts in autumn leaf. Kestrels by the dozen hang pale and translucent in the sky over church towers that were once minarets, appearing like tiny kites manipulated by invisible strings. The principal fortress is the Alcázar del Rey Don Pedro, favourite abode in his kingdom of Pedro the Cruel. From what is now the *parador* this fearsome monarch – only to be recognised in his disguise by the clicking of his arthritic knees – stole out at night to pick a quarrel with and assassinate any defenceless subject who happened to be abroad. It was here in 1492 while awaiting the fall of Granada that Ferdinand and Isabella sat side by side on their thrones to hand down the ferocious edicts by which the conquered territories were to be governed. This was a bad time to be on the losing side. King Ferdinand the Saint, whose self-imposed penances brought about his own death by dropsy and starvation, converted the Muslim survivors in this town after its conquest. Magnanimous by the standards of his day he spared those who turned promptly to Christ. Where conversion was proved later to have been insincere, backsliders were burned in batches, the king himself frequently applying the torch to the faggots after first implanting the kiss of forgiveness upon the cheeks of those about to suffer.

Zafra is a two-hour drive away up the Estremadura highway to the north. This small, bewitching town is frequently called Little Seville, due, it is supposed, to the settlement there in the past of Sevillians seeking escape from an over-severe religious climate and its all too frquent *auto-da-fés*. Here the refugees built themselves mansions in the style of their home town: white, with baroque embellishments over windows and doors painted with the unique and costly chrome-yellow pigment derived from the soil of Alcala de Guadaïra, a few miles away. This, according to local belief, not only cools the heat of the summer sun and warms the chills of winter, but possesses also talismanic qualities against the spells of witchcraft.

Like Carmona it is a town with a brilliant Andalusian surface and dark, secretive interiors. In true Andalusian style, its people lead frugal lives, are calm and slow in their movements, conduct their business transactions verbally, and settle them without written contract. Dignity is regarded as a principal virtue, and life's targets are kept simple. As in Seville, ceramic wall plaques are sometimes used to set forth the philosophy of the owner of a house. Several in Carmona enjoin kindness to birds.

Spaniards regard this town's *alcázar*, in which the *parador* is incorporated, as one of the country's most imposing, and with this I would agree, although it is smaller than most. It was built in 1443 at a time when, with the strengthening of the central government's grip, private military enterprises of this kind were becoming obsolete. In effect, this was the town house of a rich nobleman who set out to impress his friends, for, with the front line of the war against the Moors a hundred miles away, it was unlikely ever to be required to withstand enemy attack. Nor with its make-belief Moorish-style decorative battlements, its slender towers, its elegant but not too solid keep, could it easily have done so. An exquisite Renaissance patio in white marble, by the architect responsible for the building of the Escorial was added later, further enhancing the showy domestic atmosphere of the place. It is in this setting that guests are splendidly lodged.

The *parador* is pridefully named after the conqueror of Mexico, Hernando Cortes who stayed some months here at the invitation of his patron, the Duke of Feria, before his departure for the New World. Cortes, understandably, has remained a local as well as national hero, the more so because – as with the rest of the conquistadors – he was an Estremaduran man and, like most of them, of obscure and humble origin. The picture of him to be seen here presents an imperial figure indeed. As was the custom at that time, he had been given the great man's face of the day, based upon that of the Emperor Charles V, though modified by some slight tinkering with the features, and in particular by the correction of the pendulous Hapsburg lip. There is a mystery here, for in 1947 the Mexicans announced that the conqueror's remains had been exhumed in Mexico City. What had been found was described as the skeleton of a hump-backed dwarf, with a right arm withered into uselessness through syphilitic infection. Such are the deceits concealed in history.

From this point on, the road leads northwards through Merida and Trujillo and then to the east into the centre of Spain. In doing so it skirts an area of roughly 25,000 square kilometres where hardly any changes have been made to the map for half a century. George Borrow, prospecting for souls in the backlands, where he thought the 'Genuine Spaniard' was most likely to be found, came here to distribute his bibles on his 'sorry mule, covered with sores, and wall-eyed'. He would have no difficulty in recognising these villages as they are now, for, notwithstanding the prosperity based upon the tourist industry of Spain's eastern seaboard, and of cities such as Barcelona and Madrid, Estremadura remains isolated and impoverished, suffering moreover from the draining away of its human life's blood through emigration to France and to the Spanish towns.

Narrow winding lanes bring the traveller eventually to Guadaloupe, a town of great charm with old wooden and half-timbered houses, clustered round the monastery-fortress that provides its *raison d'être*. It is near enough to the geographical centre of the country to have served for a short time as the seat of government, before the establishment of the capital at Madrid. The Catholic Kings, enthroned as stiffly as figures in cathedral stained glass, held court here, issuing royal licenses for voyages of discovery or conquest to the New World, attracted to Guadaloupe not only by its location but by its reservoir of undiluted faith.

Guadaloupe's position in the forefront of Christian revival and endeavour was achieved following a sign from heaven shortly after its liberation in battle from the Moors. The Virgin Mary appeared to a countryman, instructing him to dig in a cave, where an image of her, hidden away from the invaders back in the eighth century, would be found. This he did, the image was recovered and a shrine set up. There followed a series of prodigious happenings of a rustic, homely kind. Asses reproached their masters for their ill-treatment in good Castilian, levitation was commonplace, and in one case a defunct cow, already in the process of being skinned, was raised from the dead. Pilgrims began to flock in.

From these beginnings there arose and grew through the centuries the enormous accretion of military and ecclesiastical architecture constituting the monastery. There are few more stunning experiences of its kind than to arrive here by night, dropping down from the black emptiness of the sierra, then, after the last hairpin bend, plunging without warning into the great spread of light from these buildings, their mediaeval banners afloat in a glowing sky.

The *parador* at Guadaloupe has borrowed a little history from them. It began as a hospital for pilgrims and in 1402 was issued a Papal privilege by which the first dissection in Spain was carried out, the body having been preserved in perfumed oils to which sacramental wine was added while awaiting the privilege's arrival. Its guests are housed in pseudo-mediaeval surroundings, which fail quite to measure up to those offered by the monastery itself, part of which has been converted into a hostelry. This, with the distant chanting, the aloof monks padding through the cloisters, the soft, background mutter of pilgrims' prayers, and the crashing discord of bells, *is* the Middle Ages.

In its venture into the hotel business the Church has been brilliantly successful, for nowhere in the province are guests lodged so splendidly, and nowhere do they eat so cheaply and so well. All are welcome and Guadaloupe is filled in all seasons with countrymen and women who have saved up for a year or two to come here for the good of their souls, and also to have the holiday of their lives. Zurbarán, master painter of Estremadura worked here. The monastery owns many of his canvases, and his saints wear the faces of those thick-fingered, black-clad peasants, who wander in small flocks round the Gothic ambulatory to admire the paintings of martyrdoms and miracles.

Guadaloupe, thriving on religious tourism, is an island of prosperity in the depressed economy of the province as a whole. Leaving it, the change is immediate and stark. The timbered skeleton of a once fine house that has shed its flesh stands by the roadside as a portent of what is to come; after that, only a single, rather miserable hamlet and piles of stones where others once existed are passed before Cijara is reached. One of the reasons for this last leg of the journey was the hope of seeing something of the Cijara region, generally known locally as the Siberia of Estremadura, due to its historically unhappy situation in the no-man's-land between warring mediaeval kingdoms. Nobody lived here unless obliged to. This, coupled with a recent acute loss in population, has been to the advantage of many rare animals and birds. Included among them are the Iberian lynx, and the Egyptian mongoose, which is not to be found elsewhere in Europe. Renowned as a last refuge of obsolescent birds is El Muro, a lakeside cliff listed as the breeding ground of three species of vulture, the Black Stork, Bonelli's Eagle and the Iberian Imperial Eagle. I was hoping to be able to visit this bird-watcher's paradise although it is several miles from the nearest road and only vaguely defined on large-scale maps.

The Siberia of Estremedura, roughly 60 kilometres across, contains four villages and a sprawling complex of artificial lakes formed by the flooding of the Guadiana Valley. When last counted, its total population was 2,500, but that was ten years ago and there has been a steep decline since then. A government report devoted to its predicament mentions that the direct road from Toledo no longer touches a single inhabited place for 80 kilometres. Final desolation, then, draws near, although, clutching at a straw, the report says that emigration is slowing down, 'doubtless owing to unemployment in the cities'.

Villagers without any strong ties to keep them in Cijara have pulled out, leaving those who are too old to uproot themselves, plus a hard core of devotees of the hunter-gatherer's way of life. Isolation has welded those that remain into a family group that takes a remarkably philosophic view of its situation. They are remarkably courteous and kind, even for the Spanish. When I spoke of 'people' using the normal word *gente*, someone administered a gentle correction. People in Cijara were *vecinos*, 'neighbours', and everyone, including visiting foreigners, was included in this pleasant familiarity. 'Communications leave much to be desired,' said the government report. 'Their economic resources are scant, and they rely almost exclusively upon game.' Game, however, was varied and abundant, and in Cijara they eat well. Partridge in saffron rice was on the menu at the bar, and trout could be fished from the lake in a matter of minutes. The bread baked here was the best I have tasted in my life.

Hopes of being able to reach El Muro faded. Unseasonally

in October it had been raining for days, and the view from a hilltop was of a drenched savannah through which the Guadiana River, full to the brim, had spread curlicues of water. The news at Cijara was that the direct road along the north shore of the lake had been cut off by floods and an extremely circuitous route round by the south, through Helechosa, might also be impassable. I was grateful for the excuse for this detour. Helechosa conducts a Corpus Christi ceremony in which children take up cudgels to drive out the horned and masked 'devils' that have invaded the village – a whispered suggestion that, despite the Inquisition's efforts, the old Manichaean heresy, once prevalent here, that God and Satan are co-eternal, may have survived.

But, when I went there in the rain, there were no children to be seen. Perhaps there were none left for, when a village faces the possibility of its eventual extinction, the children are the first to go. Beyond Helechosa the road came to an end. The Guadiana flowed across it into the lake where once there must have been a bridge and only a ravaged track corkscrewing up into the hills offered an alternative to turning back. At this point the river in spate carried red earth in suspension. A magenta stain was widening in the lake and, as I watched, a white bird folded its wings and dropped into it after a fish.

Beyond the rising water, cork oaks were meticulously spaced in the order imposed by nature in a landscape which – apart from artificial lakes – had been left to itself, and the maquis was as clean-cut as a well tended garden. Within a decade or two the human presence would almost certainly be gone. I wondered if the wolves would eventually find their way back, as they had in the Sierra de la Culebra in the north which I had visited in the spring. Villages containing many old houses exist where a single family remains. In one village, Boya, all the self-supporting young had been enticed away to the discos in the towns, but most of the middle-aged hoped to stay on. It was a pleasant place, amazingly reminiscent of a village in unspoiled England, perhaps in the Cotswolds, with an ancient church on the green, merino sheep cropping the grass, and cottages with flower gardens. When the talk of wolves came up, Jaime Martinez, owner of the bar, was philosophical. 'You see one now and again,' he said, 'but they don't really trouble us. They're something you can cope with. It's the wild boars that bother us. They root up everything in the gardens. You could even say the wolves are useful in a way. At least they keep the boars down.'

IN ESSEX

Essex is the ugliest county. I only went there to be able to work in peace and quiet and to get away from the settlers from London south of the river. It was flat and untidy and full of water with the Colne and the Crouch and the Blackwater and all their tributaries fingering up from the sea and spreading vinous tendrils of water into the flat land. For half the year, the wind blew in from the east, over shingle, mud-flats, saltings and marshes, and even twenty miles inland, where I first set up house, gulls drove the crows out of the fields.

I found an empty farmhouse called Charmers End in the village of Long Crendon, took a three-year lease on it and settled in. Many of the farms and villages had odd and even poetic names, Crab's Green, Sweet Dew, Blythe Easter, Fantail and Honey Wood, which I suspected of being part of a process of self-deception, for on the whole the more fanciful the name the more dismal the place. There were black-and-white cows in a shining field at the bottom of the garden when I first moved in. They were largely responsible for my choice. Otherwise, this part of Essex reminded me of the southern tip of South America where the trees are deformed, a cold wind combs the grass, and glum Indians, reserved and off-hand like the country people of Essex, are muffled in their clothes against the grey weather.

The farmer who had lived here before had grown old alone and sold his land. One day, hauling himself to the top of the tallest tree in the garden, he had drunk a quarter of a bottle of Lysol, put the barrel of a German pistol collected in the war into his mouth, and pulled the trigger. This man had liked cows, just as I liked them, but the new owner did not especially, so they disappeared soon after. The old farmer had left the place in a terrible mess. He had thrown everything that was left of his possessions out of the window but had left an old broken rocking-horse with a bunch of flowers tied to it in the kitchen. For some reason the agent who showed me the place had decided to leave this where it was. The house was surrounded by a great moat – giving some indication of the security problems of the past – and all along its banks stood big white leafless trees which, stripped of their bark and dying, would eventually fall in. It was like the Amazon. Some of the trees in the water had lost their branches, and little remained but their trunks, turned grey and slimy like submerged alligators, showing only the tips of their snouts above the surface. Those still standing provided an annual crop of an uncommon oyster fungus, collected by an Italian from Chelmsford. He called with a present of a bottle of Asti Spumante soon after I was installed.

The Post Office found me a woman to clean up four days a week. She arrived on a horse, charging up the lane and across the moat, black hair streaming in the wind, again contributing to the Latin American aspect of this corner of Essex. With her fine, aquiline features and almond eyes she could easily have been an Indian of the plains under the eastern slope of the Andes, where the natives are tall and slender.

This was Dorothea, aged 37, handsome if not quite beautiful, with a semi-disabled husband and a pretty daughter of 12.

Dorothea took control. She persuaded the pump to emit a dribble of doubtful water, removed the mummified jackdaw from the chimney, dropped a pebble by way of a test into the black and silken surface of the fluid in the septic tank, and nodded with satisfaction. The horse was a bother to her. It was impossible to leave it free to crop the grass because of holes leading to tunnels, where, as she thought, the inhabitants had once hidden themselves in the bad times of old. I said, 'I saw you on a bicycle the other day. Why don't you use it to come over here?' She replied, nodding apologetically in the horse's direction, 'Well, I just ride it when I can. It's something you have to do.'

She went with me in the car to point out the baker's, the man who might agree to cut the grass and mow the lawn, and the one who could fix up a television aerial. Assistance of this kind was easily procured in Long Crendon, as Dorothea explained, by adopting a tactful, even ingratiating approach.

We passed two men in baseball caps, one wearing dark glasses and a lumberjack shirt, chatting outside a pub. 'Americans?' I asked.

'No, locals. Carpenters up at the base.'

'They look like Yanks.'

'Well, they want to, don't they? Most of the fellows work on the base these days. If you can call it work.'

The village was a long, narrow street, straggling in fits and starts for the best part of a mile, hence its name. There was a bad smell at one end from a rubbish dump that looked like a collapsed volcano that had been smouldering for several years, and at the other from a pig farm. The houses were simple and plain, with white plastered fronts, the poorer and smaller ones thatched, some still with leaden lights. A substantial mansion standing in gardens back from the road had suffered brutal modernisation, the garden being now enclosed with a ranch-style fence. Until the previous month it had been named Hill Top, said Dorothea, but now with a new owner who had been in property development, it had become Rancho Grande. It was the only evidence that money had been spent in the village, either on preservation or ornament.

We passed three depressed-looking pubs and a grey little school with children squabbling in the playground. The church was the only building of note, with a Norman door, good stained glass and tombstones packed close in separate familiar groups as if to carry earthly associations beyond the grave.

The tour ended with a passing glance at the village hall. 'That's where I go dancing with my friend Mr Short on Saturday night,' Dorothea said.

'Your friend?'

'Well, not my *boyfriend*. Actually I don't like him all that much. We just go dancing together. Otherwise I don't find him all that interesting. I expect you heard all about Dick's accident?'

'Doesn't Dick mind?'

'Mind, why should he? He doesn't dance and he realises I have to have some sort of break. Well, I mean it's only normal isn't it?'

Later I heard the gossip: that she was the target of village adulterers, who were encouraged by Dick, her complaisant husband.

I questioned Dorothea as to why she felt she had to ride, mentioning that, according to village opinion, the horse was a bad one, with the habit of tripping over its legs.

'It's an old jumper,' she said. 'It's not so much its legs as its back. It's hit the deck a few times.'

'They were telling me you were a member of one of the Cloate families, whatever they mean by that.'

'It's a sort of clan,' she said. 'The thing they have in Scotland. Dick and I belong to it. About half the village used to be Cloates, but there's only five families left now. They say only the Cloates were allowed to ride in the old days, but they say anything.'

'What else do you do beside ride horses?'

'Well, nothing really. We're supposed to help each other,

but that's a laugh. Really it's more a question of keeping in touch. You sometimes get Cloate people who've gone overseas writing home. I suppose they feel lonely out there. Maybe you write two or three letters and then it drops.'

'Nothing else?'

'We have a sort of get-together in August. There used to be about fifty of us, but now it's down to half that. A lot of these things are dying out. I mean, times change.'

The information Dorothea provided was vague, but one interesting aspect of the Cloate personality emerged – the clan's attitude to education. Where their menfolk were concerned they saw schooling only as a means to an end. This end was usefulness and self-sufficiency. Boys took what the primary school had to offer, moving on as soon as possible to the education provided by life. In the old days, Dorothea had heard, a Cloate would build his own house. The function of a girl, however, was to please. If a girl was plain and dull, there was nothing to be done, but if she showed promise – beauty, even wit – no sacrifice was too great to develop her potential and place her on the road to success. Then she would be packed off to a boarding school – of an unassuming, yet rather special kind – in Woodford, London E11, where a village girl would be subjected to a process of transformation, so that at its end she would be hardly recognisable, even to her own family.

First impressions often mislead. My original view of Long Crendon was of a poverty-stricken, backward Essex village, of the kind often described as 'unspoilt' because there was no money for necessary improvements. Every roof, whether thatched or otherwise, carried a television aerial, but that meant nothing. Only a quarter of the houses had bathrooms, or even inside lavatories, and less than half were connected to the main water supply or the sewer. Two houses, including the Rancho Grande, and the Pied Bull – most successful of the pubs – had central heating; otherwise, when the frost set in, coal fires burned, as ever, in small grates. The locals pretended contempt for luxuries city-dwellers everywhere took for granted. Some actually boasted of leaving their windows open through the interminable Essex winter. The fact that Long Crendon remained on the surface as it was, was a matter of stubborn conservatism and resistance to change, rather than economics. Yet a hidden transformation was in progress. In 1943 the American Allies had built an important base at Effingham, some five miles away; since then, despite all local claims to a preference for the hard but worthy life, self-indulgence and luxury were making their stealthy appearance.

The Americans offered to employ every civilian in the area capable of holding down a job. They paid well and they were considerate, almost over-tolerant employers. Dorothea's Dick was one of the many who benefited from their generosity. He had been considered unemployable after his accident, but as soon as he was able to get about he was taken on at the base as a timekeeper, an occupation for which nimbleness was not required. For some time Dorothea had kept him out of sight, but one day she brought him to see me, prematurely wizened and sitting askew on a pony he controlled with one arm. The story was that while working 12 years before in an agricultural smithy, the prototype of a new combine harvester had run amok, snatched him up, neutered him, torn off a forearm, an ear and most of one foot. He and Dorothea had been married a matter of weeks when the accident occurred, and their daughter, Jane, had been conceived just in time.

I got to like Dick. Working for the Americans, according to most of the villagers, was like being on paid holiday for the rest of your life, the main problem with all the noise of the planes coming and going being where to find a place to sleep undisturbed. Dick put his endless leisure to good use. He liked people, and limped about the place getting to know everybody and picking up useful gossip. He was a treasure-house of village information, a holder of strong opinions and interested in religion.

'But you don't go to church, Dick?'

'Well, no. Most people round these parts don't.'

'And yet you're a believer?'

He gave a sly grin. 'When it suits me, I am. In the resurrection of the body, for instance. Now that's something I believe in. And I've every right to. It gives anybody like me a second chance, doesn't it? If the Bible says God can put back my missing bits who am I to argue about it?' This, I supposed, was meant to be a joke.

In my second year at Long Crendon the new farmer moved in. The black-and-white cows had long gone, and the farmer ploughed up the field and planted horse-beans, the most hideous of all crops. For thirty years the Essex farmers had been adding a few feet here and there to their usable land by tearing out hedges, but they had done it in a haphazard and disorganised fashion, whereas my neighbour was thorough. The trees across the moat were on his land, and they all came down, dead or alive, and were cut up. Those were the days when psychedelic painting was in vogue, and he rode round on a tractor painted in astonishing colours, like Sennacherib in his chariot, dealing death and destruction to nature. One of the big chemical firms was encouraging farmers to experiment with its sprays. He sprayed the banks of the moat on his side and in doing so killed off a vast colony of frogs. The resident mallards, feeding on these, also died. I watched them seized by a kind of paralysis, trying to take off. After splashing about in desperate fashion for a while they subsided and swam in slow, tightening circles. In the end they could no longer hold their heads up, and drowned. In a single year this man quite changed everything included in my view of the Essex landscape. What had looked in summer like the southern, treeless edge of the Argentine Pampas, became Siberia in the winter. This was perhaps the hardest, due to the efforts of my neighbour and his friends, of the century. Nothing held the east wind back as it blew in from the North Sea. Six inches of snow lay in the ploughed fields and the wind plucked it up like feathers from a moulting goose and dropped it into the hollows of the land. When spring came that year there were still yard-deep pockets of frozen snow lying between the bare banks at the bottom of the lanes.

Every penny Dorothea and Dick could scrape together was saved to send Jane to Woodford, but Jane was already thirteen and they were becoming desperate. Dorothea now worked three days a week at the Rancho Grande, owned by a man who had made a fortune from laundromats. Her beloved horse was for sale but there were no takers. She got permission to build on her garden and sold it off to a speculator. This was a sacrifice indeed for, endlessly enriched with the night soil from their cesspit, it produced vegetables of spectacular size and quality. Henceforth, she said, they would live on Cornish pasties with the occasional addition of sugar beet leaves. These, which the farmers threw away, looked and tasted like spinach of an inferior kind. 'Are you really sure', I asked her, 'that what you're doing is for the best?'

'We have to do everything we can to give her a proper start,' Dorothea said. 'After that it's up to her.' She mentioned her cousins, the Broadbents, accepted as the leading Cloate family. They had done well in the post-war period out of buying up and stripping the assets of several derelict estates in the neighbourhood, clearing the few remaining woods and turning the land over to agriculture. Bill and Emily Broadbent's daughter Patricia had just finished four years at Woodford, and had gone straight from it to one of the leading schools for models and faced the prospect of a dazzling future. Pictures of her were already beginning to appear in the Essex newspapers, and there was talk of contracts. I made no attempt to dampen her enthusiasm. It was hard to believe that Jane – slouching about the village with rounded shoulders, pretty in a way but with a vapid expression, and burdened with a nasal and moaning Essex accent – could ever hope to imitate her cousin.

A few days after this conversation Dorothea cut several inches from Jane's lifeless hair, tidied up her fingernails and took her to Woodford for an interview with Mrs Amos, headmistress of Gladben's Hall. She had found Mrs Amos formidable, a woman in her sixties she would have said, smooth-skinned, immaculate and precise. She was unnerved by the combination of Mrs Amos's penetrating stare, and her almost excessively sympathetic manner. All in all, there was something spiderish about her. 'But there you are,' Dorothea said. 'She gets the results.'

Dorothea had an excellent memory and in describing the interview seemed to be repeating the conversation word by word. Jane, she said, was at her worst; fidgeting, embarrassed and tongue-tied. 'She couldn't have been more stupid,' Dorothea said.

'I want to know all about you,' Mrs Amos had said. 'Are you a sporty girl? Does music appeal to you, or do you like to curl up with a book?'

But Jane just sat there and looked blank, Dorothea explained. 'She wouldn't utter. She wouldn't even look Mrs Amos in the face. There was a picture on the wall of a German battleship going down after some battle – was it the Battle of the Plate? – and she was hypnotised by it. "I'm sorry," I said to Mrs Amos. "It's just her nerves. It'll pass in a minute." I have to say Mrs Amos was very understanding. Full marks to her for that. She asked Jane what she wanted to do with her life and Jane told her she didn't know, and Mrs Amos said that was quite normal at her age, most young people didn't. She seemed to be trying to draw Jane out,' Dorothea said, 'but Jane was terribly negative. When Mrs Amos asked her what she did in the evening she said she looked at the telly. She didn't have any favourite programme, she told her. She just watched anything that happened to be on. It was all the same to her. Otherwise she went down to the bus shelter. That's what the kids do when there's nothing on the box. They just sit there and talk. Don't ask me what about.'

'So what was the outcome of it all?' I asked her.

'You won't believe this,' Dorothea said. 'She was accepted.'

'That's really tremendous news,' I said. 'You're over the worst hurdle. You must be very happy, and relieved.'

She was, and was worried now only about how she was going to come up with the money. But I was curious to know what was taught at this school beside charm.

'Well,' Dorothea said, 'that comes into it, but there's much more to it than that. I'll tell you exactly what Mrs Amos said to me. She said, "Here we introduce them to pride. Often when a girl first comes to us she has no ego, and therefore no personality and we set out to change that. When she leaves us we expect her to be full of herself, and that in a woman is the open sesame to success."'

With the coming of spring there were great changes in the neighbourhood. The Americans decided to expand their Effingham base, doubling their military personnel and building accommodation for families brought in on long-term postings. Once again, as it had been back in the forties, there were Americans everywhere. These by all accounts were smartly uniformed, outstandingly polite young soldiers, and local men who had sucked in humility with their mothers' milk were often amazed to be addressed as 'sir'.

The village began to smarten up. Essex had been discovered by the frontiersmen from London who paid dearly for arriving late on the scene. Charmers End, which nobody would pay £5,000 for when I moved in, was expected to fetch at least five times that sum by the time my lease ran out. A half-dozen rather sombre-looking lath-and-plaster Jacobean buildings were snapped up in and around the village. The newcomers stripped away plaster to expose ancient beams, knocked out partition walls to join up poky little rooms, put in cocktail bars and usually found a place somewhere for a wrought-iron Spanish ornamental gate. There was nothing to be done about a cesspit except lift the iron cover, peer in and drop it hastily back in place. The settlers from London cut down old diseased fruit trees to turn gardens into paddocks – sometimes making the mistake of buying local horses on the cheap – and rose early to exercise fashionable dogs. For the first time the Pied Bull had vodka on sale, and the village shop now stocked yoghourt in various flavours.

A paternalistic US government assured military personnel volunteering for overseas service that the comforts awaiting them abroad were no less complete than those they had come to expect at home. In fulfilment of this promise, a stream of air transports began to fly in to Effingham, laden with deep-freezers, washing-machines, pressure- and microwave cookers, hi-fi equipment, Hoovers, electric organs and even Persian carpets. Many of those for whom this flood of goods were destined had become accustomed to an annual trade-in of their possessions, replacing old models with new, and one of the major disadvantages to life overseas was that no regular outlets existed for discarded equipment. Thus the system was threatened and a surplus built up, for the houses on base were small and soon glutted with gear.

Dick was everybody's friend. When consulted by the Americans about their quandary he immediately discussed it with local shops and affluent villagers like the Broadbents. A number of these offered to help the Americans out, and slowly the flow of consumer durables was renewed. It was the commitment to Jane's future that turned Dick into a salesman. First he accepted small gifts, then a trifling commission, then finally obliged American friends by giving them a price for some article for which there was no immediate sale. This Dick would have to hold until a customer could be found. And so the process of trade developed. Dick was a reluctant and therefore good salesman, a little troubled in his conscience about the legality of what was going on, and there was a melancholic religiosity about him that was reassuring both to seller and buyer.

Dorothea and Dick continued to live on Cornish pasties and

sugar-beet tops. Dick did not like to talk about finance but Dorothea confided that, in the first few months of his operations, they had been able to add enough to the cache of money somewhere under their floor to pay for a year's schooling at Woodford. It was arranged that Jane would enter Gladben's in the coming September.

These mildly illicit activities brought Dick close to others of a more dangerous kind. He was approached by a senior sergeant newly arrived in the country with what sounded at first a tempting proposition. The sergeant had heard of Dick's connections and said that a source of supply of goods of a better kind had opened up. He showed Dick a Sears Roebuck catalogue and said that most of the items listed could be made available at about half-price.

The feeling I got was that he had already half-committed himself, but something was clearly worrying him.

'The first thing you have to do is to find out where the stuff's coming from,' I told him.

'I have. It got sent here instead of to Germany and they're stuck with it up at the base.'

'Why don't they send it back?'

'He says there's no laid-down procedure. If it's here, it's here. They've got to get shot of it as best they can or it'll stay here for ever. All they want to do is recover the cost price.'

'Nobody will believe a story like that,' I told him. 'Where is it now?'

'In Warehouse 8. I've seen some of it.'

'How does this man strike you? Do you get the feeling he's a crook?'

'He's like any sergeant. A bit tough. They get used to ordering people about.'

'I hope you're not in this already,' I said, 'but if you are, get out of it as fast as you can.'

Dick went back and told the sergeant he wanted a day or two to think about it, and the sergeant told him to keep his mouth shut.

A few days later he was back again, full of excitement and alarm.

The story was that he was out fishing in a flooded gravel-pit at six in the morning when something happened that had made him suspicious. He asked me to come and see the place, and having nothing better to do and inclined to enjoy visits to abandoned rural places, I went along.

This site was where a company had been taking out a great variety of gravel, pebbles and sand for as long as anybody could remember, and then suddenly they had dropped everything and pulled out. This had happened 10 or 15 years before, and in true Essex style there had been no attempt to tidy up before departure. Whatever was no longer of use had been left behind exactly as it was, and a half-dismantled pump protruded from the water and rails carried several shattered trucks down to the bullrushes sprouting in the verge of what was now a small lake. There were old breeze-blocks, buckled oil barrels, the base of a wheel-less vehicle sitting on its springs, and iron gates in a section of wall, wide open upon further devastation. All these objects were host to rank but vigorous creeping plants that would eventually muffle their outlines with coarse leaves and insignificant flowers.

Dick, very jumpy, insisted that we should go through the pretence of being there to fish, and we had taken rods with us. I fixed up my line and helped him to fix his. We then clambered down the bank and waded into the shallows among the bullrushes, where I noticed that he was steadier than on dry land. A moorhen scuttled away, dragging splashes across the water, and I breathed in the heavy odour of decaying vegetation and mud. It was a school holiday and two small boys had found their way down here and were hacking with knives at the bushes and seedling trees. Part of a large brick and corrugated iron building showed among the elders on the further bank. It was reached, Dick said, by an overgrown track from the main road. He had come here a few days before at about six in the morning, a good hour to fish at that time of year, and was down in the bushes by the water, baiting his hook when a big US Air Force truck came down the track and stopped outside the building. Three US servicemen got out. Dick recognised one of them as the top sergeant. They unlocked the door of the building and began to unload packing-cases from the truck and carry them in. He thought it took them half an hour to unload all the cases, after which they drove off.

'And what do you imagine it was all about?' I asked him.

'Stuff nicked from the base,' he said. 'I was shit-scared.'

'Why?'

'The sergeant. He'd have cut my throat if he saw me and thought I was spying on them.'

He then admitted to knowing of the racket that was going on, and explained how it worked. There was a fix back in the States with whoever it was handled the air-schedules by which the transports flying in always landed after the warehouses had been locked up for the night. The C-Van containers, unloaded and left in the parking bays – theoretically under armed guard – were promptly opened and up to a quarter of their contents spirited away. The consignment sheets corresponding to the abstracted goods were simply torn from the shipping documents and next morning the chief storeman cheerfully put his signature as OK.

'Why come to me about it?' I asked Dick.

'What do you think I ought to do?'

'Nothing,' I said. 'Steer clear of it. If you know what's happening, so do a lot more people and it's only a matter of time before somebody blows the whistle. Tell the sergeant anything you like and then keep away from him. If they found you mixed up in this it would put paid to your other business. And go somewhere else to fish.'

Most of the married American servicemen and their families were more than content to stay on base, and the base did its best, with considerable success, to provide all those things that made home sweet to them. Only young soldiers ventured out and when they did it was usually in search of female company among the local population. They were a godsend to the girls of Essex, which had become a sad backwater of a place for young people. The Essex girls found the Americans more polite, considerate and enthusiastic than the English boys; and in their approaches to the opposite sex, they often displayed an outmoded gallantry, sometimes evoking pretended amusement but always well received. Apart from drinking sessions in the pubs, Saturday night discos were about the only form of entertainment surviving in country places. A girl escorted to one of them by a local lad had to resign herself in advance to a loutish rather than a romantic experience. By contrast, the weekend dances organised at the base offered a model of propriety and good order.

The calm, homely and rather formal atmosphere of the social club at the base seemed to exert a tranquillising effect upon even the most unruly and pugnacious English males. Finding it impossible to pick a quarrel with their urbane American hosts, they soon gave up trying. Drinks at the base were better and much cheaper; the music was good and played on a system streets ahead of those at the discos, and the décor was tasteful and relaxing, with an avoidance of cheap effects. No one was ever overcharged at the base, and the old, sly trick practised in so many local clubs of turning up the heat to increase thirst and alcoholic consumption was here unnecessary, since American hospitality was not perverted by the profit-motive.

Above all, it was the servicemen themselves who impressed. The story had gone the rounds that before arriving in Britain they had been issued with a booklet telling them how to behave, but this struck all those who came into contact with them as an absurdity. These, the girls decided, were nature's gentlemen; handsome, clean-cut both in appearance and motive, sophisticated and rich. In the most discreet fashion, and always careful not to provoke the rivalry of their English escorts, their new American friends had shown them photographs of themselves in their civilian days, often at the wheels of enormous cars, in the glamorous environment of their homeland: Santa Barbara and Beverly Hills, the Rocky Mountains, Yellowstone Park, Miami Beach and Disneyland. Few impressionable young girls could resist such an emotional assault. It was an experience that turned many a head, including, to Dorothea's horror, that of her daughter Jane. To defeat the ruling by which any girl under the age of 17, unless accompanied by her mother was excluded from the magical Saturday night at the base, Jane – tall for her age and dressed and made up by her friends to look like an 18-year-old – was smuggled past the scrutiny at the door. She came home at midnight, smelling of alcohol and defiant. After her brief glimpse of paradise, Dorothea knew that she would never settle to monotony in Long Crendon again. But it was already July, and the dangerous weeks were coming to an end. 'Only a couple of months to go and she'll be safely out of harm's way at Woodford.' Dorothea said. 'My feeling is we're just in time.'

For a while after our visit to the old gravel-pit, Dick was under a cloud. He could not shake free from the attentions of the sinister sergeant, who refused to allow Dick to break what he claimed was an agreement, and began to adopt a threatening posture. Then suddenly the man dropped out of sight. The English plain-clothes man on permanent duty with base police went the rounds of the village with his photograph, and took a few statements, including one from Dick, but there the matter dropped. Dick learned through the grapevine that the sergeant had been arrested and packed off in handcuffs back to the States. The transports ceased to land after dark, and the volume of American luxury goods in circulation went into steep decline for a time. Some time later, as a matter of curiosity, Dick visited the old shed where he had seen the crates unloaded and found it open and empty.

'It has all been a bit of a fright,' Dick said, and now, suddenly, he was nervous about his involvement in the disposal of the base families' surplus gear. Dick had learned that such imported items were for personal use only. Somebody had broken a law, but Dick was not sure whose law it was, and who had done the breaking. The visits of the plain-clothes man occasioned further unease. The villagers interviewed would have been crafty enough to keep him out of the kitchens where any piece of machinery of American origin would certainly be on view. Still, one never knew. A man like that was trained to use his eyes. Despondently, Dick decided to play safe and pull out of the business, and then, just as his hopes for Jane's future began to recede, new prospects for commerce opened up. This time they were above suspicion.

The complex idea of status had hardly reached Long Crendon at the time of my arrival, and the alterations made by the newcomers to the houses they bought were seen by the natives as unreasoning and eccentric. Why, the villagers argued, should a man enclose his garden with a fence that kept nothing out? Why, instead of spending a hundred or two on renovating a barn, should he have it rebuilt in Norman style at a cost of £2,900?

Slowly an inkling of what was behind this madness began to seep in, and here and there a villager became infected with it. The problem was how, in their gentle and unassertive manner, were village people to acquire any of this magical property enabling a man to stand out from his fellows? Nothing a man could do to alter his house – by a lick of paint on the outside, by a glass front-door, or a chiming bell – could conceal the stark facts (known to all) of pump-water and outside privy. Almost every employable male worked at the base for a similar salary. Village life was one of total equality; all were at the bottom of the pyramid. Humility had been inherited from the feudal servility of a not too distant past. Now, suddenly, the idea was abroad that a man could be 'different' – command a little more than average respect. Nothing could be done about the house, but as Dick pointed out, the possession of a good car set a man apart, and by cutting down expenses in other directions, such a prize could come within reach of all.

American servicemen normally arrived in the country for a three-year tour of duty, and often brought their cars with them. When the time came to move on they were quite ready to part with the vehicle for a reasonable price. Dick had discovered this and acted accordingly. He came to an agreement with the Customs over the matter of excise duty, and after a period of trial and error, was able to cope with the paperwork required. Everyone knew Dick and knew that they would get value for money. Within a few months one in eight of Long Crendon's cottages had a shining American car parked at its front door.

After Christmas and Easter the third most important feast celebrated in Long Crendon was the ancient secular one of August bank holiday. At this the Cloates, for all their slow loss of power and influence, appeared together again in public as a clan and, assisted by alcohol, the old defiant spirit flickered strongly for at least several hours on this day.

On the bank holiday the people of Long Crendon, who usually preferred to stay indoors when there was no work to be done, felt suddenly and briefly the mysterious call of the open, and those who could gathered up their families to go down to the sea-shore, or on picnics amid the few trees remaining where there had once been woods. It was almost a point of honour to escape from confining walls. The local pubs which normally served, at best, a sandwich at the bar provided full-scale lunches on the bank holiday. The traditional holiday dish was eel pie, although Long Crendon was possibly the last place in Essex where it could be tasted. It was not what it had once been, since the eels were no longer caught in the Blackwater or Crouch, but imported frozen from Holland. Nevertheless, eel pie was not to be avoided on this occasion.

Several tables had been reserved for the Cloates in the pleasant garden at the back of the Pied Bull. Some of the clan had moved away from the area but had made the effort to be present at the annual reunion. Of these I knew nothing at all, nor had I had contacts with the Cloates living in the village who were notorious for keeping to themselves. I knew only Dorothea and Dick, and their cousins the Broadbents.

This was an exceptional occasion for the two families. Both Jane and Patricia would shortly be saying goodbye to the village for a while; Jane to face whatever Mrs Amos had in store for her; Patricia, having completed with distinction her course at the school for models, to join a party of them visiting Brazil, where they were to be photographed wearing the creations of a famous couturier against that pageant of water, the Iguazu Falls.

I drove Dick down to the Pied Bull and we had a drink in the bar while awaiting the arrival of the other members of the party. Soon Dorothea came into sight with Emily and Bill Broadbent, all on horseback. Patricia had broken with custom by being dropped off at the pub by the Cambridge-educated son of a local landowner, who drove her over in his Porsche.

Dick left me. I walked to the door of the bar to stand for a moment with the faint scent of eel pie from the kitchen in my nostrils, looking down on this gathering of the clan. At this level success made itself felt, and Bill Broadbent, a once handsome saloon-bar joker, prematurely aged by the good life his asset-stripping had provided, was surrounded by family toadies who had not done so well, a single gin and tonic held in every hand. These men were less prosperous than the average villager. Some were too old to be employed at the base, and some declined to do so, speaking of private means. Apart from Bill, only two had come on horseback. The Essex historian Stephen Maudsley, writing at the end of the last century, had mentioned the great-grandfathers of these men. 'Scant heed was paid to law and order in these remote parts. Scarcely a score of years have passed since the notorious Cloates of Crendon's End raided a nearby village which had given them some offence.' This seemed like the end of the road.

Jane and Patricia had moved out of the crowd and were walking together. They were fond of each other and, as had often been pointed out, however much Cloates might seem different from one another there were, as in this case, quite often resemblances that were not easy to define.

Patricia, described by Mrs Amos, as possibly her most finished product, floated, drifted, seeming at times almost to be airborne, while Jane plodded at her side as if carrying a sack of potatoes on her shoulders. Patricia's svelte body was clad to perfection. By comparison Jane appeared outlandish, almost tribal, as so many village girls were. In defiance of Dorothea's protests she had applied bleach to her hair, following this with a bizarre attack with scissors. Patricia was pleasant and gracious to all, fluttering the tips of her fingers at anyone greeting her who could not easily be reached. Jane pretended not to have seen such salutations. Both girls were smiling and, studying them as they came closer, I understood that Patricia's smile was part of Mrs Amos's art – an asset, trained and accomplished to match all the other ingredients of her beauty. Jane's smile, for all her lumpishness, was human – fallible, but sweet.

Soon after this a project came up, taking me to the Far East, off and on, for nearly four years. I had begun to feel involved in Long Crendon and its problems, and before leaving I tried to secure a base there by buying Charmers End, but the asking price was beyond my means. Nevertheless, I kept in touch with Dorothea and we exchanged letters two or three times a year. Things continued to go fairly well for them. Her first letter informed me that she had sold her horse, and that she and Dick now owned a veteran but serviceable MG. After that, their gracious but shattered house with the remnant of its incomparable vegetable patch and its cracked rear wall, went to a buyer from London and they moved into a brand-new bungalow. Their view was of other bungalows.

Dick had had remedial treatment enabling him to stand up straight, and had taken a course in public speaking. Most of her news was concerned with Jane. 'It's just as they told us it would be,' she said. 'The year's not up yet and you can hardly believe the difference. It's really wonderful what they can do.'

By the next year Jane's speech had been dealt with to everybody's satisfaction. 'You remember the way she used to mumble? I could hardly understand what she was saying myself. Now she speaks as clear as anybody. But she doesn't sound too la-di-da with it, if you know what I mean. Which is rather nice.'

In her third year Jane sounded as though she might have started to think for herself. 'She's been awarded a prize for social awareness, whatever they mean by that,' Dorothea wrote. 'I suppose we're the tiniest bit disappointed because modelling's out. She says it's not for her. Mrs Amos says she's clever enough to do anything she wants, but we shouldn't attempt to sway her. While we're on the subject did you hear about Patricia? She's always in the papers these days. Do you remember when she was just off to Brazil? Well, she married a Brazilian landowner with an estate the size of Essex. The bit in the paper said he was the seventh richest man in the world. The latest story is the marriage is on the rocks. Money isn't everything.'

In her last letter Dorothea's disappointment with her daughter seemed to have deepened. 'Mind you, whatever we've done for her, we'd do it all over again. Her father and I have written to suggest that she might consider being some-thing like a personal secretary to an MP, or a television presenter. She says we'll talk about it when she comes home for the holidays. She hasn't much to say about herself, which doesn't seem a good sign. The news of Patricia isn't so good. I sent you a cutting about her divorce from the Brazilian. Now she's married a French count with a castle in Angoulême. He's more than twice her age. Sometimes I wonder. Her mother can't see this one lasting long either. I always say happiness is what counts.'

★

When I found myself once more in Long Crendon the changes that awaited me, although more radical than expected, had not been unforeseen. It was remarkable that so dramatic a face-lift could have been carried out in so short a time. The villagers had done whatever they could to uglify the place within the limit of their resources, adding a little raw red brick here and an atrocious plastic ornament there, but it was the newcomers who had set to work to strip it of every vestige of its character. There were many of these now, and in their total isolation they formed almost an ethnic minority. In their search for the picturesque they were able to finance change from limitless funds.

Certain iniquities had been suppressed. The smouldering dump had been removed and the police had ordered the pigfarmer to bury the corpses of diseased animals. Main drainage had come to the long street at last, thus – except in the case of outlying houses – putting an end to collection of night soil by the aid of which so many superb vegetables had been produced in the past. All three austere old pubs had been sadly tarted up. I stayed at the Pied Bull. Its simple but noble façade was tricked out with coloured lights and they had hung a sign of Pre-Raphaelite inspiration showing a bull without testicles. In the past narrow, straight-backed wall benches had enforced dignity upon the patrons but now they lounged in armchairs upholstered in buttoned pink plastic. At Charmers End the moat had been sanitised and provided with a concreted landing-stage, at which a black gondola with a lamp on its prow was tied up. The house had statuary and a double garage which could be glimpsed through the sombre foliage of the *Cupressus leylandii*, now to be seen everywhere in Long Crendon.

My conviction that the village was destined to become a cultural colony of the United States had proved to be well founded, but the process seemed to have been completed in a shorter time than I would have thought possible. Two cars were parked outside many of the village houses, some of them fish-tailed monsters. Matters of fundamental custom, such as mealtimes, had been revolutionised. Throughout the centuries, country people everywhere had sat down punctually at twelve-thirty to stuff themselves with the main meal of the day, rising from the table to burn up the heavy, stodgy food by hard physical labour in the field.

Now work of this kind was a thing of the past, and gone with it for most was the traditional midday meal. Men employed at the base no longer wished to consume a pound and a half of potatoes with every meal, and soon fell in with the American system of a quick and easily digested hamburger for lunch, following the return from work at six in the evening with something more substantial; chile con carne being the current favourite. A few of the more advanced families joined with their American friends to celebrate Thanksgiving: butterball turkey and all the trimmings, flown in from the US. The local English, apart from the newcomers, were becoming less reclusive. Even in the recent past they had lived their private, separate lives behind tightly drawn curtains, in fact as well as in the mind. Now they organised get-togethers in the American fashion at which Pabst and Schlitz beer were drunk from cans and pre-cooked, containerised foods of the kind supplied by Indian and Chinese take-aways were served on cardboard plates and eaten with plastic cutlery. These accessories were smuggled out with little difficulty from the base. The memory in Long Crendon of poverty once endured was fading fast.

I found Dorothea and Dick in their bungalow. My immediate feeling was that they were no longer under a strain. A bungalow – with all the furniture polished and in place, the comforting sound of the toilet's flush, and no major cracks in the wall – can act as a tranquilliser. Dick's nervous tick, which had surfaced once every few minutes in the wrinkles round his mouth, had gone, and the doctors, in straightening him out, had added an inch to his height. Dorothea had put on a few pounds and was all the better for it. A hairdresser had brought life to the lank black Indian hair of old.

Dick was as busy as ever. Within minutes of my arrival he was summoned by telephone. He was running a little agency affair of his own, Dorothea said. Accommodation was very short in a rapidly expanding area, and he was doing what he could to help out. He had at last found the Lord. Many of his friends from the States were Baptists, and he had been born again. Dorothea put in a few hours most days, as ever, at Charmers End, not because they needed the money now with Jane more or less off their hands, but because she liked having something to do.

Jane had been home for three months. 'Isn't that earlier than intended?' I asked.

'We had a long talk with Mrs Amos,' she said, 'after which there didn't seem much point in going any further.'

'In what direction? You told me Jane had decided against modelling. What about the other possibilities? It sounded as though Mrs Amos had high hopes for her.'

'According to Mrs Amos, Jane was exceptionally gifted. She was attractive and intelligent, and she could have done anything she wanted.' She gestured resignation.

'But she didn't want to be a television presenter or anybody's personal secretary.'

'It was her whole attitude. That kind of thing didn't seem to mean anything to her. In one way, Mrs Amos said, she'd turned out better than she hoped. Another year's formation and she could have had the world at her feet. But it all left her cold.'

'Dorothea,' I said. 'I'm beginning to suspect you're to be congratulated. You have an interesting daughter.'

'Mrs Amos said you sometimes come across people you thought you could change, and they fooled you by pretending to go along, but really underneath they were going their own way all the time.'

'So Jane beat the system,' I said. 'She survived.'

33

'I suppose that's one way of looking at it,' Dorothea said. 'Anyway, we brought her home.'

'And now what is she going to do?'

'She's filling in time in the accounts office at the base.'

'And after that?'

'She'll take up nursing.'

'What could be better?'

'You won't be surprised to hear she has an American boyfriend.'

'Why should I be surprised? What is he – a pilot, or a navigator?'

'No,' she said. 'He's on the catering side. An assistant cook.'

For once in my life I was struck by inspiration. 'Would he by any chance be coloured?' I asked.

'How on earth did you guess?' she said.

It was just something that had occurred to me. I said. 'We're getting to know Jane. Both of us. What time do you expect her home? I'm much looking forward to seeing her.'

THAILAND

IN 1951 MARSHAL Phibun Songkhram, ruler of Thailand, despatched a body of experts to the US, charged with an extraordinary mission. This was no less than to discover the fountain-head of wisdom and power which, as the Thais agreed, had promoted America to leadership among the nations. They returned with the belief that this moral and material superiority stemmed largely from the drinking of whisky, the dancing together in public of men and women, and the regular ceremonial performance of the striptease.

Phibun forthwith ordered a whisky distillery to be set up. Stages were erected in towns and villages throughout the country upon which responsible persons of both sexes were to dance together. Physical contact between the couples was ruled out and the dancers would cavort round each other, waving their arms gracefully in the manner of the classic Thai dancers of old. The striptease, viewed as a purely cultural exercise was commonly staged thereafter in temple enclosures at the time of a festival, while a monk, imprisoned near by in a wicker cage, preached to the audience in incomprehensible Pali.

Thirty-five years have passed. The Thais still drink *mekong*, their version of whisky, ususally taken neat and hot – and dance the *Ramwong* on all festive occasions. Only the cultural striptease has fallen behind, rarely to be found nowadays except in the remote and more conservative parts of the country. On the whole Phibun's recipe seems to have worked out reasonably well. Thailand's economy is flourishing. It has commendable records in the field of public health and education. Its enormous birthrate is about ten times that of the United Kingdom, and the charm of the people and the varied and often extraordinary inducements offered to foreign visitors have promoted its tourist trade to the most lucrative in the Far East.

Early morning in Bangkok in the riverside garden of the Oriental Hotel. The city puts on edge in the light smog that has turned last night's moon to cotton wool. Shortly, the aspen leaves quiver at the approach of the first of the long-tail boats, powered by a 125 h.p. engine and with open exhaust, bringing commuters into the heart of the city. Many more boats follow, spreading waves of sound that seem to penetrate the skull. The Thais do not object to noise, which they associate with life, vigour, progress and success. Bangkok may be the only city where imported cars are fitted specially with extra large-bore silencers before delivery to the buyer.

With the discharge of their cargoes of office-workers, the serious business of the morning is at an end, and soon the dragon fleet comes roaring back to pick up a thousand or so foreigners waiting to be shipped away on the routine visit to the floating market.

It is an experience that illustrates R. L. Stevenson's maxim: 'to travel hopefully is better than to arrive.' The ear-splitting voyage takes the visitor behind the scenes of an oriental city in a way not likely to be repeated in the course of his stay. Here are the splendid old junks, the ghostly houses breathing out incense over the watery smells, the flooded gardens with Siamese cats swimming like otters through the flowers afloat in the yellow wavelets. A man disposes of a rat; another, net in hand, chases after a frog; a woman wrapped in a sheet washes her body with delicacy and grace; naked children hurl themselves like lemmings into the soupy water. Here, for the space of half an hour, the intricate inner life of Bangkok is exposed to the foreign eye. The true reason for the tourists' admission to this intimacy is that they are *invisible*. Every morning for so many years, and at precisely this hour, this water-borne invasion has passed through. Now not a head is turned in their direction.

At the floating market anticlimax awaits. The market as it once was has long ceased to exist. Increasing affluence makes it unnecessary for the locals to shop by boat, and the once lively scene has given place to a banal charade. The hopeful travellers are lured ashore to run the gauntlet of souvenir stalls, then herded into a slatternly zoo to watch four men traipse round with a python of immense length, before shoving it back into a sack. This is also a crocodile farm, where a few half-submerged animals remain unresponsive to the keeper's proddings with a pole. Visitors are urged to buy crocodile bags and belts produced on the spot, and a guide mentions in a jovial way that the flesh of the animals providing these is supplied to leading restaurants. 'It tastes like frog,' he says. 'You'd never tell the difference.'

This is a high spot of the average tour, but there are further excursions in plenty on offer. Bangkok contains a staggering total of 400 temples. 'But', says the guide, 'we have to be realistic and know when to call it a day.' Most visitors settle for the Temples of the Emerald, Golden and Reclining Buddhas, and that of the Dawn, and it is better after that to leave the glittering mish-mash of orientalia of the Grand Palace for another day. Having seen the film, some visitors opt for the longish pilgrimage to the River Kwai. Interest slackens a little on the Rose Garden trip, and of the ancient capital Ayutthaya, included in most tours, the guidebook notes without enthusiasm, 'outside the ruins and temples it holds little interest,' adding sombrely, 'it is one of the three gangster-ruled cities of Thailand.'

Bangkok is the Babylon of our days, yet few programmes feature more than a cautious, sight-seeing incursion into the world's most renowned nightlife. Trudging from temple to temple the subject of the famous massage parlours inevitably comes up, for despite rumoured orgies, nothing is spelled out in print. 'What do you suppose they do?' the innocents ask each other, but nobody answers with confidence.

A last-century Thai chart on view in the library of the British Museum identifies thirty-six bodily areas responding to mass-age with relief, if not cure, for many complaints, including tumours and cancer. The ancient and respected Thai healing art thus illustrated is still taught and practised in temples throughout the kingdom, and may be considered medically to rank in effectiveness with the acupuncture of the Chinese.

Its therapeutic benefits have been overshadowed, it is said, since the stationing of 46,000 American servicemen in Thailand at the time of the Vietnam war, when a profane side of the healing profession developed into an industry in which 750,000 women are now employed. In this the borderline between therapy and prostitution is hard to define. The final conclusion is that it is easily crossed.

The Patpong and Petchburi Roads are the heartland of novelty and make-belief. Bar-girls may wear absolutely nothing but a belt of silk around the waist, school uniforms or wedding dresses. In one restaurant, topless waitresses career from table to table on roller skates, while in another less inclined to mobility, they actually feed the guests. Massage parlours are scattered by the dozen throughout the area, the best-known being Atami's which accepts Diners' cards, and raises no objection to visits clearly motivated by curiosity. Externally, Atami's looks like a supermarket, its outstanding internal feature (and this is typical of such establishments) being a brilliantly lit room behind a glass screen. In this a number of ladies in pink evening gowns are seated on what must be the largest sofa in the world. Elsewhere each of these women has a number pinned to her dress, a form of identification rejected by Atami's as crude.

The secrets of the trade were recently disclosed by a young Thai woman, Suleemarn Naru, researching this weird oriental half-world for a master's thesis in sociology, whose devotion to her studies was so great that she actually worked for six months in a massage parlour with a staff of 1,000 girls. She noted that girls between the age of 12 and 22 were recruited by agents in impoverished hill villages, sacrificing themselves for a down payment handed over to their parents which – although small enough – was equivalent to the family income for a year. In the matter of prostitution, her finding was that, apart from the middle-aged practitioners of traditional massage, the majority of the masseuses were involved in this.

Chiang Mai, capital of the North, remains beneath a veneer of development Thailand's most pleasing city. Between morning and evening rush hours it is sedate enough to be explored by bike, with everything worth seeing compressed into the old town within the mediaeval walls. Parts of Chiang Mai recall scenes from old movies of China before Mao, and a glance at the map confirms that the remotest provinces of China are not far away. Men and women wearing hats like enormous lampshades hobble past under the weight of a pole balanced on the shoulders with heavy burdens at each end. Time-defaced human and animal figures, ribald and threatening or merely grotesque lie abandoned among the rubbish in odd corners. The department stores offer a range of spirit-houses to suit all pockets, from a clearance line in plastic to deluxe versions carved from teak. They are everywhere, giving shelter to the ancestral spirits of the family and to such vagrant ones as might be tempted to take up residence, just as a bird may take over a nesting box. My hotel had put up one, and so had a filling-station fifty yards down the road, both furnished with protective miniature elephants and galloping horses. The roofs of old Chiang Mai, curling at the eaves, lie upon the city like autumn leaves, and from these arise the gilt spires of many temples, spreading the faintest of haloes into the misted sky. There can be no more poetic scene than the line-up of archers, who station themselves just after dawn with their crossbows along the moat to shoot at the shadowy outlines of fish in its intensely green waters.

Among the multitude of pagodas throughout the Thai kingdom, two in Chiang Mai demand a visit, as much for the permeation of their surroundings with the aroma of ancient Asia as for their architectural distinction. Wat Phra Singh, built in 1385, enshrines one of the most venerable Buddha images, which, as a notice informs the visitor, deposited momentarily in this spot while being taken to the King of Chiang Mai, refused to move. The second, Wat Chedi Luang, is remarkable for the splendour and antiquity of its spire, guarded by a wonderful assortment of stone serpents and elephants. Both temples have been presented with a selection of majestic old grandfather clocks, which tick away resolutely in the profound religious calm, and both have set aside areas where male citizens over 50 come to sleep one night a week in order to benefit from holy emanation.

From Chiang Mai, I drove up to Mae Sae, Thailand's northernmost village, on the frontier with Burma – a place of stunning ugliness, based upon opium trade prosperity. The two countries are separated at this point by a narrow river, and I stood for a moment on its bank to watch Thai children on one side and Burmese on the other stoning each other across the water in a friendly and ineffective fashion. This area – the Golden Triangle – had been part of the territory of the Shan warlord Khun Sa, and was dominated by him until 1983. From here he controlled most of the world trade in opium and heroin. In 1983 he was finally defeated in an all-out assault by the Thai Army and driven back across the border into Burma. Here – although equally unwelcome – he remains in command of an army of some 5,000 men and controls, as he claims, the destinies of eight million Burmese Shans.

Khun Sa's successful partnership with the CIA has been described. The Shan warlord grew the opium and processed the heroin, and the CIA, in the guise of wholesaler, flew this into Vietnam, the handsome profit thus derived helping to finance the covert operations of those days. This once valued ally is now a thorn in the American side. He has recently proposed a deal by which he guarantees to cut off virtually the whole of the world's heroin supply at source in return for US economic aid totalling 95 million dollars a year for five years.

At Mae Sae, hilltribes people, women and children, some weeping and in rags were crossing the bridge from Burma. Their lot is a sorry one, whether in one country or the other, for they are without nationality, and it was highly likely that this particular group of refugees would in due course suffer eviction from Thailand as they had from Burma. They are unpopular on both sides of the frontier, the common complaint being that their slash and burn method of cultivation is detrimental both to environment and climate. It is an argument that ignores the fact that the hilltribes, with a current population in Thailand of 830,000 have always been there, although it is only in recent years that marked climatic changes have been recorded.

The climate of such tropical countries depends for its stability on the presence of rain forests, and an often catastrophic drop in rainfall follows their destruction. On the whole the hilltribes try to avoid the labour involved in felling large trees, contenting themselves with the cyclical clearance and cultivation of land upon which secondary forest has taken a decade or so to restore a measure of fertility to the soil. The clearances that change the climate are those carried out by logging firms and coffee and rubber planters. In 50 years nearly two-thirds of the big trees have gone. The nation is, therefore, two-thirds of the way along the road to climatic disaster.

Whatever the true facts may be, the wretched hilltribes carry the can, and are often the victims of brutal treatment by the state. In 1987, it was announced that 2,000 tribal people were to be 'repatriated' (i.e. shoved back across a border that for them did not exist). The spokesman added that 160 families had already been cleared in the style of the Scottish Highlands of the last century, and their villages burned. In February of this year a further 5,000 hilltribes people were ordered to pack up and move down into the plain to facilitate a private company's reforestation venture upon what was regarded as their ancestral land.

Tribal wretchedness has been increased by a crackdown on the small-scale, although widespread, production of opium, grown as a cash crop with which to pay for rice. Thus Khun Sa's competitors in North Thailand have been wiped out, although by all accounts the big-business narcotics trade carries on as before. Happily, at this moment of crisis, a new income from tourism is helping to keep the hill-farmer's head above water. Last year 120 package-deal operators in Chiang Mai despatched 100,000 clients into the mountains in search of primitive and often strenuous pleasures. 'Jungle adventures', as they are termed, may include such imaginative trimmings as a mile or two of transport by bullock cart, or on the back of an elephant, or in a sampan, but there is a fair amount of foot-slogging involved. There may be the occasional glimpse of an impressive snake, and once in a while an encounter with bandits, as a result of which, on one occasion in 1988, fatalities were sustained. Trekkers are promised guidance to villages rarely visited before. Here the deal may include a pipe of opium smoked with the headman, and a rudimentary massage by one of the tribal maidens who has been rushed down to Chiang Mai for a crash course in the art. To the excitement of the local tourist industry, a border conflict between Thailand and Laos flared up at the beginning of February and the most enterprising of the Chiang Mai operators laid plans for a 'battle experience' tour in which trekkers could have experienced the audial excitement of distant cannon fire. Within days, however, the war was called off. As reported in the press 1,000 shells and rockets rained down in a ceremonial bombardment of the previously vacated area under dispute, after which the generals of both sides, their staffs and their wives got together for a conciliatory night of revelry, hot whisky-drinking and the *Ramwong*.

Down in the relaxed and hedonistic South the hair shirt is gratefully laid aside and visitors surrender themselves to the beach ritual in the usual way. Thailand has learned little from the fate of the Spanish Costas. Thirty years ago Pattaya, now the leading resort, was a fishing village with fretwork-adorned fishermen's shacks, a few mad little seaside castles built by the rich, and painted boats strewn among the nets drying on the immaculate sand. It is now the most expensive as well as the most garish of Thai cities with 400 hotels, guest-houses and condominiums covering the site of those once engaging scenes. Despite its jazzarenas, its glittering nightlife, and its many widely advertised 'pampering facilities', Pattaya, even according to the local newspapers, is far from being what it was. Coming straight to the point, the *Bangkok Post* complains that the penalties imposed by the management of the several hundred bars upon bar-girls who absent themselves momentarily from normal counter duties for a pampering session with a customer have been unreasonably increased. Fines of 100 baht have shot up to 400 baht (42 bahts to the pound), while an unheard-of 1,000 baht are demanded for a few moments of sexual satisfaction as compared to a reasonable 300–400 baht paid until quite recently 'for an evening of entertainment'. The newspaper goes on to lament the loss of the old easygoing atmosphere in the city's nightspots, particularly when police in uniform enter a bar to hustle for drinks: 'They are driving so many customers away because foreign tourists become uneasy when they see an armed official consuming alcohol when he should probably be on duty.'

Ruling out Pattaya with its pampering and its gun-slinging

cops, I went instead to Phuket, Thailand's largest island, down close to the border with Malaysia – a younger arrival in the field of pleasure. Here I stayed at a comfortable but isolated hotel, in appearance half-way between a pagoda and a railway station, with mock-Tudor half-timbered additions in which artfully painted concrete stood in for wood. The central feature was a series of still pools in the lobby, which, at a touch of a switch, could be set in motion to feed a river flowing through open doors over a flight of concrete steps into a lotus pond below. Everything had been thought of here to further the guest's pleasure down to the orchid laid on the pillow at night, attached to two wrapped peppermints and a quotation – sometimes from Shakespeare – in praise of sleep. The only trouble was there was nothing whatever to do and nowhere to go in an immediate vicinity of sand-dunes and stagnant ponds from which I was assured a leisure complex of unprecedented dimensions would shortly emerge.

In Patong, a few miles further along the coast, something like this had already happened. It had been first in the field of development, and here had arisen a concrete jungle of the most fanciful kind. In a rabid assortment of architectural styles, the pacemaker seemed to have been modelled on a Dayak long-house with a soaring, gabled roof under which the wooden idols of Borneo might have been stored. There were a number in this style. There were also a little suburb of snow-proof mountain chalets built for Swiss occupation under this re-fulgent sun, a German *speishaus* with a sweating employee in *lederhosen* at the door, what looked like a Spanish model prison, and for the Brits, the usual nostalgic pubs.

Nothing much in Patong seemed to be working at the time of my passing through, for the sewers were being replaced and 100 yards of swamp spread from a burst water-main. Pyra-mids of building materials obscured all the views, such as they were, while newly opened-up terrain on all sides was spiked like a fakir's bed with iron reinforcements awaiting the con-crete. In the background, tremendous earth-moving machines charged about like an armoured brigade in action. A dried-out part of the town contained scuttling whirlwinds full of calcine dust, through which the visitors struggled, handkerchiefs clamped to their noses. From the invisible bay below a despondent howl arose to announce the presence of the long-tail boats of Bangkok.

Beyond Patong, the newer resorts, Karon, Kata and Naihan had some way to go before reaching this extreme. Nevertheless, here too, the shape of things to come was to be discerned in the new roads slashed through the contours of the landscape; the ironed-out dunes; the drained marshes; the streams corseted with cement; the hills sliced away.

Of the unique charm of South-East Asia where it borders the Andaman Sea, little survives in Phuket but what is to be found at Mai Khao – a long and deserted beach north of the airport, which, with its hinterland, has mysteriously been spared. For a while the road leading to the mainland via the Sarasin Bridge runs within a mile or so of the shore, to be reached by any track taken to the left. Here a seascape of oriental antiquity remains. The beach is feathered by the mossy shade of huge cassuarinas, from which fishing owls as large as eagles come planing down to the waves in the early hours of the evening. Within hearing of the planes taking off, painted storks mince in casual fashion among the lilypads of a shallow lake. In the rainy season, beginning in July, orchids flower in the branches of every tree. When I was there in February none were in flower, but this was the month when the turtles come ashore at night by the hundreds to deposit their eggs, and in the morning their scuffled tracks – strangely industrial-looking in their regularity – are everywhere to be seen.

KHARTOUM
AND BACK

THE PEOPLE WHO should know differ strangely as to which is the longest river. The *Times Atlas* casts it vote in favour of the Amazon, the *Encyclopedia Britannica* says the Nile, while the *Guinness Book of Records* cannot make up its mind. Whichever the winner in this photo finish, one thing is certain: the importance of the Amazon in the human scheme is slight, that of the Nile huge. The one, majestic and aloof, has no history, enriches no land, supports only a handful of fisher-men. The other is currently responsible for the existence of 50 million people, and even in the time of the pharaohs may have supported a population half that size, which, ruling out China, would probably have exceeded the number of the inhabitants of the rest of the globe.

The Nile brought glittering civilisations into being, wholly dependent upon the annual bounty of its floods, and a single year's withholding of its waters from the parched lands await-ing them would have been enough to obliterate an empire. 'Egypt', said Herodotus, 'is the gift of the Nile.' And not only Egypt but that 3,000-mile-long ribbon of fertility which un-coils through the deserts of the Sudan, where local wars of extermination have been fought when an occasional drop of a few inches in water levels meant that there was not enough food for all.

Khartoum, capital of the Sudan, seemed a likely starting-off place for explorations of the Upper Nile. It turned out to be a somewhat caved-in town with an embalmed colonial flavour, an occasional leper in sight, isolated grand hotels, and a Sudan Club where the many British expatriates that remain appeared to spend much of their lives. The Chinese had built a sumptuous Friendship Hall and glutted the town with Double Happiness matches – now serving as small change – while the Japanese kept the broken streets filled with yellow Toyota taxis. A thousand elephants had died to stock main-street shops with banal ornaments carved from their tusks, and the skins of such endangered animals as leopards, cheetahs and crocodiles were on offer at bargain prices.

I stayed at a new hotel in the centre where the novelty and the charm of Orient fully compensated for faltering Western technology. A little Arabic, not well learnt so many years ago, had been resuscitated for the occasion, and this permitted a proper exchange of courtesies with spotlessly robed fellow guests queueing for the lift. 'Peace on you.' 'And on you peace and the blessings of God.' 'They say today that if you wish to reach floor three you must press button six.' 'Let us do that. *Inshallah* we shall arrive.' '*Inshallah*.'

The doorman swept off his hat in the way Sudanese servants probably did 30 years ago. Fifty yards from where he stood smiling and bowing, a beggar advertised his plight by a strong-voiced cry, 'God is merciful,' repeated with unflagging conviction every 10 seconds throughout the daylight hours. According to a printed warning it was as strictly forbidden to photograph him, or any other 'debasing sight', as it was a power-station, a military establishment, or a bridge.

Down on the waterfront the scene was a lively one. Khartoum is built at the confluence of the Blue and White Niles, the first gathering its waters in the Ethiopian Plateau; the most distant source of the second being the Kagera River in

Burundi, some 1,500 miles to the south. It came as a surprise to find that one river is actually blue, and the other, if not quite white, at least a palish green. It is regarded by many visitors as an emotional experience to discover a spot on one of the sand-banks where this separation of colours is clearly visible, enabling the pilgrim to stand with one foot in each river.

Hotels and government buildings impose a stolid conformity along the city waterfront – one could be anywhere – but at Abu Rof, just outside the town limits, the Nile comes into its own, and could almost be mistaken for the Ganges. Here people strip off to wash down, having pushed their way down to the water through the herds of cows and goats that are brought to drink. Here, taxi drivers back their shattered Toyotas into the shallows to sponge off the dust, and here – inevitably – the donkey-drawn municipal water-carts are brought to be filled. This is a playground to which men bred in deserts are attracted by the mere presence of water. They sit here in rows in barbers' chairs to have their heads shaved, and before the lathering begins the barber adjusts the mirror to enable his customer to enjoy the reflected scene of all that is happening down by the river at his back.

Abu Rof fosters the intense sociability of lives lived outside in what is for the most part of the year a good climate. Neighbours carry out their beds to sleep on the beach, which is furnished like a communal room with domestic objects, chairs, the occasional sofa, a kitchen stove, most of these softened in outline by pigeons' droppings. The villagers swap tall stories, pray a little, brew up tea, and polish each other's shoes, and turbaned and immensely dignified men gather in clear spots among the domestic litter for a game of marbles.

The backdrop to this amiable scene is the brown ramparts thrown up by the Khalifa and held with hopeless courage for an hour or two against the cannon fire of Kitchener's expedition sent to avenge the death of Gordon and to recover the Sudan. Kitchener's gunboat, the *Melik*, with its paper-thin armour and single three-inch gun, is still tied up a mile or so upstream.

Sheikh Hamid el Nil's cemetery, and the tomb of this holy man, whose name implies his mystic involvement with the river, is a short taxi-ride away. It has become the centre of a dervish cult, hardly more than tolerated by Islamic orthodoxy, which views gymnastic devotions with the same uneasiness a practising Anglican might feel in the presence of Holy Rollers at worship. I drove out on Friday evening, when all Khartoum relaxes, to see the dervishes whirl. About 100 of them had marched in under their flags and were engaged in a preliminary workout. The drums crashed, and the dervishes began to jerk and twitch.

There was nothing exclusive about the occasion. Any by-stander could join in, and many did. A hard core of devotees whirled in professional style, but the onlooker caught up in the spirit of the thing was free to improvise. The drums imposed their own tremendous rhythmic discipline, but within this framework anything went. One pranced about, leapt, gal-loped, whirled until eliminated by vertigo, howled, shrieked, frothed at the mouth if possible, while the dervishes cracked their whips and lashed out with their canes. It was to be enjoyed by all; all good, therapeutic mania, like a 'Come Dancing' session with 10 marks out of 10 for contestants who could throw a trance or work themselves up into a fit.

My driver, who had been standing by his taxi, soon began to suffer minor convulsions and, after grabbing at the steering wheel through the window in an effort to hold himself back, suddenly tore loose, picked up a stick, and went bounding away. A few minutes later he appeared again, exhausted and reeling, but spiritually renewed. 'If you believe in God, sir,' he said, 'why do you not join us?' It was an experience he thought I ought not to miss.

I had no objection when he suggested a visit to the nearby tomb of the Mahdi, liberator of the Sudan from Gordon and the 'Turks'. It proved to be a garish edifice of recent construction, reminding one of a space-ship on its launching pad. Kitchener destroyed the original tomb. He had the Mahdi's body dug up and went off with the head with the intention of turning it into a drinking cup, deterred only from doing this by Queen Victoria's startled outcry. Winston Churchill refers with distaste to this incident in 'The River War'. He speaks of the Mahdi's 'unruffled smile, pleasant manners, generosity, and equable temperament'. 'To many prisoners he showed kindness . . . to all he spoke with dignity and patience.' His limbs and trunk were flung into the Niles. 'Such', says Churchill, 'was the chivalry of the conquerors.'

The driver obtained my admission into the enclosure from which non-Muslims are normally excluded, on the promise that I would join him in a prayer, and I duly stood with him and did my best to recite the words of the Arabic formula.

The Nile is rarely easy to approach. In the Sudan, river steamers only operate for about a quarter of its length, and roads following the valley are usually out of sight of the water. I had arrived with an introduction to the owner of a motorised felucca, but he had gone out of business, and the only man prepared to offer long-distance transport was a Mexican white hunter who offered 25 days' hunting for £15,000. He mentioned as an inducement that on a recent expedition a client had had the good luck to shoot a bongo, an exceptionally rare species of antelope, only to be taken in the Sudan.

It would have been nice to go to Juba, capital of the deep south, to visit at least the fringe of the extraordinary papyrus swamp known as the Sudd, and stay in Juba's hotel where colonial nostalgia is so acutely felt that friends who had been there were prepared to guarantee that Brown Windsor soup was served with every meal. There were severe impediments to this project. In the Sudan communications are coming close to total breakdown, and this vast African country offers a foretaste of the likely predicament of the Third World when, in the end, petrol ceases to flow.

The beautiful lady in the tourist office broke the news to me that such were the fuel shortages that the plane to Juba could be held up there for as long as a week, or, at worst, a month. Shortages of this order might delay, once I got there, the proposed return by river boat, and it was hard to come by precise information as to what was happening in the south because the telephone lines were out of order.

Every world traveller will assure you that the Sudanese are the nicest people you are ever likely to meet, and I was beginning to agree. It was Saturday morning and there seemed to be a faint whiff about the place of the aphrodisiac smoke of acacia wood burnt in certain rituals on Friday nights. Young ladies in flowered chiffon saris came and went, smiling and giggling, shaking hands and touching their hearts, while the lady in charge of the office broke her depressing news.

'You could go by car,' she suggested, 'but you may have to queue eight hours for petrol.' She added that the car would cost £125 a day, mentioning that the journey to Juba occupied at least five days in each direction, and that 250 gallons of petrol would have to be carried. It was a moment, if ever there was one, to seek refuge in the art of the possible.

I ran to earth the only man in Khartoum with a Land-Rover for hire; he found enough petrol to fill his tank and for two spare cans, and we set off with the object of travelling as far south as this meagre ration would allow. An asphalt road took us to Jebel Aulia, where we crossed the dam built in 1934, which was covered as if by graffiti with the great names of British engineering from those far-off colonial times. Here fishermen, casting their nets under a screen of herons and fishing eagles, were taking Nile perch from the water. These they bartered with the villagers for such things as firewood and eggs. Beyond Aulia the road, marked as confidently as ever on the map, turned into a tangle of interlacing tyre tracks in a near-desert. Its surface was as flat and hard as a cricket pitch and once in a while we drove into a drab village, overtopped by a chocolate and green minaret, with the mirage lying like stagnant water, and creeping back as we charged up the streets.

Such villages, just beyond reach of the Nile floods, were so poor that even the vultures had given them up. Nothing, absolutely nothing, was ever thrown away. The rains came in autumn, the villagers grew a single crop of sorghum, and after that their lives teetered on the edge of survival for the nine months to the next rains.

When we stopped for a midday snack a chance remark by the driver put the whole predicament of the underfed four-fifths of the world population in stunning perspective. Schooled in the proprieties of the well-nourished fifth I made a move to gather up our litter. He was horrified. 'Leave everything,' he said. 'The goats will deal with the orange skins, even the paper, and the Arabs will turn the beer-cans into cups. Come back here in an hour, and you won't see a trace of anything.' Since the vultures had lost hope and gone away, animals that had died from natural causes lay scattered about these villages quite intact, but mummified by the sun.

We turned away to the east, passing without warning across the frontier between arid savannah and the brilliant fertility of the nearly two million acres of the Gezira, the great garden of the Sudan filling the triangle south of Khartoum between the Blue and White Niles. A glum prospect of mud huts afloat in the mirage still showed through the rear window, but ahead was a soft bedazzlement of green fields moated with running water, and sparked with the refulgence of brilliant birds; great wading storks in absurd postures, ten kinds of kingfisher, green cuckoos and crimson bee-eaters, insect-hunting from the telegraph poles where they perched in their hundreds. The Nile valley, throughout the length of its passage through the arid lands, is the paradise of birds, drawn to its water and the teeming insect life of its marshes and its saturated earth.

It was intended back in the twenties that the Gezira project should provide cheap cotton for the Lancashire mills, but each year less cotton is grown for export and more food for home consumption, although the Gezira still provides most of the national income. It is not quite the success story it was, and production in most sectors is in decline. The management of water on this scale is a complex affair and technological breakdowns are compounded by a brain-drain to the affluent Gulf States. Water levels are maintained by specialists at pumping stations and irrigation regulators, who are required to be in constant touch with one another through the telephone network. This has begun to break down, so that canals frequently overflow and land is damaged by excessive flooding.

It is said, too, the canals are no longer kept as free as they should be from weeds. This not only reduces the efficiency of irrigation, but has provoked a marked increase in the incidence of bilharzia. I was told that 80 per cent of Gezira children before the age of 10 now suffer from the disease, and the anaemia and chronic diarrhoea it entails. The shells of the snail that acts as host to the parasite in the intermediate stage of its development were to be seen everywhere in the mud excavated from water-courses.

A quick forage round the market was to produce enough fuel, a gallon here, a gallon there, for a two days' trip to the north, and our first stop was at the sixth cataract of the Nile, where the river slips between burnished coppery hills and a miniature gorge. The description cataract over-dramatises a fall in the water, rippling over pink stones hardly more than a few feet high; but here the boats taking part in Kitchener's river war had to be dismantled once again to be reassembled only a few yards further on (nuts and bolts had sensibly replaced rivets in their construction), and there is a local legend that here they were bombarded by Mahdists who remained miraculously immune from the Maxim guns by reinforcing the chainmail they wore with pages from the Koran.

There were wide, tranquil waters above the babble of the cataract, with palms, beanfields and birds and butterflies galore, and little girls were tugging goats by the ear, one by one, down to the water and actually persuading them to drink. Here I ran into the corruption spread by tourism even in this remote place. A year or more back, before petrol shortages had closed them down, an agency had been accustomed to send parties of trippers to this enchanted spot, and a local peasant, under the pretence that he owned the land, had levied a toll on access to the river. Watching from his lookout he spotted the Land–Rover's approach and hurried to lay branches across the path, charging £1 per head before he would remove them. It was the first and the last time that I heard the hateful word *baksheesh* in the Sudan.

The track leading to the north followed the railway line and in the space of an hour we passed the wreckage of two derailed trains. They had become a centre of local pilgrimage, and while we were examining the second train several goat-herds came into sight from behind the rocks to make a cautious, tiptoe approach as if for fear of disturbing a sleeping, but potentially dangerous animal. One of them picked up a stone and threw it at a mangled tanker-truck, and the sound of the stone striking metal was shrill and bleak in the dry air. They came up and shook hands with us repeatedly, delighted at the relief from the terrific monotony of their lives offered by the wrecked train and the sight of fresh faces.

In this vicinity, at the approach to the important river junction at Shendi, we found ourselves among 100-foot-high mounds of immense ironstone boulders, heaped together in such a way that it was hard at first to accept that they had not been built by human hands. Scattered over the sand the shapes resembled squat armless Venuses, 100 tons of sand-polished sculpture by Henry Moore, sand-logged dinosaurs, black iron shards, and meteorites.

Shendi, at one of the old crossroads of Africa, had always lived off the river traffic and the caravan routes crossing the Nile at this point. It had been an emporium of ivory and slaves, particularly the slave-girls brought down from Abyssinia, those highly valued harem items whose jet-black skin was – as an early writer put it – as cool to the touch as a toad, mentioning that a toad was sometimes kept on hand to enable the would-be purchaser to convince himself of the truth of the claim. Shendi had fallen into a decline highlighted by the loss of one of its ferries. It had been out of action for a year, although the spare parts necessary to get it going again had been delivered some months before, remaining in their crates by the river bank where they had been dumped from a lorry, and probably forgotten.

Here a pull-in for market traffic offered the huge and expensive luxury of Pepsi Cola, English cigarettes (high-tar content for the Third World), a packet of which cost an average Sudanese worker a day's wages, and hardboiled eggs by way of a snack. Children were waiting to seize upon and suck the discarded shells.

A hard day's drive brought us by evening to the site of the ancient Nilotic kingdom of Meroë where we camped for the night among the low pyramids – there are about 200 in all, clustered in groups over the low hills. They remain so well preserved, so clean-cut in their outlines that a few of them could be mistaken for follies built here by some Sudanese Victorian eccentric. The obvious clue to their antiquity lies in the fact that so many have lost their tops, dismantled in search of treasure by an early Egyptian military expedition tricked by an impostor into coming here in search of gold.

Throughout most of its course through the Sudan the Nile is surprisingly difficult to reach behind the green mosaic of its gardens and its innumerable irrigation ditches. All this invaluable land has remained in the same families for many generations, producing a precisely calculable return and a sufficiency of food for all, based on a stable equation of birth and death. Antibiotics have destroyed this equilibrium. Until now epidemic sickness has carried off most of the children of the Third World in the first year of their lives. Now they survive to compete with each other for food supplies that have reached their limits. Up to four crops a year are raised at Meroë, but there is no way of coaxing more food from the soil, and even the volume of water supplied by the Nile has come close to its limit. Too many heirs divide the family plots into smaller and smaller segments, and too many peasants are already struggling to survive on the produce of a rectangle of land the size of a suburban front garden. Malaria, typhoid and hepatitis have been almost eliminated, but only at the expense of strengthening the hand of starvation.

There seems to be no remedy in sight for this situation, which is allied to another long-term threat in the Sudan – that of desertification. There are more mouths to be fed everywhere, not only in the Nile valley itself but in the vast arid areas of semi-desert that border it. A few years back the greatest drought of this century coincided with the quadrupling of world petrol prices. The annual grasses failed to come up because there were no rains, and the herdsmen, impoverished by the loss of their stock, and no longer able to buy kerosene, began to cut down the last of the trees. No one is more keenly aware of the function fulfilled by the trees than the desert nomad, but he was up against the wall. The acacias and the desert apples were turned into firewood, and the desert was on the move again.

The first symptoms of this creeping sickness of the earth were to be seen at Meroë, where sands were blowing into the green fields by the river, and one saw lorries stuck in sand-drifts where only two or three years back there had been a surface as hard as concrete. A few weeks before my driver had made the trip up to the north, passing a spot between Karima and the Egyptian frontier. Last time he had been in the vicinity there had been a grove of date palms there, with a bit of a garden producing a few cucumbers, with a well and a donkey turning a water-wheel. Of this nothing remained but a few palm fronds sprouting like feather dusters from the top of the dunes.

I flew to Cairo, passing over the Aswan High Dam and the 300-mile-long lake it has created. Lake Nasser came as a surprise. The mind's eye had presented an immense version of a highland reservoir, and I was unprepared for this great sprawl of water, for its headlands, capes, its inlets and creeks by the hundred – even its fjords – all of them alien and out of place in this dry and incandescent land. Egyptians will say of this much-advertised solution to all their problems that it has turned out to be a mixed blessing, and there is an undertone among them of murmurings and doubts. A typical Third World thirst for industrialisation, cost what it may, has been satisfied by the dam and the electricity it has generated, and it would be unfair to suggest that many of the factories brought into being have been as disappointing as the one that produced so many millions of headless pins. The question is whether in the long term Egypt's capability as the most lavishly endowed of all agricultural countries may have been placed at risk.

The natural rhythms based for thousands of years on the annual flooding of the river and the soil's renewal by the silt deposited by the floods have been disrupted by the dam. Artificial fertilisers, expensively produced, will be required as a substitute for the silt, but the perennial irrigation – which replaces the annual flooding, and drying off – has entailed problems of drainage which can only be solved by an expensive system of deep drains, which Egypt cannot afford. In the absence of drainage the build-up of salt carried in the river water will lead to a decline in the soil's fertility. It has recently been discovered that the loss of silt has accelerated the river's flow, eroding the banks and threatening to undermine the bridges.

The peasant shakes his head cannily, and the fisherman wrings his hands. This year the cauliflowers were smaller, and this year fewer fish are being taken. The fisherman blames his poor catches on a change in the water and claims, too, that many fish that once came down from the upper reaches of the river are now held back by the dam. He is probably right. What advanced technology provides with one hand, it may be taking back with the other.

It was remarkable to find the river at Cairo, rather more than

100 miles from the sea, not noticeably wider than it had been at Khartoum, 2,000 miles closer to its source. The dry season had laid bare a wide border of mud, and this had been invaded by colonists who had staked out gardens, while slime-covered figures down by the water's edge were filling buckets with precious mud, to be carried away.

In Cairo one was trapped in the noise, the convulsive despairing crowds, the entangled traffic of an urban population of nearly eight million imprisoned in a city designed to house a third of that number. Virtually nothing but luxury flats has been built since Nasser's reforms drove the speculators out of land into property. High-rise blocks, Centre Point-style, have gone up by the hundred, many of them left empty, although frequently changing hands at ever-increasing prices. A million of the homeless of Cairo now squat in its great cemetery where they share the tombs with the dead. The traffic follows no rules other than those of total war, and as the Islamic faith fosters a belief that one's destiny cannot be avoided, crashes are frequent and spectacular. Because most garages, lacking the space to house them, decline to recover crashed vehicles, they are normally shoved off the road and abandoned.

Egyptians tackle all their problems with ingenuity and resource. I saw a Volkswagen crushed absolutely flat used to plug a hole in the wall of a department store. Larger wrecks had been expanded by the use of hardboard, and taken over by homeless families. When fatal crashes happened, the bodies were sometimes, if space allowed, pushed under the car, reverently covered with flowering branches, and left for the arrival of the police – which might be long delayed.

Those who wish to escape the bustle and the clamour of the capital are recommended by an official guidebook to make a move, as soon as they have seen all the sights, to Helwan, 18 miles away on the banks of the Nile, described in *Tourist Information Egypt* as 'this city of sunshine, health and beauty . . . always noted for its marvellous dry climate, and for its mineral waters . . . one of the famous health resorts of the world'.

A leading article in the *Egyptian Gazette* dated 11 February 1981, brought the record up to date: 'Unauthorised property development is continuing unabated in Helwan. The value of government land appropriated by private property speculators there is estimated at £500,000. With impunity they bring in the bulldozers, level down whatever lies in their way, and arrange their bricks and mortar with such panache that unless you know, you would never guess that the whole operation was a flagrant breach of the law. With alacrity the more brazen among them put up fences and signs warning trespassers, and then sell off further tracts of land to a second generation of speculators.

'One individual who seized the hill situated by the continuation of Riyadh Street built an attractive villa at the top and planted an attractive garden. Water and electricity were laid on, rubble and rubbish were discreetly dumped on the other side of the hill. He then started selling off the rest of this well situated piece of land. He is now abroad, but assures everyone that he is now rich enough to buy and bribe his way through any legal proceedings that may be put in his path.'

The writer then went on to speak of the pall of smoke lying over the town, discharged by the string of factories that had been built along the river. I went there and was reminded of my experience of the eruption of Vesuvius back in the forties. People who had come to Helwan for the sake of their health were groping their way about with handkerchiefs held over their mouths, leaving their footprints in the grey fallout that covered the promenade and extinguished the flowers in the celebrated gardens. The view of the Nile might have been through a dirty curtain. The remedy, said the *Gazette*, was to compel factories to pay their corporation tax 'and to fit chimneys on the equipment which is polluting a district once famous for its balmy perfumes of jasmine, date and guava trees'. It seemed to doubt that much would be done about it.

Upmarket package tour operators switch their attention to Egypt in winter. The news was of all the hotels in Luxor and Aswan chock-a-block, of the Valley of the Kings glutted with multitudes, of fashion models being photographed on the knee of every god at Karnak, of *Son-et-Lumière* and of belly-dancing, barbecues and even sangria at Abu Simbel.

Minya, accepted as the capital of Middle Egypt, where there are antiquities enough to be visited, is no longer in fashion, and I went there, staying at the old Savoy. The hotel is full of sepia photographs and nostalgia, and possesses a new dining-room ceiling pierced with 830 illuminated holes, representing stars, which has so far not quite succeeded in drumming up new business. There was pigeon in saffron rice on the lunch menu, followed by a majestic sweet called 'eat it and thank God', but the peace of the surroundings was disturbed by an upper-class Egyptian woman who grumbled loudly at the absence of a buffet. A waiter quietened her with a mish-mash of the negatives pervading a language which insistently tempers deprivation with hope. *Ma'aindish* (I have none), *ma-fish* (It's off), *khallas* (finished), *bukra inshallah* (tomorrow, God willing).

No town by the water in the good old days was conceivable without its half-mile of promenade, and Minya had this to offer, although the parapet dividing it from the river was now used to dry washing, many of the garments on display being colourful in the extreme, some extraordinary. Across the water a vast cemetery extended for miles, with thousands of tombs, some dating back 4,000 years. I arrived at the moment when the males of a funeral party were about to embark for the further shore. Local custom excludes women from the final scene of the human drama, and they were left to screech and tear at their garments.

The Nile here, and in all the other towns forgotten by winter visitors, was the river of the Victorian painter in water-colours. There was nothing in the scene that would not have been witnessed 100 years ago; girls in garnet velvet robes carrying watercress on their heads, the low horizon of palms scythed by sharp, white felucca sails, a buffalo with a heron picking at its ear, fishing boats painted with holy tombs, trees of wisdom and crescent moons, a child playing on pan-pipes to advertise the huge eel he had for sale, curling like a python from his wrist. For those who crave peace it was here.

The pyramids start at El Faiyum. Few of these southern pyramids are visited by tourists, although they are remarkable enough, in particular the steep, white fortress shape of El Maidum. El Faiyum uses an ancient system to raise its water from the Nile and the town is full of the unearthly sound of water-wheels grinding on their wooden bearings, resembling only the underwater song of whales. The oasis contains a shallow lake, 25 miles in length, which entices wading birds to leave the safety of the river, and here they fall to cohorts of Italian sportsmen in ambush.

A party of thirty Romans – most of them fantastically uniformed for the sport – had just come in for their midday meal at the Panorama Hotel when I was there. The morning had been a good one. The Italians, having brought provisions including spaghetti, cheese and even spring onions from Rome, did not eat the birds they shot, but sold them to an Egyptian dealer, who killed any that were still alive before thrusting them into a sack. One of the sportsmen told me he had shot about 100 *anitre* that morning, but his ducks turned out to be sandpipers, avocets, phalaropes and ruffs – many of them of great rarity by our standards. He had bagged quite a few small birds such as wagtails, too, but these the dealer discarded contemptuously, flinging them into the water. The total bag for the morning weighed 70 kilos, totalling possibly 1,000 birds, and the group expected to shoot as many again when they went out in the early evening. It was the best place they knew of its kind anywhere in the world, but they thought it was too much to expect things to go on much longer like this. Three or four years, at most.

North of Cairo the Nile divides into two channels, one reaching the sea at Rashid, near Alexandria, and the other at Damietta, about 40 miles from Port Said. From these two main courses spreads the vast fan of the Delta, the greatest vegetable garden on earth, which is in its way a secret place, hardly visited by anyone without business there, ignored by the tourist.

The Delta is beautiful in all its parts. A soft light, sharpened with a little sand, billows over the fields and haloes the peasants at work with their buffaloes. The canals breed their own mists, and there are naked boys everywhere stalking moorhens with their nets, and delving for catfish in the mud. Ninety per cent of these children suffer from bilharzia.

For much of the estimated 40 million years of its life, the Nile has been depositing silt in the Delta. This jet-black, crumbling, crystalline, almost vivacious substance bears no resemblance whatever to the grudging soil tilled by the English gardener. It grows all the familiar vegetables in sizes that are so monstrous that a good Delta cabbage has to be picked up in both arms, and one can see a man bent under the burden of an enormous cauliflower carried on his shoulders. Methods of cultivation remain primitive in the extreme, but they are totally effective given a bottomless reservoir of cheap labour. I covered 500 miles of Delta roads without seeing a plough in action. The earth was being chopped and patterned everywhere, by peasants using the adze, which, say the landlords, is 'kinder on the soil'. Water is shifted daily by the thousand million gallons, from river to canal and canal to ditch, but there are 100 waterwheels turned by a donkey for every pump. These are supplemented by gangs of freelances who scamper from property to property shouldering the device known as the Archimedean screw, used to move small quantities of water. The severe time and motion principles of antiquity prevail here. No one in the Delta falls asleep, Mexican-style, with his hat over his face.

Arrangements are feudal, even by comparison with, say,

some of the less-developed rural areas of Latin America. Outside Damanhur, near Alexandria, a gang of men were waist-deep in stinking water, cleaning the sludge from a canal with their hands. They were working at great speed, urged on by two overseers on the bank above, and when one of the men began to show signs of fatigue, and began a blubbering protest, an overseer picked up a large stone, threw it, and hit him in the chest. The man began to scream, came charging up the bank, and grabbed up an adze in a threatening manner, but was soon overpowered. For his insubordination he was told that a quarter would be deducted from his day's wage, the equivalent of £1.60. 'If you want to eat, you must work,' the overseer said. He was quite happy to discuss this incident, and labour relations in general, with an utter stranger. Unemployment was very high, he said, and his firm were able to pick and choose when it came to employing labour. They would only use men prepared to drive themselves hard. When asked why dredging equipment was not used, he said the high cost of fuel made it uneconomic. For the price of a gallon of petrol a man would do more than the machine.

There was no shame, no concealment, about such transactions, no desire to avoid publicity. They were the facts of life in the Delta, recognised and accepted, likely to have drawn only a foreigner's attention and comment. The overseers were not psychopaths but ordinary men doing a regular, respectable, no less well thought-of job than, say, greasing cars. A half-hour later I saw a gang of young children, guarded by a man with a switch, who were engaged in clearing stubble from a field. The man was delighted to stop for a chat. He was benign-looking and genial. We wished each other peace and the mercies of God, shaking hands and touching our hearts. He told me that the youngest of the children was about eight, and they were paid the equivalent of 20p a day, starting work at 7 a.m. 'I love them all,' he said, lashing out playfully at a nearby slacker. He prided himself on knowing how to get the best out of children. 'Encourage them,' he said. 'Kid them along, praise them when they do well.' He held up the switch and shook his head disapprovingly. 'I really hate to have to tickle their hides.'

The Delta population doubles every few years. Everyone has heard of the Pill, but despite the urgings of President Sadat's wife it is rejected by the very poor. Children here, just as in the slums of Naples, are a source of income, and as they undercut the price of adult labour they can find employment however short work may be. The driver lost his way in the labyrinth of mean streets of Mahalla el Kubra, and we were instantly adopted and taken into the confidence of an assortment of males sucking at their hookahs outside a café. One of our new friends provided facts and figures. He himself, he said, seemed to spend most of his life out of work, but his two daughters in their late teens had jobs in the brickyards of El Rashid, where they were paid £1 each a day. Three of the younger children, ranging from 5 to 12, did odd jobs in the rope factory. Nothing too strenuous, he said, and it kept them out of mischief, and brought in another 80p. His wife's contribution raised the family income to a level which at least filled all their stomachs. She did the daily shopping for a rich woman, who was so fat, he said, that she could not stand up, only kneel, and even then she had to be supported.

Fat women in these small Nile-side towns were everywhere to be seen, and a man had just come into sight manoeuvring his enormous wife, like a piece of stately furniture, into a position where she could be propped against a wall across the road and left. He came over and introduced himself in English as a high-pressure welder, producing a sheaf of testimonials given him by companies he had worked for in Britain and West Germany. His wife had been joined by several elephantine friends, dressed like Madonnas of the Florentine school in black biblical robes. They wore patent-leather shoes with gold buckles, and small girls in attendance, squatting as necessary to wipe flecks of mud from their sparkling footwear, completed the feudal picture.

It was a scene without appeal for the welder, on a month's

leave from Hamburg. The hookah, pulled from a neighbouring mouth, was thrust between my teeth, while he plied me
with all the questions indispensable to the protocol of such
meetings, and exposed the secrets of his own unsatisfactory
life in Mahalla. 'What is your affliction [work], sir? Don't talk
about daughters, but how many sons have you? How is King
George? I love Miss England. The ignorant woman over there
is my wife. She eats every day one kilo of nuts, and on Friday
four pigeons.'

At El Rashid – once Rosetta, where they dug up the famous
stone by which ancient Egyptian hieroglyphics were de-
ciphered – the mouth of the river was finally reached. Cold
Mediterranean rain was spattering on the yellow water and in
the muddy streets, but it did nothing to damp down the
animation of an intensely oriental setting. Perhaps there is
something in the story that the Gypsies passed through Egypt
on their way to Europe, for the streets were full of objects,
carts, barrows, market-stalls, even the occasional wraith of an
American car, painted in exuberant Gypsy style, largely with
rambling roses. El Rashid gathered the harvests both of the sea
and the land, a bustling, prosperous place where business and
pleasure had reached a civilised agreement. A fleet of taxis
(half-fare travelling on the luggage rack, a quarter in the boot)
brought buyers and sellers from all the villages, and they went
about embracing each other and roaring with laughter.

The deals done, a man could seat himself in one of a row of
golden thrones for his shoes to be polished, while dictating a
letter to a scribe, nibbling at a calf's foot from a charcoal
brazier, or perhaps having his blood-pressure taken by a
doctor who operated from a 1938 Studebaker, with a blow-up
of an electro-cardiograph plastered by way of advertisement
over his back window. Camels were debarred from the town's
centre, but while I was there, one had managed to sneak
through and pass down the main street, and was cropping
geraniums.

In the background the Nile moved in its last sluggish curve to the sea. Its great rival, the Amazon, is 150 miles across at its mouth, containing the Island of Marajó, roughly the size of Belgium. One could sit in a golden, plush-bottomed throne in the muddy square of El Rashid and look across the waters to the Nile's further bank, which might have been 200 yards away. There were five months to go to the end of the dry season, by which time not a drop of the waters gathered in Ethiopia or the mountains of Equatorial Africa would reach the sea. A little would have been wasted, but the rest would have been taken up by a million gardens, their boundaries touching each other for nearly 4,000 miles. A river of life indeed.

AMONG
THE BULLS

'WHEN THE HORN went in I felt absolutely no pain,' Tomás Campuzano said. 'I suspected this animal of defective vision from the first, but failed to take proper precautions. It was like being hit by an express train. I was airborne, somer-saulted and landed face down, shocked and acutely surprised. I rolled over, saw one of the boys take the bull away with the cape, and the blood fountaining out. Still no pain. They shot me up with morphine in the sick-bay and then took me to Zaragoza hospital, where I spent a month.' Tomás showed me the tremendous scar left by this close encounter with death, scrawled like an undecipherable signature up the inside of the thigh from knee to stomach. He joked continually. 'If you are going to suffer a *cornada*, then Zaragoza is a good place. They have the best horn-wound surgeons in the country.'

Among the toreros of Spain, Tomás Campuzano is accepted as the most ready to tackle 'difficult' bulls, the euphemism for those with exceptionally large horns or suspected by the experts who look them over before the fight of potential unpredictability in action. For this reason there are few who have received more horn-thrusts (five to date) from the terrible Andalusian bulls with which, as a fully fledged matador, he is so often called upon to match himself. He takes part in up to fifty fights in a season. Last year was outstandingly successful. A torero who has given an impressive display with a bull may be awarded as trophies one ear, both ears – or, in exceptional cases, even the tail of the vanquished animal. In the 1986 season, despite a wound that nearly dislocated his sword arm, Campuzano collected a grand total of eighty-six ears and eight tails for a series of uniformly brilliant performances.

He started informal training at the age of seven at whatever bull-farm could be persuaded to allow him to practise his cape-passes with a calf, and appeared as a professional in the ring at the legal minimum age of 17. Now aged 30, and earning about £7,500 per fight, he has reached the height of his career, a modest, friendly man who smiles a great deal, and has remained unspoiled by success.

Tomás was born in Gerena, about 10 miles from Seville. It is the archetypal Andalusian hilltop village, put together from stark, white, geometrical shapes, raised above a prairie of pale wheatfields, patched here and there with great brassy spreads of sunflowers. In Gerena the narrow streets are calm and immaculate. Dignity of appearance and personal style is much cultivated. Men walk slowly, held erect, and few women are to be seen. It is a spare, silent place, a last refuge of the Spain of the past. Almost the whole of the hill's summit is occupied by the low-lying, blind-walled palace of José Luis García de Samanieco, the Marqués of Albacerrado, who owns all that is visible from his rooftop of the almost Siberian landscape of this region of Andalusia, as well as one of the great *ganaderías* of fighting bulls.

Tomás, whose father was once a shepherd on the estate, has moved down with his family to take over one of the large new houses at the bottom of the village. It is a place to which he returns continually between fights, and where he is a living legend, a poor boy who has shot to the top of what in rural Andalusia still remains the most glamorous, and the most honourable of professions.

The new Campuzano house is an extended and softened version of the seventeenth-century peasant dwellings that present austere profiles to the village from the top of the hill. A big sitting-room holds modern furniture of the best quality, gathered under a vast chandelier, but with the retreat from simplicity there has been a loss of strength. Otherwise custom prevails. When I visited, the voices of women and children could be heard faintly beyond the ornate doors, but only men with a certain solidity were present: Tomás's father, still moving as if in control of sheep; an exceedingly genial brother who manages Tomás's affairs; a couple of old sun-cured uncles leaning upon their sticks. The mother flustered in with coffee on a tray, flashed a nervous half-smile and withdrew. Tomás's wife – clearly, from her photograph, a beauty of the highest order – did not appear.

This, in some way almost oriental, gathering was dominated by the huge mounted heads of two of Tomás's most difficult and memorable bulls, whose challenging eyes it seemed hard to avoid. Tomás said that they were masterpieces of the taxidermist's art, and that the facial expression – different in every bull as in every man – had been most successfully preserved. He invited me to join him on the landing half-way up the staircase, at a point where the most fearsome-looking of these animals, Abanico by name, could be viewed from precisely the angle at which Tomás had been exposed to its stare six years before in the ring at Málaga. 'I'm off to Madrid on Monday,' Tomás said, 'and whenever I go on a trip I stand here and look into this brute's eyes, and tell myself, at least they can't throw anything at me worse than this one.'

At this point the subject of fear came up. It seemed a doubtful one to raise with a man generally accepted as among the most courageous of all toreros, but he cut across my attempts at tact. 'Was fear something you could come to terms with?' I asked. 'No,' he said, 'never.' The fact was that it got worse and worse, strengthening with each increase of a man's responsibilities. From the day he got married the fear increased, and now that his wife was expecting a child, it was closer again and more insistent. In summer, he said, when he could be fighting twice a week, a bullfighter's family was constantly overshadowed by fear. While the fight was on no telephone calls to the house could be made by friends – to keep the line clear for any emergency – and only close relatives were invited into the home, to maintain what amounted to a silent vigil. They were exceedingly devout, and crucifixes and rosaries hung everywhere about the home. Another minor bullfighter who had drifted in said, 'We take our troubles to the Virgin of Macarena. She's a Sevillian – almost a member of the family you might say. Imagine two fights in two days. Naturally you're praying half the time.'

The estate house of the Albacerrada bull-breeding farm is two miles up a country road from Gerena; a clean-cut example of purest Andalusian architecture. Decoration is outlawed, the atmospheric quality of these surroundings depending upon white, crystalline façades and the blue mossy shade of cactus and eucalyptus. Adjacent is a small, high-walled ring in which the cows from which the bulls are bred are subjected to a series of tests, known collectively as the *tentadero*. *Tentaderos* take place at frequent intervals during the summer months and have come to be treated as a social event, inevitably watched at Albacerrada by the Marqués and a few of his intimates. It is explained that the number of those present on such occasions is kept to a minimum to avoid distracting the animals under test.

When I arrived the testing was already under way. I looked down from the rim of the small arena at a rider on a padded horse, steel-tipped pole in hand, waiting on the far side of the ring for the entrance of a cow under test. The Marqués had just expounded the bull-breeder's theory that taurine courage is transmitted through the female of the species, and that the male only adds strength. For this reason, only two-year-old cows are subjected to serious testing, and they are certainly no less fierce than the bulls.

The wall of the ring was painted a most profound and refulgent yellow, with the overhead sunshine rippling and showering down its uneven surface. The wall colour was intensified by that of the sand, and there was a yellow reflection in the faces of the onlookers. After a while the unearthly quality of the light seemed even to effect the mood, endowing this scene with a feeling of separateness from the surrounding world. A religious hush had fallen; the spectators were motionless and silent. An element of ritual was discernible here, a flashback perhaps to Celto-Iberian days and sacrificial bulls.

A small black cow came tearing out into the ring, slid to a standstill and swung its head from side to side in search of an adversary. It was big-horned, narrow of rump, all bone and muscle; faster in the take-off than a bull, quicker on the turn and with sharper horns. 'Ugly customer,' a herdsman whispered approvingly in my ear. The horseman thwacking the padding of his horse with the pole, called to the cow and it charged, crossing the ring at extreme speed, head down, horns thrust forward in the last few yards, thumped into the quilting over the horse's flanks and threw it against the wall.

Time and again, it skewered up ineffectively with its horns while the horseman, prodding and shoving down with the shallow, testing *pic*, scored the hide over its shoulders. Failing to get through the padding it trotted off, then turned back for a second charge. The watching herdsman noted points in their books under four headings: courage, speed, reflexes, staying power; and communicated what might have been approval or disdain with inscrutable signs.

It was this performance with the horse and the cow's indifference or otherwise to the prickings of the *pic* that sealed its fate; but when the serious business was at an end, fun for all followed with the cape. Tomás Campuzano had arrived to help the local boys add polish to their technique, conducting a series of passes with a mathematical exactitude that seemed sometimes to border on indifference. The onlookers smiled dreamily. Those that followed the master seemed agitated by comparison and a young Venezuelan bullfighter who had come along appeared a little out of his depth with a beast of this kind, or perhaps the cow was learning quickly from its mistakes.

Surely, I asked myself, the keen-eyed selectors could ask for nothing better than this animal with its limitless vigour and thirst for aggression? But the experts detected weaknesses overlooked by the outsider, for rejection followed the completion of its trial. And so in the course of the morning six aspirant cows came and went. It was a spectacle providing its own special brand of addiction, preferred by many enthusiasts to the commercial bullfight itself. Spain's leading painter of bullfighter posters, present on this occasion, later admitted that he never missed a *tentadero* if he could help it. Both he and Don José Luis, although a little stiffened by middle age, gave brief but confident displays with the cape and came off intact, although the Marqués's boxer dog (always addressed in English) broke into the ritual calm with yelps of hysterical anguish at the sight of its master exposing himself to such danger. Of six cows, four rejects were subjected to the ignominy of having a few inches lopped from the end of their tails after the test. In this way they were marked for the slaughter-house. The two accepted, to be kept for breeding, had the dangerous ends of their horns removed. Both operations – the second performed bloodily with a saw – were carried out forthwith and in view of the onlookers.

From the ring we moved back to the estate house for a snack served in the yard. This took traditional form: thick, solid potato omelettes cut into cubes to be eaten with the fingers, slivers of hard farm cheese, white wine of the last year's vintage (still a little murky) from the estate vineyard, which, spurred on by Don José Luis's assurance that it contained only five degrees of alcohol, guests downed like water. The informality of such occasions is much appreciated in Andalusia – and referred to approvingly as *simple*. To this slightly feudal environment Tomás Campuzano had been admitted as an admired friend. Part of the reward of a famous bullfighter is an escape into the Nirvana of classlessness.

The bulls inhabit an untidy savannah of old olives, thorn and coarse grass entered a few hundred yards from the estate house. There are upwards of 600 of them kept in two separate herds, the four-year-old *novillos* and the five-year-old bulls in the full vigour of life. Throughout the summer months their numbers dwindle steadily as the bulls are sent off, six at a time, to fight in the big city rings where the management can afford to pay for the best. For a *corrida* of six four-year-olds, the Marqués expects to be paid three million pesetas; for the five-year-olds the price is four million. He loses money on the bulls, he complains, but keeps afloat on the slight profit the estate makes from sunflower oil, wheat and olives.

All guests are taken as a matter of course to inspect the herds. They ride in a trailer drawn by a tractor from which fodder is distributed in times of dearth, and which is therefore acceptable to the bulls. The trailer has high steel sides and is heavy enough not to be turned over by a charge. The tractor's engine is always kept running because the bulls have learned to associate its sound with food. Still, the excursion is not quite in the same bracket as a trip through a safari park because a fighting bull is more aggressive than anything encountered in the wild, and if annoyed is liable instantly and unforeseeably to charge the offending object, whether animate or otherwise. A Spanish treatise on the subject of bulls speaks of the bull's docility on the ranch. 'It is more than likely', it says, 'that the vast majority of fighting bulls would allow themselves to be stroked. To attempt this one must put away the almost insuperable fear that their presence and proximity inspires.' None of those present on this occasion seemed inclined to put the author's theory to the test.

Chugging behind the tractor into the bull pastures was accepted as a minor adventure. The bulls stood, heads lowered, a few yards away, to watch our approach with steadfast, myopic eyes. Their relative invulnerability has relieved them of the necessity to develop acute vision, but their hearing is exceptionally acute. Thus we probably appeared no more than a vague, invasive shape, but lulled by the soft clatter of the diesel and its promise of mash, they did nothing about it. It rains hardly at all in summer, and the bulls spend the day in ceaseless foraging for pasture, moving always very slowly and with great, ponderous dignity. The animals in each herd settle quickly to mutual tolerations, undoubtedly realising that an inbred policy of no-surrender means the death of one of the disputants of any quarrel that is allowed to arise. They learn quickly. When Don José Luis's boxer decided to try his luck with a five-year-old, the animal soon realised that the dog was too fast to be caught by the horns, so, adopting an invitingly passive stance, he lured the boxer within easy reach and removed several of its teeth with a kick.

Under the protection of the tractor and its soothing noises no scene could have been more arcadian and nothing more appropriate to this Andalusian setting than the bulls, viewed either in majestic silhouette against the green-grey wash of olives or as they wandered ruminatively, deep in the strong tide of sunflowers that had burst through the fences of their enclosure.

'Whatever the financial loss, the bulls are my life,' the Marqués said, having taken us at the end of our visit to the palace for an inspection of his most treasured possessions. Once again I found myself confronted with mounted heads. These were of two Albacerrada bulls 'pardoned' following extreme bravery shown in the ring; one in Madrid in 1919; the other in Seville in 1965 – an historically unique event. Despite some reluctance on the part of the traditionally minded authorities of the Maestranza (as the ring at Seville is known), they were obliged by the insistent demands of the crowd to break their rule. And so the Marqués's bull *Laborioso* (hardworker) was returned, appropriately fêted and garlanded to the herd. It had taken seven thrusts of the *pic*, and had overturned seven horses, three of which had to be replaced. Its wounds were healed through massive injections of penicillin, and it lived on until 1976.

Bullfighting, practised in one form or another since Celto-Iberian times, not only in towns but in innumerable villages throughout Spain, began to fall into decline in the post-war period. Spanish attitudes were much changed by the tourist influx. New rings were opened in many northern areas where bullfighting was previously unknown, but the uninstructed demand of a ninety per cent foreign audience was for pure spectacle. Bullfighting taken straight was seen as tedious so bullfoonery was often added with the provision of clowns and dwarves in bullfighting gear who threw custard pies in each others' faces, or the procedure might be livened up by performing dogs. Since the foreigners hardly knew one bull from another it was an opportunity for disreputable breeders to supply sub-standard animals at cut prices, and there were cases of low quality, underpaid bullfighters refusing to tackle bulls without artificially shortened horns. This was the period when ambitious but inexperienced youngsters (known as *capitalistas*) were paid small sums to invade the ring and join the fight, sometimes with tragic results. Bullfighting began to suffer from the competition of football, and promising village boys aspired to become pop-stars rather than matadors.

Rock-bottom may have been reached in 1981 when the concluding corrida of the Seville season had to be put forward a day because it coincided with a home match by Seville FC, the promoters realising that otherwise the ring would have been empty. Of this melancholy occasion a leading newspaper critic wrote: 'Thus the present decadent season draws to its end. It has offered little but boredom for the public, and bad business for the promoters, with half the seats unsold.' The bulls, said the critic, had been uniformly atrocious: small, lame, numbed-looking, and inclined to totter about like calves on shaky legs. The sad and insipid bullfighters spread boredom like a disease. 'When they trundled on the sixth bull, I said to my colleague,

"Perhaps I'll take a nap. Wake me up if anything happens." He didn't because he, too, fell asleep.'

From this disastrous year, there was a steady recovery. The commercial backers had come to understand that it was a matter either of drastic reform or, for them, the end of the road. They paid more for their bulls, and for their bullfighters; got rid of the clowns, suppressed the circus antics of such as El Cordobés, and his imitators and then attracted a new generation of matadors. As a result, 1985 was adjudged 'brilliant' and 1986 'excellent'. As part of this renaissance, a bullfighting school opened near Seville in January 1987 with 16 young pupils ranging from 9 to 16 years of age. The event was sufficiently important for it to be attended by the representative of the Ministry of Culture responsible for what is officially entitled 'the taurine art', who spoke enthusiastically of the performance of the children in their encounter with bull-calves of appropriate size.

Alcalá de Guadaïra, site of the bullfighting school for promising boys, is a small, white pyramid of houses dominated by a vast Moorish fortress defending the old approach to Seville. Otherwise it is notable for mining the high-grade sand, supplied to bull-rings which can pay the steep price for it, and for the richly chromatic earth that provides the yellow paint for Seville's baroque buildings, and for the interior of the Marqués de Albacerrada's miniature amphitheatre. This place suggests the persistence of an ancient half-submerged bull-cult, for once again the mounted heads are everywhere, and every tavern and bar is glutted with fight-posters, photographs and prints. Within hours of arriving in Alacalá I received an invitation from an olive-growers' association: 'We're having a bit of a fiesta up at the inn this evening. Just a few friends. No more than a glass of wine and a sandwich. We'll probably kill a bull.'

The school is in the honeycombed building next to the ring itself; a single dim room cluttered with scholastic objects, exercise books, desks, a blackboard, plus piles of harness, plastic matador's swords, and a miscellany of horns. The largest of these is fixed to the front of a formidable contraption like a handcart on bicycle wheels used for chasing would-be *banderilleros*. Special respect, and possibly some magic virtue, attaches to these particular horns, as they were removed from a bull killed in a fight with another bull.

Students receive instruction for two hours a day on three days a week, about a third of this time being devoted to ring tactics and the rest to practice in the ring. Funds have been allocated to the school by the Ministry, but, through 'delays in legalisation', these have not yet arrived. Since it cost the equivalent of £75 to hire a second-class fighting cow for two hours (a first-class cow costs twice this sum), there is little practice with animals, and a great deal of make-believe in which masters, horns in hand, pursue their pupils all over the empty ring.

Joselito Ballesteros, aged 9 but looking hardly older than 7, gave an impressive demonstration with the cape, shaking it in a taunting fashion, and making defiant bullfighter noises at his father, one of the teachers. The father, shoulder hunched, head down and horns thrust forward, scraped with one foot in the sand in the manner of a bull who is about to attack. In due course he was despatched as Joselito lunged forward with his imaginary sword, an *estocada* loudly applauded by the bystanders. In another part of the ring the mature student of 16 skipped aside to avoid the charge of an instructor manipulating the simulated bull on wheels, raising himself on tip-toe to plunge the pair of *banderillas* into a padded leather surface where the neck muscles would have been.

'In this profession, as in others,' Ballesteros the father said, 'everything depends on an early start. Joselito started training at 5. At the moment he can hardly see over an animal's back, but he could be giving private performances by the time he's 14. He can't be accepted as a professional for four more years after that.' Ballesteros described the principles inculcated by the school. 'The art of the ring is wrapped up with moral attitudes,' he said. 'We keep a close check on their behaviour in the day school as well as in the home. We are engaged in the development of artists and believe that art is inseparable from life.'

'How many children like this can expect to become great bullfighters?' I asked.

'Five per cent.'

'And how many will die in the ring?'

The question startled him, and his face crumpled.

'When they're properly trained, as these boys will be, there's nothing to worry about. It's the old-timers trying for a comeback, and the kids that will do anything to get a start. The bulls cut them down, but they don't make the papers. How many of them go that way? There's no knowing.'

He seemed depressed at the turn our talk had taken. Perhaps it was something he wanted to put out of his mind. The boys were dancing round us with their capes, striking attitudes of defiance, sizing up phantom bulls, coming close to the imaginary horns. Now the master's attention was taken up, a little horseplay had been brought in.

'Above all we teach our boys to master fear,' Ballesteros said. 'That's the most important thing of all.' Almost plaintively he added: 'You see, the horns are very sharp. It's bad for them if they get scared.'

The more I saw of these Spaniards of the deep south the more it became clear to me that it was a misapprehension to believe that their feeling for bulls was anything less than an almost obsessional admiration and respect. Near Alcalá a handful of olive-growers had clubbed together to pay an enormous price for a bull to be killed at their annual fiesta. Whatever their excuse, this could not have been anything but a sacrifice to ensure a good harvest, and understandably, only the most splendid of animals could be offered to the gods. Noble is the adjective never out of Spanish mouths when they speak of the bulls, to whom they frequently attribute such human qualities as candour and sincerity. This is F. Martinez Torres, himself a bullfighter, on the subject of courage: 'The bull is the only animal in creation that is not daunted by any wounds he receives. He does not possess the treacherous or bloodthirsty instinct of other animals that crouch unseen and spring on their prey from behind. He attacks nobly from the front. Face to face, there is no animal that can beat him.'

This is only part of the story, for the bull is capable of enduring friendship, and never forgets a face – or a voice. 'There have been some bulls,' Torres tells us, 'which during the fighting, on being called by the herdsman they knew, have broken off the fight and trotted meekly over to the place where their former custodian stood, allowing him to stroke them from inside the fence, or at times in the arena itself. When he has finished doing this, they have returned to fight with the same fierceness as before.'

The hard-bitten professionals of the Spanish press, bull-lovers to a man, are saturated with the pathetic fallacy. Here is a passage from Antonio Lorca's account in *El Correo* of a *novillada* for young bulls in Seville at the time of my visit. Lorca cannot stomach vulgarity and believes that the bulls feel the same. 'Such a bull as this demanded at least a token authority to direct its noble charge. A real fighter would have provided inspiration and, faced with a tasteless fidgeter, it showed indifference, even impatience.'

Manuel Rodriguez of ABC, also covering this event, noted that the fourth (inevitably 'noble') bull gave the matador Fernando Lozano two warnings of the danger he placed himself in through misuse of the cape. Rodriguez too, abhorred vulgarity, 'Elsewhere they might have thrown cushions. Here in Seville we correct such lapses with an icy silence.'

Back to Lorca. 'Four bulls received huge applause from the crowd as they were dragged from the ring. As for the fighters, it was a mediocre harvest of a single ear. Again I ask myself the question, is a bullfighter born, or made? From what we saw yesterday I can only conclude that he is born. Nevertheless, it is his duty to himself and to us to continue to grow. Shame it was to see great bulls thrown away in this fashion.'

A SMART CAR
IN HAITI

Wₕₑₙ ₁ ꜰɪᴙꜱᴛ went to Haiti there were 6,000 generals in its army out of a total force of 20,000, and now one of the survivors of this legion of high-ranking officers sat at the bar of the modest but charming Hotel Meurice, watching the world through a whisky glass he rotated in such a way that its cut facets projected golden spearpoints of reflection on the ceiling and walls. The general was rubicund and genial, very black, as most army officers were, but with a bronze burnishing of the cheekbones of the kind that in Haiti advertised the good life. He was at the hotel to deliver a fresh supply of Papa Doc Duvalier's 'gold' postage stamps, commemorating the fifth anniversary of Papa Doc's assumption of the title of President for Life. Mr Johnson, the owner, was required to top up his stock, and also display a stamp on a newly designed showcard on his reception desk. He was expected to persuade at least 50 per cent of his guests to buy a stamp, costing the equivalent of £8. The general asked me if I had made my purchase, and I excused myself saying that I had only checked in that morning. 'Be advised by me,' he said. 'Acquire all you can. This is philatelic rarity that will soon double or treble in value, and you are getting in at the bottom of the market.' He gave me a beautifully engraved card. *Vincent Deshayes. Général de L'Armée.* 'You are a friend,' he said. 'Come to me privately if you desire to make a substantial purchase at a good discount. You will make a killing.' He drained his glass, patted me on the shoulder, picked up his swagger stick, and sallied forth into the impeccable Haitian day.

Mr Johnson watched him go, hatred and gloom expressed in what could be seen of his face, which was largely swathed in bandages. He was just out of hospital where he had been detained for a week after an encounter with one of the general's subordinates who had beaten the living daylights out of him. The captain had side-swiped Johnson's car in passing in his Jeep, and Johnson's fatal mistake had been to sound his horn in protest. The captain pulled up and sauntered across.

'What's your name?' he asked in French.

'Johnson. I run the Grand Hotel Meurice.'

'Someone's screwing your wife.'

'I hardly think that,' Johnson said.

The captain raised the baton he was carrying. 'Say, "Someone's screwing my wife."'

'Someone's screwing my wife,' Johnson agreed.

The officer then struck him a number of blows about the body and head, flattening his nose and breaking an eardrum and several ribs. The beating, Johnson said, was bad, and the hospital if anything worse. Luckily he was not in need of medicine because there was nothing but aspirins. Food had to be brought in, and his wife, called in to look after him, slept on the floor beside his bed. 'That's it so far as I'm concerned. I'm calling it a day,' he said. But I knew him too well, and I knew that next year if I came back he would still be there, a prisoner for life of the charm of this strange and beautiful island.

Even the beating and the hospital had not been the end of Johnson's troubles. Haiti depended for survival on US aid, most of which went to foot the bill for the salaries of fictitious generals and the military equipment they were supposed to require, leaving little over to be spent on essential services. At this moment Haiti was suffering from its worst water shortage in history. Newspapers reported that women were rising at two in the morning to walk to the mountains to carry home their water supply for the day. In Port-au-Prince robbers raided hotel swimming pools, and while Johnson had lain groaning on his bed of pain a well-organised gang, having first drugged his dog with bread soaked in rum, had syphoned away 30,000 irreplaceable gallons.

Two days after my arrival the marauders were back. Johnson rushed up literally tearing at what could be reached between the bandages of his hair to say that once again they had knocked his dog out with overproof rum, and cut down and gone off with the finest of his specimen trees. This had been planted by the rich creole who had owned the place and who collected arboreal rarities. I remembered it as having a thick glossy trunk with many wart-like protruberances, and flowers that attracted clouds of sombre moths. The thieves had carried it away, Johnson said, to convert into charcoal, second only in value in the absence of all other combustible material, to food itself – which in any case Haitians were slowly learning to do without.

We looked down from the veranda into the swimming pool where a small snake was twisting desperately in the 18 inches of curdled water in its bottom, and then, a little to one side, at the naked stump where Johnson's tree had once spread its opulent shade. Johnson's single visible eye glistened in the opening of the bandages. 'I have to get away for a time and simmer down,' he said. The number of misinformed tourists attracted to Haiti in these days made it hardly worth keeping the hotel open; in any case his French wife who enjoyed *les affaires* could easily manage. Besides this he had a project in mind. 'I've lived here 20 years,' he said, 'and the time's come to put a few thoughts on paper.' Someone had just discovered a pocket of black men who spoke Polish. They proved to be descendants of the defeated legion of General le Clerc – Bonaparte's brother-in-law, living as charcoal burners on a mountain-top in the Departement du Nord. It sounded like promising material for his book, and when he suggested that we might run up there together, I immediately agreed.

Johnson's pride and joy was his Facel-Vega, an ostentatious and over-elaborate French car of which only a few hundred had been made to special order. It was studded with the gadgetry of its day, little of which continued to work after exposure to the primaeval servicing arrangements provided in Haiti. The lights did not switch on, the power-steering had failed, and the electrically operated windows on which the air-conditioning depended had suddenly fallen and could not be raised. The worst trouble with the car was that the mere sight of it was offensive to the police and the miscellaneous thugs supported by those in power, who believed that only they should ride in comfort. It was inevitable that any squad car or collection of motorised tontons-macoutes noticing the Facel-Vega parked in the street should do what they could to scrape a fender as they passed. This, Johnson said, would be the first opportunity he had had to get out on the open road and put the car through its paces.

The next day, a Sunday, we set out in hope, although over-shadowed by the news that the road to Cap Haitien on the north coast, where we had hoped to stay, had become inpracticable for all but a jeep. The general opinion was that we might get two-thirds of the way, but we had been driving for less than an hour and had only just passed St Marc, 35 miles from Port-au-Prince, when the road ahead disappeared among what looked like bomb-craters, and we turned back. 'Looks as though we shan't be seeing the Poles,' Johnson said, and I agreed, suddenly realising that all the bare and bitter landscape of northern Haiti studded nevertheless with so many delect-able, wildly coloured and ramshackle little towns such as Marmelade, Limonade, Petit Paradis, Limbo, Phaëton, Plaisance and Ditty, some of which I had seen, and some not, had passed for ever beyond my reach.

But at least St Marc was left to us, on the frontiers of the lost world, wearing its coat of many colours. Long-limbed, bare-foot girls in white dresses and wide Edwardian hats roamed the streets which were painted with all the colours of yesteryear: greens to rest the eyes after the hot plain, saffron, cerulean, ultramarine, and reds in all stages of reduction by the sun to a final nostalgic sepia. The girls floated towards us as if moved by a slack tide. At the far end of the street a number of tiny Lowry figures were tugging on a rope to pull a gingerbread house upright. A man drifted past caressing the head of a fighting cock shorn of comb and wattle, carried under his arm. The street was scattered with scampering black pigs, and somewhere behind a ruined clapboard façade a piano tinkled out a hymn.

REJOICE! said the single word over the door of the bar. We went in and were instantly, and without ordering, served by a negro of huge solemnity with a fried banana apiece, upon which he ladled a dollop of shrimps. With this went blue tumblerfuls of the pale and ensnaring Haitian rum. The girls lined up in the doorway and followed our every movement with their splendid but melancholic eyes. One used her muslin scarf to polish a small area of the Facel-Vega's wing, then smiled shyly at her reflection. Swept along by the rum, Johnson began rummaging in his stock of folklore and myth. 'One of these days you may turn up out of the blue and find all our rooms taken,' he said. 'Should this ever happen let me warn you not to go to a boarding house run by a nubile woman. They have this habit of falling in love with any white man and putting menstrual fluid in his food. It works, and you'd find yourself in quite a predicament.'

In Haiti you were expected to believe anything, and no story of werewolves or enchanters was too fantastic to be true. Foreign residents like Johnson, who had done a long stint on the island, were more credulous than the natives themselves. There was something about the fey and dispirited postures of the girls at the door that prompted a question. 'Have you ever seen a zombie?'

'On more than one occasion,' Johnson said, as I knew he would. 'They are characterised by an appearance of extreme lethargy, as well as their way of speaking through the nose.'

'Any chance of my ever seeing one?'

'That would largely depend upon you. Ask yourself, have you an open mind? A professional sceptic is a man in blinkers. If we had the time I could show you extraordinary things, as for example a *mapu* tree that is the home of a spirit. You are bound to laugh but it is a phenomenon scientists are in two minds about. Do you remember the celebrated Ti Bossa?'

'I've heard of him.'

'This was the voodoo priest who put President Magloire in power. As you know, he had forty wives and could render a man invisible purely by pouring a small amount of a certain white powder over him.

'Didn't Magloire give him a Cadillac?'

'The island's first. It's still up there in the mountains. His people built a temple round it and they still sacrifice a white cock to it every Saturday.'

'Now that's something we should see,' I said.

A narrow lane led down to the sea, and a boat painted with a cabalistic design, its bottom stove in, sat in its shadow on the beach. There were hardly any small boats left on the island now, and three ebony-black fishermen were just about to launch a raft to fish for sharks. Slow, rakish tropic birds joined wing-tips with their reflection in the cobalt sea. A boy sat cutting mother-of-pearl to make brooches from a pile of helmet shells. He came up with a sample of his work in the hope of a commission. A brooch carved and polished with a routine Dahomey head could be finished in the day and would cost one gourde. There were seven gourdes to the dollar. '*Pas cher*,' he said.

Johnson suggested we might as well go back to Port-au-Prince, then take the so-called international highway up through the mountains to Belladere. We had both come to the conclusion that if we wanted to see anything of the fast-vanishing countryside of Haiti, it was now or never. The map promised us 40 miles of tarmac, but at Poste de Flande, roughly half-way, the international highway seemed about to give up the ghost.

For months not a drop of water had fallen from the skies of Port-au-Prince, but here the rain fell in sudden opaque showers between intervals of brilliant sunshine. We groped our way cautiously through streams and round landslides. Sometimes road and river-bed would be united for a hundred yards and large, greyish kingfishers went hurtling past on both sides of the car, and we could see little fish darting away from the front wheels. All the trees had been cut down and when the sun came out the tall, ragged poinsettias on the eroded hillsides made the day seem hotter. In rural Haiti only one couple in ten can afford to get married in church, but those who still do clothe the ceremony in dignity and panache. A bride on her way to her wedding who went splashing past on horseback in a great muslin foaming of veils and skirts was preceded by a dozen capering drummers. The name of this village was 'Peu de Chose', which in a way described it well.

The small town that followed was a piece of nineteenth-century Normandy recreated in the tropics. A clapboard version of a French church wore its spire askew like a comic hat. It was supported by a mairie, a closed-down École de Jeunes Filles, a pigmy château patched with corrugated iron, and a magnificent Parisian pissoir enobled by its positioning at the top of a flight of wide steps. A herd of dwarf cows occupied the square, where they browsed of the fallen blossoms of the flame trees. We stopped to watch the approach of a ghostly black version of a French grandee with white Napoleon beard, cutaway coat, panama hat, spats and malacca cane. A girl had set up a stall near by, and sat smoking a cob pipe, her skirts pulled halfway up her black thighs. She sold single and half-cigarettes, olive oil by the spoonful and dried fishes' tails at one cent apiece, and cuffed away sparrows that alighted for a quick peck at the fish. The 2,500 generals had been treated well by their backers, but these were the poorest people in the Americas.

We went into the empty Café du Centre which was fitted with booths to which strips of buttoned leather upholstery still adhered. There was a faint reek about the place of coffee and Gauloise cigarettes which I accepted as an illusion since these things were no longer to be found in such a place. Through the window we watched the Sunday afternoon formal promenade of dignified black men in winged collars and their wives who wore hats tied in place with motoring veils.

'This', said Johnson, 'is a copy of France as it once was. You won't hear Creole spoken here. These people actually believe themselves to be French. Take that old man with the white beard we just saw. I know him. He has papers to prove he's a descendant of the Duc de Brantôme. There's another family here that goes back to Lamartine. Forget about Papa Doc Duvalier. This is the real Haiti. This is the heart and soul of the island.'

A small boy had brought our rum, but now I saw a woman I took to be the proprietress approach. She was an exceedingly beautiful mulatta, of the kind they described here as *jaune* with the palest of golden skin and soft chestnut hair. This was the end product of generations of selective breeding by a rich family struggling towards their white ideal. Anywhere but here she would have passed as white, and only her huge, Pre-Raphaelite eyes betrayed her racial secret. She smiled and beckoned with her finger. '*Venez voir les oiseaux*,' she said.

We got up and followed her through the back of the bar into a garden overlooking a wide swamp spread through the valley under a black mountain. A half square mile of the swamp was covered with flamingoes, possibly a thousand of them, and at this moment – perhaps because someone had fired a gun – they were beginning to take off. Slowly, as the coverlet of birds was stripped back it was converted into a pink cloud which floated away between two low peaks and was lost to sight.

A circular thatched hut of the kind you saw everywhere in Haiti had been built in a corner of the garden. 'Is this the place where they hold the cock fights?' Johnson asked.

'We do not have cock fights,' she said. 'The people come here for their celebrations.' She had switched easily into English.

She went ahead and we followed her into the hut which was much larger than most. It had been decorated as if in readiness for carnival, still several weeks ahead. Cut-out paper shapes dangled from the thatch and the floor was covered with intricate designs traced out in flour, recalling the complex wrought-iron patterning of the last century. The roof was supported by a number of poles, from each of which hung large drums. Pictures of the kind that might have been painted by children with a taste for the bizarre stood on the floor all round the walls: intertwining snakes, staring eyes, a dancing skeleton, Jonah captured by his whale. 'Voodoo,' Johnson said. 'In this of all places. I'd never have dreamed of it. They're certainly advancing their frontiers.'

Childish fantasies were followed by a row of Haitian gods. Johnson catalogued them with a kind of proprietorial relish, while standing before them, the woman curtsied to each in turn. Baron Samedi, lord of the underworld – shown here as an undertaker, in top hat, dark glasses, coat with starched cuffs, white gloves and cane. Ogwé, wearing his admiral's uniform, guardian of good manners. Ogón, sword in hand, god of war. General Brutus, patron of adulterers, who assumes human form to molest young girls. Maitress Erzulie, goddess of love, a dark-eyed Madonna with a sword appropriately thrust through her heart.

The café-owner spoke to each in Creole. Her white skin glistened in the thin shafting of light through the walls of the hut. Addressing the images she smiled continuously in a cajoling fashion as a saleswoman recommending a doubtful product might have done. 'Now I have introduced you,' she explained to us.

'And these are the gods you pray to?' Johnson asked.

'We don't pray,' she said. 'The Haitian gods don't listen to prayers. They are very businesslike. We hold a celebration, we feed them and we dance to them, and in return they give us their help.'

'Could they be persuaded to do anything for us, if approached in the right way?'

'Of course,' the woman said. 'They are very reasonable. If you fear death you should leave a bottle of rum for Baron Samedi. Ogón will defend you from your enemies. You can repay him with cheroots.'

'I think in both our cases an offering to Maitress Erzuile might be more appropriate,' Johnson said. 'What do you suggest?'

The café proprietress pondered a moment. 'She's a woman,' she said. 'You can't go wrong with cold cream.'

'I'm sure you're right.' Johnson told her. 'Perhaps you could obtain some for us. We will leave the money.'

At this moment a workman clattered in with a bucket of whitewash and a long-handled broom. He put these down, picked up a stick and struck out at the biggest of the drums, filling the hut with doom-laden reverberations. The woman crossed herself and started to berate him, and we left them and went outside and stood looking down over the town. It had been raining and the rain had stopped, and now the sun filled the view to overbrimming with bright reflections. Naked children splashed joyfully in a brief torrent running in the street. A woman washed clothing in a pellucid puddle. A bell clanked and a little procession of hatted church-goers paddled past, shoes in hand.

We went down to the Facel-Vega. There were no tontons in this poor, devout place, and a small crowd had gathered in ecstatic admiration of the car. Someone had made up a little garland of white flowers, and this now encircled the firm's emblem, a sprinting greyhound, which embellished the radiator. Johnson passed it over to me to sniff. It was very fragrant. 'The spiritual life here seems to be quite intense,' he said. 'It would have been nice to stay a little longer. But with our problem with the lights I think we should be making a move.'

RONDA

P EACE, SO RELENTLESSLY denied the traveller on the Costa del Sol, descends instantly when, just beyond Marbella, he turns off north onto the Ronda road. This is marvellously deserted. Ronda – kept (allegedly by a hoteliers' conspiracy) short of accommodation – rids itself of the bulk of its visitors at the end of every day. A few cars passed me on their way downhill to the coast, otherwise there was little sign of life in these splendidly empty mountains.

Five miles short of Ronda I pulled in at a roadside café. It was precariously sited close to the slope of a steep valley, and a previous customer's car, unsuccessfully parked, had rolled fifteen yards downhill into a corral with some donkeys. From the organised life of an area now described as the California of Europe I had suddenly crossed an invisible frontier into the improvised Spain of old. The man who ran the place made me an omelette of potatoes studded with mountain ham – very dense and dry, to be correctly eaten with the fingers. He poured himself a glass of blueish wine and sat down with me to share the view. A huge bird – eagle or vulture – flapped into sight over a nearby peak and planed down the valley. I asked him why there were no houses, and he said it was because this had been bandit country. There had been bandits in these mountains as late as the forties. One of them had ridden in here one night for what turned out to be his last meal before falling into an ambush laid by the Civil Guards.

While this conversation was in progress a large and handsome nanny-goat had stationed herself at the back of my chair. Now, with great delicacy and precision, she leaned forward, picked up a piece of my bread and began to chew. 'Hope the goat doesn't bother you,' the man said. 'She's a friend of the family. Often pays us a visit.'

'She doesn't bother me in the slightest,' I said. 'She's a fine-looking animal. What's her name?'

The man looked surprised. 'Not being a Christian,' he said, 'she doesn't have one. We just call her the goat.'

I thanked him, patted the goat on the head and left. Ten minutes later as I drove over the top of the sierra and down through the outskirts of Ronda the landscape burst into life. There were hens and pigeons and litters of scuttling black piglets in the open spaces. A mother snatched up her baby from the verge of the road, a horseman wearing leather chaps and a big hat galloped after an escaping cow, and a traditional turkey-woman controlled her flock with a seven-foot whip.

The great Arab gate called the Puerto Almocabar bars the way at the entrance to the town. It is flanked by massive towers and through it a perfect white Andalusian street of matching houses curves up into the heart of Ronda. The road narrows among the Gothic and Moorish buildings at the top of the hill and then descends to the New Bridge over the theatrical gorge of the River Guadalevin, with glimpses through ornamental grilles of cyclopean boulders rearing up 300 feet from the trickle of water in the bottom. Across the bridge the town opens into the Plaza de España, a charming if haphazard square smelling of geraniums and saddlery, with shops like caverns, a country coachman plying for hire on the box of a vehicle like a tumbril, and men with sonorous voices calling the numbers of lottery tickets for sale.

Here, through a fine, ruined archway is the town's carpark where the cars line up under a backdrop of the old town across the river, its white houses crammed like a seaside terrace along the edge of a 500-foot precipice. On our side, Don Miguel's restaurant juts out over the gorge at its narrowest and most fearsome point, recalling a scene in Tibet. I asked the knowledgeable attendant about eating there, and he replied, 'You could do worse. Personally, I never set foot in the place. I suffer from vertigo and it makes my head swim.'

In all, it was a memorable first encounter; a small corner of Spain miraculously preserved, hardly changed, as it seemed, since the editor of *Murray's Handbook*, a difficult man to please, wrote of it in 1880: 'There is but *one* Ronda in the world.'

By now it was 8 p.m., with the sun waning in power at the bottom of the sky, and an evening refulgence diffused from surfaces of bare rock, and a nacreous speckling of clouds to warm the whiteness of the buildings. The best of Ronda is built along the edge of the Tajo, rising to nearly 1,000 feet, looking at this hour like a vast amphitheatre saturated with fading light, men on donkeys and mules immediately below among ancient, abandoned houses with trees growing through their roofs, a herd of sheep running as nimbly as cats, a threshing floor ringed with stones like a miniature Stonehenge, and in the distance, the sierras being pulled apart, range from range, by the mist.

The Tajo provides the reason for Ronda's existence, for apart from this incomparable natural defence why should it have occurred to anyone to settle here? Only the unreliable irrigation provided by the Guadalevin river offers relief in an environment largely copied from African deserts. The cliff abetted the inhabitants in their struggle against marauding armies, but the living was poor. Before the new affluence promoted by tourism, Rondeños picked olives, raised pigs and cured ham. Before the war, day-labourers might hope to find employment for 100 days a year, and the daily wage could be as low as 3.50 pesetas at a time when there were nine pesetas to the US dollar. Andalusia was described at that time as the poorest region in Europe, and there were Andalusians, as reported in the newspapers of the day, who literally starved to death. Hence the chronic and permanent banditry. Hence the garrotte, set up two centuries ago outside the Church of Los Dolores in Ronda, where desperate peasants who had taken to robbery were brought to be strangled in batches of four – as recorded in macabre fashion by the figures carved in the church's porch.

Unendurable poverty, and its long legacy of hatred, determined the atrocious aspects of the Spanish Civil War in Andalusia. It is widely asserted that the cliff in Ronda was the scene of the episode described in Hemingway's *For Whom the Bell Tolls* in which local supporters of the Franco revolt were compelled by cudgel-armed peasants to run the gauntlet before being tossed over the edge. There is no clear-cut evidence that this actually happened, and the subject is avoided in local discussion, but it is not denied that many hundreds of civilians were murdered in the town. With its capture by the nationalists, republican sympathisers were punished, as elsewhere in Andalusia, with extreme severity. Broadcasting from Seville, the Nationalist General Queipo de Llano had said: 'For every person they [the government supporters] kill, I shall kill ten, or perhaps even exceed that proportion.' There is no doubt that he meant it.

Panem et Circensis was the Roman recipe for civil peace, and there can be no doubt that even when bread is in short supply in Spain, fiestas, the Spanish equivalent of circuses, are provided in abundance.

I arrived in Ronda half-way through the annual September festivities which, although scheduled in the handsome official programme to take place between the 8th and 14th of the month, had been inflated by tacking a full extra week of jollifications onto the front. What was on offer was a marathon of pleasure guaranteed in the end to reduce revellers to a state of exhaustion. Every day of the interminable two weeks was crammed with such attractions as displays of horsemanship; shows put on by folklore groups invited from numerous countries; a concert by *cante flamenco* singers; pageantry by lovely ladies in old-style costumes; a carriage-driving contest; military parades to the music of stirring bands; a pentathlon; an 'interesting' football match; a bicycle race; a procession of giants and 'big-headed' dwarves; a comic bullfight in which aspirant toreros dressed as firemen would squirt each other with fire-hoses while being butted round the ring by aggressive calves; and finally, two versions of the real thing, a *novillada* fought with young bulls and the celebrated annual *Goyesca* in which all participants are attired in the bullfighting regalia of the eighteenth century.

Those who are still on their feet at the end of the long festive day are expected to make a night of it at the feria, outside the town, in operation from 1 a.m. until dawn. Here *casetas* (temporary cottages) are for hire where families entertain their friends, sherry flows like a river in spate and professional gypsy dancers and guitarists can be called in to keep the party going.

Alarm is often voiced at the inroads made by expanding fiestas into the serious business of living. Here is Don Rafael Manzano, director of the Alcázar of Seville on the subject of that city's spring fair – now, according to Don Rafael, completely out of control – which Ronda has set itself to imitate if not surpass. 'Until recently only rich people with no work could stay up and enjoy themselves all night. Now everybody tries to. If the parents stay up, so do the children, as part of their democratic right. The result is that my own children fall asleep over their books at school. As a nation we are in danger of forgetting that there is work to be done.'

The main attractions of the Ronda fiesta are staged in its bull-ring – the excuse for the fiesta itself being to commemorate the birthday of Pedro Romero, a Rondeño who became the most famous bullfighter of all time. Romero invented the modern style of bullfighting, conducted largely on foot. At a time when life was notably short and brutish he lived until the age of 90, having faced his first bull as a boy of eight, and having killed some 6,000 animals in all. Pedro Romero attracted the attention and admiration of Francisco Goya, and the archaic costumes worn in the annual bullfight in homage to both men are based on the paintings from his *tauromaquia* collection in which some paintings depict Romero in action.

The bull-ring, scene of so many of Romero's exploits, is one of the oldest, the largest and the most elegant in existence. Its exterior with the exception of the splendid baroque main gate, featured in the film of *Carmen*, appears of massive African simplicity, giving the illusion of an enormous, white, slightly flattened dome, dominating the centre of the town.

The museum it contains offers a wide though eccentric variety of bullfighting memorabilia, with occasional bizarre items such as a pair of matador's pantaloons displaying the blood-stained rent through which the wearer accidentally skewered himself with his own sword. What is probably the first bullfight poster published advertises the appearance of Pedro Romero, who, with his *cuadrilla*, would kill 16 bulls, the promoter promising that slothful or reluctant beasts were to be animated by savage dogs. The Goya prints are interesting, all the more so because lengthy descriptions clarify activities which otherwise might remain obscure. Could captured Barbary pirates have been forced to fight in the ring in Goya's day? Several prints show dark-faced bullfighters in turbans and flowing robes defending themselves somewhat hopelessly with their swords. In one case they are mounted pitifully on donkeys – which the bull effortlessly demolishes. These prints, the captions assure us, are based not upon fact, but upon the painter's imagination. Nevertheless, one wonders. Ronda is devoid of self-conscious displays of the trappings of antiquity. The monuments from the Roman, Arabic and Gothic occupations associate in a comfortable and matter-of-fact way with the buildings of our day; the Minaret de San Sebastián next to an ironmonger's shop, facing the bakery at the top of the Calle Salvatierra, and, at the foot, the princely façade of the Salvatierra Palace itself in an environment of bars. History is taken for granted everywhere. The permanently crowded bar La Verdad (Truth) in the Calle Pedro Romero has an ancient Arabic inscription running all round the doorway leading to the kitchen. It reads: 'There is no conqueror but Allah', a remarkable declaration of outlawed faith in a town where the Inquisition once ruled. So much is forgotten, so much overlooked.

José Paez, author of a book and many newspaper articles about the town, accompanied me on a final stroll through the streets. It was the last day of the fiesta and there were girls by the hundred in Sevillian-style costumes, roaming in groups, clicking their castanets, dancing and singing in their high-pitched voices. Sometimes a man went with them as they passed from street to street, banging a drum, leaving no corner or alleyway unvisited, as if beating the bounds of the town. José agreed that what we were witnessing must be the vestiges of some bygone ceremony by which the town had been cleansed of evil influences. The dancers seemed moved by compulsion, communicating a little of this to onlookers or passers-by in their vicinity. As the current of excitement took possession, women put down shopping bags and abandoned babies in prams to join in, and once in a while a man, correctly dressed for the routine of an office or bank, would stop to dance a few steps. It was a moment when one saw the fiesta in a new guise, not merely as the vehicle of popular enjoyment, but – at least in part – as a ritual left over from pre-history, once seen as essential to the wellbeing of the community.

Our walk ended in the splendid and gracious Alameda Gardens, laid out in 1807 by a mayor who hit upon the ingenious and wholly successful method of raising funds for this project by imposing stiff fines upon citizens heard to blaspheme. Ronda is full of wildlife, and it was present here in concentrated form. The pines wore haloes of winged insects, chased by innumerable miniature bats, many of them said to roost in the balconies of the post office. Enormous diurnal moths hung like humming-birds in suspension before the flowers they probed with a long proboscis. José, a student of nature, has produced a most interesting theory after a study of the behaviour of vultures which appear at this time every year without fail to circle in the sky for an hour or so before flying off. It was at least 50 years, he said, since the horses killed in the bullring had been dragged to the edge of the cliff and thrown over for disposal by the vultures. Nevertheless, every year the birds brought their young here on their first flights to pass on to them, as he supposed, the knowledge of the place where once there had been food in abundance and which might possibly provide food again.

We strolled to the edge of the cliff. The sun had just set and shortly, stripped of its light, the sierras would lose both colour and depth. Within half an hour night would suddenly fall, and the mountainous shapes, reduced to a sharp-edged cut-out against the still-luminous sky, would come very close to the town, filling the gardens with the hootings of enormous owls.

José said, 'I regard this town where I was born as an earthly paradise, and although I have travelled in many countries I always return to it with gratitude and relief.' After a moment of thought, he added, 'People come to this spot to commit suicide. Sometimes I ask myself, why do they not look at the view and change their minds?'

THE BOLIVIAN
TREASURE

ACHACACHI IS A beautiful, squalid town under the high peaks of the Bolivian Andes. I was up there looking at the fearsome one-man tin-mines that are a feature of the area when the Aymara guide, Jorge, picked up a rumour that a *huaquero* had found treasure on an island in Lake Titicaca. *Huaqueros* are professional grave-robbers, of which there are hundreds – possibly thousands – in Bolivia and Peru. The perils of their profession compel them to flit from site to site, shrouding their doings and whereabouts in secrecy. According to the report, this man was to be found at the moment in the village of Suma, near the shore of the lake. No one could provide his name, or be quite sure even where the village was. We drove 100 miles north along the lake road in the direction of the Peruvian frontier, asking all the way, and eventually found it.

Suma was a cluster of brown huts at about 14,000 feet, under the Sierra de las Muñecas – a string of ice-peaks thrusting up abruptly from the great grey spread of the Altiplano, important enough for Jorge to bow to as they came into sight. We ran into an instant complication. The village was celebrating an important feast. 'The Indians are ceremonious,' Jorge said. 'It would be ill-mannered to approach them directly and ask for this man. If they invite us we must drink and dance with them a little. We should enter into the spirit of the occasion and gain their confidence. Then I will ask.'

We left the car and walked down to the village, with the scattering of llamas and yellow dogs on its outskirts, and men and women dancing in its centre. A man crawled through a two-foot-high doorway to intercept us hospitably with a platter of *chuchawasi* bark, chewed locally to confer telepathic powers. This it was in order to reject. The village, he told us, was celebrating the second funeral of a man who had died six months before. Until this day his spirit had continued to live in his house, but now it was to be escorted to the grave already containing the body, given a tremendous farewell party, and begged not to return. Such villages possess a single shop selling nothing but the fancy-dress required to cope with an unending succession of ceremonies, and now we approached the dancers: a hundred or so drunken men and women, plumed, masked and festooned with glittering baubles, holding each other up and traipsing round to the squealing of flutes. The village priest had had himself carried out in a chair, his face bandaged like a mummy's against the sun, to observe these goings-on, while the villagers – a number of them with bottles in their hands – rotated round him like the moving figurines on a Bavarian clock. The carcase of a sacrificed llama was suspended upside down from a frame, and newcomers arriving to join the dance dipped their fingers in the small puddle of its blood, then daubed it on their foreheads.

It occurred to me that a priest, always the best-informed man in such localities, might be able to help us in our search for the *huaquero*, but Jorge vetoed my appeal for his assistance. He had learned that the priest had been sent to coventry after criticising the villagers on the score of their over-sophisticated sexual practices. As my guide admitted in their defence, the Aymaras were 'subtle and romantic' in their lovemaking. A further worsening in relations between the Indians and the Church had occurred over the details of the present fiesta. The priest had insisted that the dead man, a notorious evil-doer, should be buried in unconsecrated ground. He had overriden the villagers' appeal for the grave to be dug in the closest possible proximity to those of persons who had led impeccable lives, to allow the evil to be diluted with the good. Our involvement with him, Jorge said, would be seen as tantamount to consorting with the enemy.

Jorge found the *huaquero* through a go-between he happened to dance with, who made the man sound elusive and difficult. What did we want with him? No more than to see whatever it was he had found, before he had had time to melt the gold down. The go-between said that before having any truck with us or anybody else, the *huaquero* would have to be assured of our sincerity. This could only be done by seeking the advice of Tio, the Devil, who would demand a sacrifice of tobacco, coca leaves, alcohol and a llama's foetus.

The outlay was small enough, and was agreed, but a slight problem arose in the matter of the foetus (regarded in Bolivia as the indispensable accessory of magic operations of all kinds) for which demand always exceeds supply. The two men went off together to make enquiries as to where one could be had. Jorge was nervous about leaving me alone among the drunken, machete-waving celebrants. 'Don't move,' he said. 'Be very polite to them. Go along with anything they say.'

I watched the gyration of Indians dancing round the priest in his bandages and dark glasses. A glacier full of sharp winking reflections broke out of the mist, then a blizzard blotted it out. The wind kicked and thumped at the walls of the huts, and the flutes squealed shrilly. An Aymara wearing chain-mail with fragments of mirror-glass tied to it danced up with a jug of alcohol and splashed a little on my lips. Then Jorge was back, trailing after him the *huaquero*, a small, haunted man, the first grey-haired Aymara I had ever seen. He held a carrier bag given away by a La Paz store. A foetus had been found, and the bag contained the sacrificial item I had just paid for. Paranoia flickered continually in his expression. *Huaqueros*, Jorge explained, were like this. They led stressful lives, obliged continually, like the tin-miners, to fork out money to keep the Devil sweet, and to meet their end through the collapse of a tunnel, while burrowing into some ancient burial mound.

The *huaquero* shot me a hostile glance, clambered into the back of the car, and we set off for the lake, about five miles away. As we breasted the summit of a low hill it came into sight, clouded purple by the plankton in its depths. There was no wind here, and through some optical illusion bred of ice and sky, the surface curved smoothly like glass sheeting down to the horizon. Three reed boats were tied up in the shallows. The fishermen had taken their catch up to a nearby shack to be cooked, exchanging some for spirits, so that by the time we arrived they were all drunk.

We sat down with them to grilled trout, and the *huaquero*, clutching his carrier bag went off in the direction of a cluster of huts where it was to be supposed the treasure was hidden, and where Jorge said he would conduct his sacrifice. Presently he was back, but it was clear from his expression and indignant gestures that something had gone wrong. A rattle of depressed gutturals passed between them, and Jorge explained that Tio had rejected his offerings. In consequence he had now decided not to show us the gold objects – one of them he mentioned was a jewel in the form of a butterfly. These were now destined to be melted down for the few grammes of the metal they contained. He had brought along something to help appease our curiosity, and saying this, he unwrapped a paper parcel to reveal a foot-long ceramic jaguar. This he would not allow us to hold.

It was a moment that provided one of the great surprises of my life, for in the museums of Lima and La Paz I had never seen anything remotely resembling this object. It was impossible that this blue terracotta figure, decorated with hieroglyphics, could have originated in Bolivia. The pottery of the Incas, who had dominated the area, has been described as trite. The

Mochicas of the great preceding civilisation produced portrait-vases of incomparable genius, but they were concerned with the surface of things. The jaguar was the product of a different brand of inspiration and a different mind. This could only have been the work of a Mayan artist, in search of spiritual essence rather than outward appearance, who had set out in this case to interpret malignity concealed in animal form.

The question was how had the jaguar come to be where it had been found? Honduras in Central America, the nearest outpost of the ancient Mayan civilisation, was 2,500 miles away, and although Mayan traders are supposed to have moved freely between Yucatán in Mexico and Panama in the south it is hard to believe that any trader of those days could have accomplished the terrific journey to Bolivia, offering, moreover, articles for sale that could have had little appeal for a people with alien canons of taste.

The only solution to this enigma, if one existed, seemed to lie with the art historians of La Paz. I asked the *huaquero* if he was willing to sell the jaguar, to which he replied that he would not accept money for it, but would agree to an exchange for a suitable watch. I was wearing a wrist-watch of reasonable quality but this he rejected as being too small. Unhappily, Jorge's watch, too, was small by his standards and an offer of the two watches for the jaguar was turned down out of hand. It was clear that value in this case was equated with size. Separating thumb and forefinger he measured out about two and a half inches. This was to be the minimum diameter of the dial, which had to be coloured red or blue. He told us that such watches, hugely prized among the Aymara, were on sale on the market stalls of La Paz. This I knew to be true, and that the price was about the equivalent of £4.

It was a wretched predicament, for I could see that the man would settle for nothing less. The offer of all the money we were carrying, amounting to some £50, plus the watches, was received with a contemptuous smile. It was two days to La Paz and back. In the meanwhile Jorge said, the man might have changed his mind. Moreover, *huaqueros* could only save themselves from the robbers, who continually stalked them, by covering their tracks and staying on the move. 'Whatever arrangement we make with this man,' he said, 'he will not be there. We shall never see him again.'

The *huaquero* rewrapped the jaguar in the newspaper and put it back in his carrier bag. Refusing a lift, he turned away and walked off, leaving behind a mystery never to be solved.

'He saw you were excited,' Jorge said, 'so he believed it must be valuable and he wished not to let it go.'

'And what will happen to the jaguar now?'

'No one else will want it. It was interesting only to you. He will keep it for good luck, I think. If the luck turns bad, maybe he will give it to the Devil.'

GOA

THE FIRST TIME I went to Goa I stayed in its capital, Panjim, in the charming old Hotel Central. Among its many attractions was the fact that the windows, constructed at a time when glass was hard to come by, were made from tiny squared-off panes of mother-of-pearl from oyster shells. A talking mynah I assumed to have escaped its cage had taken up residence in the garden and sometimes greeted me cheerfully in English, although with a marked Indian accent. Another endearing feature was the atmosphere of trust fostered by the absence of locks on any of the doors. When at the time of moving in I commented on this no one seemed surprised. They had never bothered with locks, the manager said. No one would touch any of my possessions. Nevertheless, he thought it a wise precaution to keep the splendid windows closed when I left the room, purely to keep out the crows. These, he said, had the bad habit of collecting objects like sunglasses with which to decorate their nests. They were the only thieves in Goa.

This was shortly before 1961 when, after four hundred years as a Portuguese colony, Goa became an Indian state. Now, 30 years later, there had been some small tightening up of security, but it was largely, along with traffic-lights and super-markets, a matter of keeping up with the times. Holiday-makers from the outside world occasionally got into minor brawls among themselves, but the beer was too weak to promote real fury, and Goa remained on the whole an oasis of calm. The sun shone with undiminished vigour for six months in succession; the cost of living was low, so naturally the foreigners crowded in. This year, the hotels were full so I took an austere villa in a development that had gone up almost overnight; the builders were sweeping up the wood-shaving when the agent handed over the keys. So there were keys in Goa, at last. It soon transpired that they were something of an afterthought. Doors fitted with mortice locks were still not easy to find. In the style of an old-fashioned godown, they were fitted with massive sliding bolts, secured with a heavy padlock. For the first few days, tenants like myself wrestled with them, but sooner or later we succumbed to the confiding environment and ceased to bother about our possessions.

Baga beach was only fifty yards away over a rise of sand-dunes. Baga is one of twenty-four local names for the Goa beach as a whole which unwinds by the sea like a strip of immaculate desert, stretching for 100 kilometres from north to south of the small state – a distance a determined walker, allowing for river-crossings, might hope to cover in three days. This is something of a survival, and a reminder of what beaches in other continents may have been like before the age of pollution and the shores' imprisonment in concrete. There are no unpleasantnesses on this strand: no plastic jetsam, no tar-balls, no oil-encrusted gulls' corpses – not even seaweed. Unsullied sand stretches for mile after mile under a backdrop of feathery tamarinds, bamboos and wind-wracked pines. Where they can be conveniently launched, the fishermen have lined up their boats. These have the gaunt profiles of Viking ships. They are black, their bows painted in primeval designs of blue, yellow and white. Sometimes – since the fishermen are all Christians – they have white crosses added in relief. Friar Domingo Navarete, the Dominican who stopped here in 1670 on his great journey from China back to Lisbon, wrote of them (and they have in no way changed), 'Those are very odd boats, they have no nails or pins, but the boards are sewn together with ropes made of coco, (and though) the water enter'd by a thousand holes . . . the Moors assured us they were safe . . .'

In the morning the beach would be left to the seagulls scuttling after land-crabs, only rarely disturbed by the racing passage of a boy on a bicycle fitted with a sail. Later, sari-wearing ladies of the Baga Beach Club would arrive for their exercises, superbly athletic, but always graceful as they chased their frisbees in all directions. Occasionally, a party of hippies might turn up and while away the time moulding statuary in the sand. At about 5 p.m. the Beach Club ladies, escorted by an instructress, were back for a quarter-hour's practice in meditation, after which splendidly erect and all in step, they would walk back up the beach in single file – colourful isosceles triangles in motion, within minutes of 6 p.m. a European lady always appeared, to face the going-down of the sun in the correct yoga posture.

The life of the beach remained divided from that of the hinterland – worlds apart – each with little knowledge of the other. Some native Goans claimed that they had never visitied the beach and many that they avoided it at the time when the winter visitors were in possession. Nudism was much practised – although it always seemed to me that it was done discreetly – in certain areas where temporary foreign colonies had formed. Victorian values are defended in the Goan hinterland and some months back a party of scandalised country-folk expressed their disapproval of the moral laxity of foreigners by smearing cow-dung over a bus in which a party of German tourists was travelling. Subsequently, *Goa Today* published an article under the heading 'Naked Apes', in which it bewailed the impotence of the police to do anything to remedy the situation, for, despite all the prohibitive notices that had been erected, it turned out that in India it is only an offence to remove one's clothing in public in the furtherance of a lewd or indecent act.

The paper complained not only of the foreigners but of a category of domestic tourists who treat the beaches at Anjuna and Vagator as if they were part of an open-air peep show, and even go there to take snapshots of unseemly foreign goings-on. Goans do not wholly approve of the animal high spirits displayed by some of their Northern Indian visitors. They show particular dismay at the conduct of week-enders from Bombay or Delhi who often wear comic noses or dress up as Mexican bandits brandishing water-pistols disguised as six-shooters. When reprimanded by the police over such antics the standard reply is, 'Please excuse, we are only letting down hair.'

The drug problem and its spread from foreign visitors to the Indian population causes more concern. 'Don't dabble in drugs,' warns the notice at the entrance to Colva Beach. 'It is a social evil and crime punishable with 10–30 years R.I.' This means what it says. 'R.I.' is rigorous imprisonment – frequently to be endured in the Reyes Magos hilltop fort, rumoured to allow visits only once a year at the Feast of the Three Kings. Those applying at other times are turned away with the recommendation to pray for divine intercession in the beautiful blue and white Portuguese church at the foot of the hill.

A mile or two back from the shore traditional Goa awaits. By comparison with India as a whole, it is underpopulated. It is possible, as nowhere else in the sub-continent, to find oneself quite alone among green fields and woods. It is agricultural country, full of calm, rustic scenes from the past. The friendliness and hospitality of the people is tinged with a certain gravity picked up, it is to be suspected, through their long association with the Portuguese – least ebullient of the Latin races.

Sightseeing is comfortably done by buses which wander everywhere along the country roads. There is no better sample run than to take a trip from Dabolim airport to one of the northern resorts. This should be broken for at least a couple of hours to explore the capital Panjin, which remains in part as Portuguese as Lisbon, serves authentic Portuguese food in its restaurants, and posseses cafés in which customers still sip port and listen to *fados* on Saturday nights.

Such journeys are best started in the cool of the morning to experience the sight of buffaloes in the paddies, dragging their ploughs through the mist, and churches and temples sparkling along the edge of ghostly lagoons when the sun breaks through. The shoulder of a mountain looms in the vapour. Peasants in straw hats are bent double to transplant rice. Cranes take off. This scene appears to be more the work of a classical painter of old China than an Indian landscape. Magnificent old Portuguese estate-houses dominate some of the villages, and the concentration of baroque churches is greater here than in Portugal itself. Catholics and Hindus live in comfortable association, with little evidence of the barriers of caste and religion which are still prevalent in other parts of the country. A few miles from Calangute on the north shore, a small roadside temple in dedicated to the Nāga (snake) deity. I was invited in by the English-speaking priest, who was sorry not to be able to show me a sacred snake, as the last one had died of old age, and they had not been able to replace it. 'We have limited resources,' he said. 'There is a bigger place down the road where you may see a good example.' The Nāga temple also kept rats, which he was happy to display. These, and the snake when they had one, were fed on rice and milk. They were very peaceable, he said. He was eager to dispel the possibility of doctrinal confusion. 'It is not worshipping rats, we are. More it is an expression of solidarity with animal creation.'

Calangute is set in shaded gardens, planted with areca, pepper-trees and coconut-palms. Here people lead open-air existences, occupied with such unhurried cottage industries as the production of coconut fibre and its transformation into rope. A woman pokes at the embers under an enormous witches' cauldron boiling the day's rice; a man gives his white goat a morning scrub-down, then stands back to admire the result; children, gobbling like turkey-cocks, race round the playground of an infant school called Toddledom; bells summon to the services of the church. The environment is saturated with sober pleasure.

The centre of the village, being close to the beach, is dressed up for the benefit of the tourists, with astrologers working from auto-rickshaws; sincere-mannered purveyors of tribal bric-à-brac; a sidewalk pharmacist offering remedies for fits, gas, itching of the extremities, cholera, loss of memory, and sudden fright; and a resident holy man who lives by the display of his deformities.

Tucked away behind the souvenir shops, Calangute's little market must be one of the liveliest anywhere. It is full of long-snouted, darting piglets, and small, delicate, docile and beautiful cows, who stuff themselves without ill-effect on discarded packaging material and empty cardboard boxes (buy one a handful of spinach and it will follow you about like an affectionate dog). The local people come here not only to shop, but for the day's quota of excitement; for the ritual tussle between buyer and seller, the venting of minor indignations, the triumph of the small bargain, for the noise, the smells, the laughter, the hour's freedom from household chores.

The Souza Loba restaurant is within easy reach down a sand-clogged track leading to the beach, and many shoppers burdened with their bundles make for it for a cold beer or a pre-siesta snack. Despite its local renown, it is a self-effacing place, concerned single-mindedly with the preparation of good food, and oblivious to visual appeal – almost even to comfort. Tables and chairs rock, piratical cats scramble in through the windows (a guard with a cane makes no more than a pretence at striking out at them), and a dark, lacy butterfly may come planing down to suck at some stickiness on the table-cloth. It is hard to find a seat, waiters rush about shouting 'soon it is coming' – a routine and usually empty promise. The food, nevertheless, when it at long last arrives, is a symphonic fusion of Portuguese and Indian culinary art – just as reported.

What was astonishing on the occasion of my visit was that, after a profoundly exotic meal, the waiter should reappear to place before me a large helping of Swiss roll, leaking jam into a puddle of congealing custard. This, along with the rusted aspidistras of the surroundings, was clearly part and parcel of a cultural intrusion from the old India of the British Raj. The Goans at the next table had been served a similar mess and were tucking in with obvious relish. The waiter explained: 'Swiss roll better for bodily organs after intake of spiced food.'

'And you don't have anything else?'

His smile was kindly, but firm. 'In Goa we are all eating Swiss roll.'

He seemed to be keeping me under surveillance for a while until a customer called him away. An exceptionally handsome sacred cow had stationed itself under the window in readiness for the occasional windfall, but I waited until the waiter was well out of sight before taking action.

THE LAST BUS
TO MARMELADE

I EASILY SURVIVED three extended trips to Haiti during the reign of Papa Doc, but when Baby Jean-Claude picked up his crown my feeling was that the end was at hand. Blessed are the poor, says the Book, but it could hardly have been commending this kind of poverty. The newspapers spoke without surprise or shame of a normal situation in which two families were reduced to sharing the ownership of a single sheep. In the fishing villages along the north coast all the boats had long since fallen apart, and the fishermen now cast their nets with poor success from long rafts tied together with home-made sisal rope. There was nothing to be done about it, and no hope for the future.

For all this, the mysterious charm of Haiti, deriving from the innate nobility and debonair style of the oppressed majority of the population, remained intact. Despite the ravages of neglect it was still a beautiful place, with an indulgent tropical grace, now only half-concealed by ruin.

Three incidents occurred in rapid succession, which, taken together, led me to suspect that I was on the island for the last time. The first arose as a result of the Haitian urge to cover blank spaces, such as the adobe walls of the cabins in which many live, with decorations of a spirited and fanciful kind. The best examples of this urge for self-expression were to be found in villages accessible only on mule-back or on foot. Once in a while a fine example turned up in a town, and I came on one in Carrefour, a seedy outer suburb of Port-au-Prince.

A man, probably fresh from the country, was painting the white-washed wall of his garden. This he had transformed into a scene, as if viewed from above, of a lively river pouring through flower-ornamented banks, with a variety of fish frolicking in its wavelets. My arrival coincided with that of two policemen in a squad car. One held the man while the other went into the garage across the road, returned with a canful of sump oil and with this obliterated the artist's work. My mistake was to photograph the occurrence. The police-man with the can came over, gestured to me to give him the camera, took out the film and threw it into a hedge. 'Take this as a warning,' he said.

The second discouraging incident took place next day, within a mile of the same spot. It was a rowdy street-scene after dark. A man rushed out of a bar clutching his neck with both hands, blood trickling through his fingers. He kicked at the door of the car and I got out. 'Someone just cut my throat,' he said. He took a hand away to show a slash over the windpipe which drooped open like a pendulous lip. In the case of fatal severance of the jugular vein, blood fountains. In this instance it dripped. 'Get into the car,' I told him. 'I'll run you over to the hospital.'

At the hospital there was little sign of life. The nightly power-cut had affected this part of the town. Torchlights could be seen bobbing about in the rooms like grave-robbers at work in a cemetery, and a weak current provided by a hospital generator pulsated in a single bulb suspended over the recep-tion counter. For a time nothing happened, then I rang the handbell and an old man in pyjamas shuffled into view. I asked him who was in charge, and he said, 'I am, but we're not taking in any emergencies. Come back tomorrow.'

'This man's dying,' I said.

The would-be patient, who had collapsed into a dis-embowelled armchair and was bleeding darkly, gave a loud groan, and took his hands from his neck to expose his wound. The old man looked at it. 'Superficial,' he said. 'Take him to number 10 rue de Réunion. They'll fix him up. I have to give you a note, and the fee will be five gourdes.'

The man in the rue de Réunion was a sail-maker who carried out the small repair necessary in ten minutes. 'I don't make sails any more these days,' he said. 'The hospital sends me all the business I can handle. I get a better result than any surgeon when it comes to sewing them up. It's the practice that counts.'

The third incident sprang from multiple beginnings all rooted in the misadventures of my friend Johnson. Previously I had always stayed at his hotel, the Meurice, but now he had closed down so I was forced to put up at the Splendide. As soon as I could I went over to listen to his troubles, arising from a long-standing feud with the authorities, which he could only lose. For the fiftieth time he assured me that he was at the end of his tether. At the time of my last visit three years before, he had been beaten by an army officer almost to within an inch of his life for sounding his horn in protest after the officer had knocked in a fender of his car. Johnson's fatal mistake had been to complain to the Ministry of Justice, since when he had never been left in peace. Now, when we met again, I was shocked at his appearance. I saw him for the first time since the bandages had been removed. His head hung slightly to one side; one eye was half-closed in a sad imitation of a wink. He told me that he found it physically impossible to smile.

Although it was midday, his formerly energetic wife was still in bed. She had nothing left to do with her life, he said, and had given up. We went into the garden where the last of his beautiful specimen trees had long since been cut down by invaders for transformation into charcoal. Everything was now smothered with weeds, many of them producing striking flowers. The swimming-pool, although there was no one to use it, was nearly full and remarkably clear. 'Don't they steal the water these days?' I asked.

'Of course,' he said, 'about 500 gallons a night.'

'You could empty the pool,' I suggested.

'I'm not allowed to.'

'I should have thought the pool chemicals make the water undrinkable?'

'They've invented a new law against them. It's called wanton intoxication of resources.'

'What happened to your old Facel-Vega?'

'It had to go in the end. They had an army jeep going round the streets looking for it. Every time I left it parked anywhere they backed into it. A general bought it for 2,000 gourdes.'

'Theft under another name,' I said.

'The price of a good bicycle. If ever I open up again, the general says he'll be happy to go into partnership with me.'

'What made you close down?' I asked.

'They kept up the pressure,' he said. 'In the end they had a policeman out in the street all day keeping the place under surveillance. Every time a guest showed at a window he exposed himself.'

'So you're pulling out at last?'

'I have to,' Johnson said. 'The only thing that's been keeping us here is my step-daughter. She works with one of those aid organisations up in the north. Place called Marmelade. I hoped you'd come. We had bad news this morning. There's a bridge on the point of collapsing, and they're stopping the bus service the day after tomorrow. That means she'll be cut off. We have to find some way of getting a message through to her. I'd go myself, but they won't let me leave town. We're in a terrible jam.'

The bus left the bus station at five o'clock in the morning – in Haiti the most active hour of the day. Johnson had protested. 'Why should I drag you into this?' But in reality I had nothing better to do with my time. It was an excuse to see a part of the country that was new to me, and I was happy to be able to do something for this poor, martyred man to whom I had taken a liking.

A placard was propped against the bus's side. *Dernière Visite à Marmelade*, and for the benefit of those who couldn't read, a vigorous crayon-drawing beneath the lettering explained why. It showed a bridge sagging askew over a river with a bus upside down in its bed. A row of survivors wept and gesticulated on the bank and torrents of their blood ran down to mingle with the water. The dramatic incident thus illustrated had never happened, but it was something that *might*. Travellers waiting to be borne away to other destinations had gathered to admire the notice and take farewells of operatic solemnity of those condemned to confront the perils of this particular trip.

Ten hours followed through the exhausted sun-varnished landscape of Haiti before we reached Marmelade. The clouds piled over the gunmetal mountains were as rounded and solid as plaster fruit, but never covered an implacable sun. Negroes with famished bodies and iron faces watched motionless as the bus rattled past through the streets of villages where they sold bisected cigarettes and advertised coffins for hire. The passengers crossed themselves, sweated and groaned, and the chickens, hanging in bundles from the roof-rack, slowly died. At the suspect bridge everyone got out and crossed on foot, and the bus followed, nudging its way cautiously over the sloping surface. When we were about to set off, a passenger wrenched a chicken from one of the bundles and threw it to the driver as a reward.

I tracked Claudine Johnson down in her office in a parched, wooden street, paralysed in the hard afternoon sun. The office was an oasis of cheerfulness and endeavour in the wilderness of a small town that had turned its face to the wall. 'She needed a cause,' her father had said of her. 'She believes she's found one and nothing matters to her but that. She provides a respectable front for a racket. The US sends in hundreds of tons of aid – chicken wings, second-grade beef, used clothing – all of which goes on the black market. My daughter's allowed to distribute dried milk which nobody wants. They're making a laughing-stock of her.' She was small, neat and precise, with a ready smile, well-kept hands, every hair in place. A beaker full of powdered milk stood on her desk. She told me that she carried out an analysis on a sample taken at random from each delivery. 'It's something I'm very particular about,' she said.

She had read her father's letter and I spoke of her parent's anxiety at the fear of her increasing isolation, stressing their hope that she could get away for at least a short visit to Port-au-Prince on the bus leaving next day.

'How long are they likely to take over the repair of the bridge?' she asked.

'Things don't move fast in Haiti,' I said.

'No, they don't,' she said. 'Still, it's surprising how much you can learn to do without. For example – electric light, the telephone, and water most of the time. I suppose if it comes to it we can do without the bridge. There's always a way round. We have a lot going on here at the moment. In a few minutes I have to go off for talk with Aide Catholique. They're the Haitians we work with. We're on the point of a breakthrough. There's a fair chance of being allowed to expand our operation into the Departement du Nord.'

'That sounds like good news.'

'My organisation will go on handling the dried milk as before for the time being, and I'm taking over the distribution of discarded spectacles. Clothing and meat are coming through nicely now, but we leave that to the Haitians. It's good for them to share the responsibility. I might conceivably be able to get away for a few days, but no more.'

'As a suggestion, you could take the bus tomorrow, and catch a plane back via Cap Haitien.'

'It's a possibility,' she said. 'I'll have a word with the people I work with and see what can be done.'

She left to go to her meeting, and I to check in for the night at a hotel absurdly entitled Le Relais du Grand Duc, the only solid building in Marmelade. It dated from the time when the stony, emaciated fields surrounding the town had produced, in the late seventeen hundreds, the richest crop of sugar in the world. The dukedom in which it had been included, conferred on one of his favourites by the Haitian Emperor Christophe, had been seen as ludicrous even in those days. The Relais possessed thirty-eight rooms, but I was the only guest. It was perfumed throughout by the dark, ancient wood panelling all its walls. There were cut crystal handles on the doors, and four-poster beds, and its façade was decorated with a time-worn and faded coat of arms depicting a negro in a cocked hat, wearing a sword and riding on the back of a pig.

A chicken wing from Oklahoma, fried up with a local plantain, constituted an unexceptional evening meal, but it was washed down with fragrant and delicate Babancourt, the island's only product of distinction, and arguably the best rum to be found anywhere. While savouring a flavour inherited from the imperial days of old, a sound caused me to glance up and find a fair-skinned and well-dressed young Haitian smiling down at me. He gave me his hands, introducing himself with a bow as Winston L'Agneau. A neatly engraved card described him as *Chef du Secteur, Milice Populaire François Duvalier*. From this I gathered that in this remote corner of the country the tontons-macoutes maintained, even officially, a presence. The beautifully laundered white shirt, open at the neck, allowed a glimpse of a small gold cross on a chain. When the smile faded his expression seemed tinged with melancholy. 'It is my great pleasure to welcome you to Marmelade,' he said. His accent suggested schooling of the better class in France, some acquaintance with the policies of Richelieu and the poetry of Lamartine. 'I am a petty functionary,' he said, 'charged temporarily, due to the absence of a colleague on sick-leave, with the tiresome milice formalities in our town.'

He had arrived for a purely routine inspection, as he put it, of my passport. This he hardly glanced at before handing back. He then asked for my laissez-passer, which, he said, he was compelled to stamp. I told him I had no idea that they were still required.

'Normally that is so,' he said. 'Unfortunately they see fit to designate this a military zone. For reasons we do not understand these regulations are still in force. We think that it is because they have forgotten to change them.'

'What do I do about it?'

'It is no more than a formality, but I would be compelled to hold your passport while you go to Cap Haitien to apply for this document.'

'I have to take the last bus to Port-au-Prince tomorrow. Do you see any hope of my getting there and back in time.'

'No,' he said. He laughed apologetically. 'The office is already closed. Tomorrow is Saturday. Here we have the English weekend. It will open again on Tuesday. I will write a note so that you will be attended to immediately. I am really sorry. It is so ridiculous for you.'

'You know Miss Johnson, don't you?' I asked.

'Who does not know Miss Johnson for the good work she does among our people? She is admired and respected by us all. Miss Johnson is a lady we all love. Every man and woman in our town.'

'And does she need a laissez-passer before she travels anywhere?'

'Even Miss Johnson will require one. I must tell you our country is tied hand and foot by bureaucracy. These officials are like flies round a honey pot. We Haitians suffer from them as much as our friends who visit us from other countries.'

It was a situation in which a skilfully proffered bribe might provide the only solution, but bribery itself was a fine art to be left strictly alone by those unpractised in its protocol. 'Monsieur L'Agneau,' I said. 'It's impossible to explain to you how much it means to me to catch that bus. I'm booked on a flight to Europe on Monday. Is there nothing you can suggest?'

The smile changed his face again; now it was a cautious, secret one. He caressed the ball of his thumb with the tips of his first and second fingers in a delicately suggestive Mediterranean gesture. 'Please realise I am sympathetic,' he said, and I wondered if he was using the word, as persons with a French background often did, in a way that failed to reproduce its English meaning. His eyes wandered from my face momentarily to take in the emptiness of the room, then returned. 'You are officially in this town only because your name is in the hotel register,' he said.

'But it isn't,' I said. 'They gave me a slip to sign.' At this moment I was struck with the thought that a way of escape might have been left open for me.

'That is interesting,' he said. 'In a bureaucracy there are bureaucratic muddles. Perhaps no entry has been made in the book. If this is so, I think that for you something could be done. You are unknown – a stranger passing through. For Miss Johnson it is different. She is in everyone's eye. Many people would be sorry to see her go. We hope she will stay.'

At almost exactly the same time next evening, Johnson and I drank a rum together by the side of his emptying pool.

'You'll have to resign yourself,' I said. 'You won't be seeing her for a while.'

'You mean they won't let her go?'

'Not easily, no. The real fact is she doesn't want to go. If it's possible to imagine anyone coping with life in the Haitian backwoods, she probably even enjoys herself.'

Johnson threw up his hands in one of his acquired French gestures, signifying surrender and resignation. 'Well, at least we know. What do I owe you for the bribe?'

'Think nothing of it,' I said. 'It was only a small contribution to the fellow in the hotel reception. The one tense moment was when it looked as though I might be stuck in the Cap for a week.'

'That would have been quite an experience.'

'Yes,' I said. 'Not one to be forgotten in a hurry.'

SIAM AND THE
MODERN WORLD

THAILAND, UNTIL 1953 generally called Siam, went modern just before my first visit there, later that year. The order went out that the nation was to cease looking to the past and to take the future in a firm embrace. Hat Yai, a provincial town in the south within a few miles of the Malaysian frontier, was chosen for an experiment in instant modernisation, and I went there to see what was happening. There was a tendency in Siam for the words 'modern' and 'American' to be used interchangeably, so, when the decree was published for Hat Yai to be brought up to date, most Thais accepted that it was to be Americanised. Little surprise was aroused when the model chosen for the new Hat Yai was Dodge City of the eighteen-sixties as revealed by the movies.

In due course the experts arrived with photographs of the capital of the wild frontier in its heyday, and within weeks the comfortable muddle of Hat Yai was no more. Its shacks reeling on their stilts were pulled down, the ducks and buffaloes chased out of the ditches, and the spirit-houses (after proper apologies to the spirits) shoved out of sight. It became illegal to fly kites within the limits of the town, or to stage contests between fighting-fish.

Where the bustling chaos of the East had once been, arose the replica of the main-street made famous by so many Westerns, complete with swing-door saloons, wall-eyed hotels and rickety verandahs on which law-abiding citizens were marshalled by the sheriff to go on a posse and men of evil intention planned their attack on the mail-train or the bank. Hat Yai possessed no horses and the hard men of those days rode into town in jeeps – nevertheless, hitching-posts were provided. For all the masquerade, Hat Yai in the fifties bore some slight accidental resemblance to what Dodge City had been a century before, and there were gun-fighters in plenty in the vicinity. It was at that time an unofficial rest-area for Malaysian Communist guerrillas from across the frontier, tolerated simply because the Thais lacked the strength to keep them out. The communist intruders were armed to the teeth, and Thai law-enforcement agents – part of whose uniform included Davy Crockett fur caps from which racoon tails dangled – were few in number. Reaching for one's gun was a matter of frequent occurrence in the main-street saloons. Although it was largely a histrionic gesture and few people were shot, newcomers like myself were proudly taken to see the holes in the ceilings.

The arrival of the movies played their part in the vision of the new Thailand. In a single year, 1950, hundreds, perhaps thousands of movie theatres opened up all over S.E. Asia, the first film on general release being *Arsenic and Old Lace*. With this the shadow-play that had entertained so many generations of Thais was wiped out overnight. A multitude of mothers throughout the land worked tirelessly at pressing back their daughters' fingers from the age of five to enable them to take stylish part in the dance dramas such as the *Ramayana*. From this point on it had all been to no purpose, and the customers who befuddled themselves in the saloons with *mekong* whisky, drunk hot by the half pint, were waited upon with sublime grace by girls whose performing days were at an end. Real-life theatre demanded the imaginative effort of suspending disbelief; gangster movies did not.

Investigating the threatened disappearance of the puppet-show, a Bangkok newspaper reported that it had only been able to discover a single company, surviving somewhere in the north of the country, working in Thai style with life-size puppets manipulated not by strings but by sticks from below stage. It took 40 years to train a puppeter to the required pitch of perfection in this art, and it seemed worthwhile to the newspaper to bring this company down to Bangkok to film what was likely to be one of its last performances.

This was given in the garden of the paper's editor, Kukrit Pramoj, and attracted a fashionable crowd of upper-crust Thais, plus a few foreign diplomats, many of whom would see a puppet-show for the first and last time. So unearthly was the skill of the puppeteers, so naturalistic and convincing the movements of the puppets, that, but for the fact that their vivacity surpassed that of flesh and blood, it would have been tempting to suspect we were watching actors in puppet disguise.

After the show most of the guests went off to a smart restaurant, filling it with the bright clatter of enthusiasm that would soon fade. Such places provided 'continental' food – the mode of the day. In this land offering so many often extraordinary regional delicacies, found nowhere else in the world, successful efforts were now made to suppress flavour to a point where only a saporific vacuum remained. Kukrit, then, as ever since, a champion of Thai culture, made the astonishing admission that he knew nothing of the cuisine, now only to be savoured at night-markets and roadside stalls. In a flare-up of nationalist enthusiasm he announced his determination to put this right. He made enquiries among his friends and a few days later I received an invitation to lunch with him at the house of a relation, a prince who was a grandson of King Chulalongkorn. The prince, said Kukrit, employed a chef trained to cook nothing but European food, and he could not remember when – if ever – he had tasted a local dish. Entering into the spirit of adventure he had tracked down a Thai cook with a popular following in the half-world of the markets, to be hired for this occasion. And so the meal offered, for him too, the promise of novelty and adventure.

The prince lived on the outskirts of Bangkok in a large villa dating from about 1900. It was strikingly English in appearance, with a garden full of sweetpeas – grown by the prince himself – which in this climate produced lax, greyish blooms, singularly devoid of scent. He awaited us at the garden gate. Kukrit leaped down from the car, scrambled towards him and, despite a government injunction to refrain from salutations of a servile kind, made a token grab at his right ankle. This the prince good-naturedly avoided. 'Do get up, Kukrit, dear boy,' he said. Both men had been to school in England and, apart from their easy, accent-free mastery of the language, there was something that proclaimed this in their faces and manner.

My previous experience of Thai houses had been limited to the claustrophobic homes in which the moneyed classes took refuge, shuttered away in a gloom deepened by a clutter of dark furniture from the menacing light of day. The villa came as a surprise, for in the past year an avant-garde French interior designer had flown in to effect a revolution. He had brought the sun back, filtering it through lattices and the dappled shade of house plants with great, lustrous leaves, opening the house to light and diffusing an ambience of spring. We lunched under a photo-mural of Paris – *quand fleurit le printemps* – and a device invented by the designer breathed a faint fragrance of narcissi through the conditioned air. The meal was both delicious and enigmatic, based we were assured on the choice of the correct basic materials (none was identified), and auspicious colours according to the phase of the moon. Kukrit took many notes.

The entertainment that followed was in some ways more singular, for the prince told us that he had inherited most of his grandfather's photographic equipment, including his stereoscopic slides, and he proposed that we should view them together – 'to give you some idea of how royalty lived in those days'.

King Chulalongkorn, who reigned from 1868–1910, was a man of protean achievement. On the world stage he showed himself to be more than a match for the French colonial power that entertained barely concealed hopes of gobbling up his kingdom. At home he pursued many hobbies with unquenchable zest; organising fancy-dress parties and cooking for his friends, but, above all, immersed in his photography. He collected cameras by the hundred, did his own developing, and drew upon an immense family pool of consorts and children for his portraiture. We inspected photographs taken at frequent intervals of his sons lined up, ten at a time in order of height, for the king's loving record of their advance from childhood to adolescence – all of them, including the six-year-old at the bottom of the line, in a top hat. Toppers had only been put aside in one case when four senior sons had been crammed into the basket of an imitation balloon.

The queens and consorts were even more interesting, and here they were seen posed in the standard environment of Victorian studio photography; lounging against plaster Greek columns, taking a pretended swipe with a tennis racquet, or clutching the handlebars of a weird old bicycle. Fancy-dress shots, of which there were many, bore labels in French – the language of culture of the day – L'Amazone (Queen Somdej with a feather in her hair grasping a bow); Une dame Turque de qualité (the Princess of Chiang Mai, with a hookah); La Cavalerie Légère (an unidentified consort in a hussar's shako); La Jolie Cochère (another ditto, in white breeches and straw hat, carrying a whip). The impression given by this collection was that the Victorian epoch had produced a face of its own, and that this could triumph even over barriers of race. Thus Phra Rataya, Princess of Chiang Mai, bore a resemblance to Georges Sand, Queen Somdej had something about her of La Duse, while a lesser consort, well into middle-age, reminded me of one of my old Welsh aunts.

The prince put away the slides. Like his grandfather King Chulalongkorn, and his great grandfather, King Mongkut – who was an astronomer, and invented a quick-firing cannon based on the Colt revolver – he had a taste for intellectual pleasures. He showed us his Leica camera with its battery of lenses. Candid photography was in vogue at the time. By use of such gadgets as angle-viewfinders it was possible to catch subjects for portraiture off-guard, sometimes in ludicrous postures. There was no camera to equal it for this purpose, said the prince. As for his grandfather's gear, it took up rather a lot of space, and he would be quite happy to donate it to any museum that felt like giving it house-room.

We strolled together across the polished entrance-hall towards the door, where my attention was suddenly taken by what appeared to be a large, old-fashioned and over-ornate birdcage, suspended in an environment in which nothing belonged to a period earlier than the previous year. I stopped to examine it, and the prince said, 'Uncle lives there.'

Although slightly surprised, I thought I understood. 'You mean the house-spirit?'

'Exactly. In this life he was our head servant. He played an important part in bringing up us children, and was much loved by us all. Uncle was quite ready to sacrifice himself for the good of the family.'

The prince had no hesitation in explaining how this had come about. When the building of a new royal house was finished, a bargain might be struck with a man of low caste. The deal was that he would agree to surrender the remaining few years of the present existence in return for acceptance into the royal family in the next. He would be entitled to receive ritual offerings on a par with the family ancestors. Almost without exception such an arrangement was readily agreed to.

'How did uncle die?'

'He was interred under the threshold. Being still a child I was excluded from the ceremony, which was largely a religious one. Everyone was happy. Certainly Uncle was.'

I took the risk. 'Would a Western education have any effect at all on such beliefs?' I asked.

'That is a hard question,' the Prince said, 'but I am inclined to the opinion that it would be slight. It appears to be more a matter of feeling than conscious belief. Education is an imperfect shield against custom and tradition.' We stood together in the doorway and the cage swayed a little in a gust of warm breeze. 'In some ways,' the prince said, 'you may judge us still to be a little backward.' His laugh seemed apologetic, 'In others I hope you will agree that we move with the times.'

TAHITI AFTER
GAUGUIN

W IEDLER, MY CONTACT in Tahiti, had come to the island forty years ago, married a local lady and was now a happy member of a vastly extended Tahitian family. He lived in Papeete, but we had made the trip together to Huahine, one of the six principal Tahitian islands where Wiedler was trying to effect a reconciliation between a favourite nephew and his wife, who had gone home to her mother there. The nephew, a smiling bronzed Adonis with marvellously tattooed torso and thighs was waiting for us in the gardens of the hotel. This had been built on the site of an ancient Polynesian temple of which many vestiges were scattered about. Rivulets of clear water curled through the grounds, mirroring the reflections of passing girls, swathed stylishly in their *pareas* and decked with frangipani. The morning was untidy with blossom which the girls were brushing with a certain reverence from the paths, and a sea of many colours showed through the branches of trees. The white line of a reef was drawn just below the horizon, and the distant surf added its muttered commentary to our discussion. Gauguin faces were everywhere to be seen.

The problem was that Ricky – as the nephew called himself – was employed in the new black pearl industry on a remote island in the Tuamoto group, with a lagoon 46 kilometres across but a population of only 128, and his wife was bored. There was no television. The cabins supplied by the company were fitted with solar panels producing enough electricity to work a video, and there was a good selection of cassettes, all on violent themes. Apart from that, the only distraction was churchgoing on Sunday. The wife had agreed to stay on if their housing could be improved by the addition of a picture-window. This would have to be imported at great cost from the States, and extreme dexterity and seamanship would be required to manoeuvre it in a small canoe through the opening in the reef to reach the village. Ricky had raised the further objection that once in place the window would generate intolerable heat, and that the ever-present sand would prevent it from being slid open or shut on its runners. There the matter rested. In any case, Ricky added, he was heartily sick of the view of the sea.

The positioning of this hotel had been selected with great care, offering not only marine prospects of the most glamorous kind upon which Ricky seemed glad to turn his back, but an inland view of an extinct volcano known in Tahitian as Pregnant Woman Asleep – which indeed well described it. This, and the other ancient volcanoes, from which the islands are formed, provides a unique feature of the Tahitian scene, for here there are no eroded surfaces and no bare rock. Every peak, pinnacle or precipice is mantled by a tight carapace of ferns, appearing from the distance as a carpet of the deepest green.

Considerable imagination is shown in such places to keep the visitors amused. Beyond the normal 'activities', trips are arranged on Huahine to view the colossal eels, spared, it is supposed, by an ancient taboo, inhabiting a shallow local stream. Guests with the strength to do so are urged to try their hand at lifting one of these confiding monsters – weighing up to 30 lb – from the water. On Raiatea they will drop you off on a desert island, provided with a survival kit that includes in the season of hurricanes a rope to tie yourself to a tree, and leave you there as long as you like.

Bora Bora's speciality is feeding sharks – an experience described at the hotel as *impressionant*, which indeed it is. The Tahitian boatman chooses a likely spot and you lower yourselves into the water. A lifeline is fixed to the canoe, but this carries little conviction. 'Nothing can happen to you,' the boatman, swimming ahead, calls back, adding jokily, 'I have a special deal with the sharks.' He floats a bucket full of kitchen scraps for distribution, and after grabbing a handful, scatters them in the water. Instantly we are enclosed in a swirling envelope of fish of all degrees of beauty and freakishness. Eventually a shark shoulders its way through the screen of lesser fish to take what is on offer, which it does in a hesitant and somewhat listless fashion. On this occasion we saw six in all, the smallest perhaps 5 foot and the largest 7 foot in length. The boatman said that he had heard that an incautious feeder had once lost a hand, but that had been somewhere else, and long ago.

In contrast with the endless variety and vivacity of the life of the lagoon, the fauna of Tahiti is unremarkable. There are no snakes or frogs, few birds and butterflies, and the quadrupeds are represented by edible, vegetarian rats and by an occasional wild pig. I was shown what its owner claimed was the unique survivor of the native vegetarian (also edible) dog, an insignificant tailless and almost hairless beast. This was normally fed on coconut, but there must have been a break somewhere in the ancestral chain, as I later surprised it licking furtively at a piece of fat.

Of the six islands, Moorea, Huahine, Raiatea, Bora Bora and Maupiti are inevitably less changed by our times than Tahiti itself. Populations are small, and on the whole committed to a happy-go-lucky subsistence economy. These lesser islands – Bora Bora apart – receive relatively few visitors. They are largely to be explored by bicycle or on foot and have retained a substantial element of the old Polynesian charm.

Huahine and Raiatea – the sacred islands of the old civilis-ation – are littered with the vestiges of those ancestral shrines known as *marae* and there is something about these monoliths and packed rows of standing stones – despite the lagoon water rippling over the coral near by – that endows them with a strangely Hebridean feeling.

Nevertheless, Tahiti itself, away from its single main road, must be scenically as charming as ever, and a few hundred yards up into any of the valleys radiating from the central peak, the explorer plunges into forests of almost Amazonian opacity and grandeur. The accepted beauty spot is still Matavai beach, where Captain Cook came ashore in 1769, and nothing has been done to despoil it. William Hodges, artist to Cook's second expedition, painted it in 1773, and this year it remained with its cassuarina trees, its stream, and its tracery of cliffs lifting into the mists, just as he saw it. Only a Tahitian Venus with lightly tattooed buttocks drying herself after a dip was absent. Here, Cook's crew, besieged by the garlanded island girls, learned of the existence of free (and instant) love, tore the locally valuable nails from the planks of the *Endeavour*, to offer in token of their gratitude, and caused the ladies much amusement by insisting that the natural conclusion to these encounters should be conducted behind the screen of nearby bushes.

This, too, was the landing place in 1797 of the missionaries sent by the London Missionary Society, who, as entranced as Cook had been by their reception, and the setting, asked for the bay to be given to them. The request was immediately granted by the local chief, who had no concept of private property, and was later disconcerted to learn that he and his people were debarred for ever from trespass on the area. The evangelists were a strange assortment, picked by the Society on the score of their probable usefulness to an uninstructed people and they included a harness-maker, a bricklayer, a farrier, a weaver and a butcher and his wife. None of these had ever left England before, and few their native villages. It was four years before any of them learned enough of the language to preach a sermon to a puzzled though sympathetic audience. The Tahitians built their houses, fed them, and provided them with servants and labourers galore, but after seven years not a convert had been made. The device which eventually established their unswerving rule is described in a letter home, written by one of the brethren, J. M. Orsmond: 'All the missionaries were at that time salting pork and distilling spirits . . . Pomare [the local chief] had a large share. He was drunk when I arrived and I never saw him sober.' Orsmond describes the compact by which Pomare, reduced to alcoholism, would be backed in a war against the other island chiefs on the understanding that his victory would be followed by enforced conversion. Since Pomare was supplied with firearms to be used against his opponents' clubs, victory was certain. 'The whole nation', Orsmond wrote, 'was converted in a day.' Then followed a reign of terror. Persistent unbelievers were put to death, and a penal code was drawn up by the missionaries, and enforced by missionary police in the uniforms of Bow Street Runners. It was declared illegal to adorn oneself with flowers, to sing (other than hymns), to tattoo the body, to surf or to dance. Minor offenders were put in the stocks, but major infringements (dancing included) were punished by hard labour on the roads. Within a decade the process by which the native culture of Tahiti had been extinguished was exported to every corner of the South Pacific, reducing the islanders to the level of the working-class of Victorian England.

J. M. Orsmond crops up again on Moorea where he is remembered with anguish until this day. After their mass conversion it was hoped that the Tahitians might be induced to accept the benefits of civilisation by being set to work on sugar plantations, and to create these a Mr Ayles, formerly a slave overseer in Jamaica was brought over, along with the necessary mill equipment. The enterprise failed, and Mr Orsmond, believing that 'a too bountiful nature on Moorea diminishes men's natural desire to work', ordered all breadfruit trees to be cut down. By this time, the population of Tahiti had been reduced by syphilis, tuberculosis, smallpox and influenza from the 200,000 estimated by Cook to 18,000. After 30 years of missionary rule, only 6,000 remained. At this point the French arrived to take over. Given the circumstances it was the best possible solution. The brethren were driven from their kingdom, and thereafter the gradual recovery both of numbers and joie de vivre was under way.

Back to the Tahiti of our days – dating according to Wiedler from the epoch-making events of the early sixties. These included the coming of television, the siting of an international airport at Papeete and, above all, the decision by the French to begin nuclear testing on the atoll of Mururoa, 700 miles to the south-east of Tahiti. In 1962, Wiedler said, a Tahitian had been fined for speeding on a bicycle down the main street of Papeete. By 1963 when the Pacific Experimental Centre (CEP) responsible for the tests had taken over much of the city's centre, the reckless cyclist belonged to another century. An army of technicians arrived from France, and the islands were drained of able-bodied males required for the workforce. Many of these came from villages where they still lit lamps at night to drive the ghosts away, and only such things as sugar, rice and basic articles of clothing were bought with money. From this relaxed environment the young islander faced one in which, paid the unthinkable wage of four US dollars an hour, he was introduced to credit facilities, urged to buy whatever he fancied, and expected to drink beer. Up till then he had been accustomed to spend the odd hour, whenever the mood took him, fishing or perhaps cleaning up a manioc patch. Now he clocked in at 6 a.m., learned to jump to it when given an order, and put in a strenuous eight-hour working day. The population of Tahiti had more than doubled, almost overnight, to 123,000, and new arrivals had to be shoved into whatever living space could be found for them. Now, living standards are the highest in the South Pacific, and so are the prices. A packet of cigarettes costs the equivalent of £3. Coconuts, washed up by the thousand along the Tahitian beaches, fetch more in the market of Papeete than they do in London. Love – still as free as ever on the islands – is highly priced and dangerous in the capital.

The changes brought about by sudden wealth and its many obligations are more fundamental than generally realised. *Le Monde* noted the Tahitian tradition by which males aged between 16 and 25 years are expected to spend their time in pursuit of pleasures – usually love affairs. This period at an end, most of them settle down to marriage and raise up to ten children in exemplary fashion. The undisturbed island society is a crime-free one, in which people still make up excuses to give things away. Standards of public health are nowhere higher, with a negligible infant death-rate. Currently, 50 per cent of the population of Tahiti as a whole is under 20, and by 1990 the average age of this juvenile half is expected to fall to 16.

There have been 88 nuclear tests to date, but when, as is bound to happen, they come to an end, what is to happen? A slackening in demand for labour has already caused severe unemployment, leaving too many young workers unable to pay for addictions fostered by the consumer society. In October 1987, an attempt by the dock-workers' union to compel employers to take on more hands failed when the military were called in to unload the ships. This set off riots in which 100 leading shops and business premises in the heart of Papeete went up in flames, and 1,000 gendarmes and foreign legionnaires were flown in to restore peace. It is perhaps characteristic of Tahiti that no casualties were sustained in this upheaval.

I had another meeting with Wiedler and his favourite nephew, who had been in Papeete at the time of the riots. 'It was better than the movies,' Ricky said, but doubt showed through the pretence of relish. His wife had been urging him to look for work in the capital, but now she had changed her mind and they were returning, fairly contentedly, to their atoll. She was to have her picture-window. Ricky was confident that in the end she, too, would have enough of the view, and then he would get a local artist to paint a picture over it of the Boulevard Pomare, Papeete, with the plane trees from France, and the cars parked all along the front.

BARCELONA AND THE
FOREST BEYOND

WHEN, SHORTLY AFTER the war, I lived for a time on the then untouched Costa Brava, I was sometimes approached by a fisherman wanting a lift into Barcelona. The fishermen only went there out of dire necessity, usually in fear and trembling, to buy fishing tackle unavailable elsewhere, and the car-sickness from which they always suffered was accentuated by nerves. The fishing-tackle shop was down a side street leading off the Ramblas, and I usually dropped my passenger on the corner. Barcelona was Sodom to the austere and clean-living fishermen, and I knew that my friend would be carrying his money sewn into the lining of his jacket, and that his hand would be on the weasel paw charm in his pocket. This, on the frontiers of the zone known as the Barrio Chino, was a brazen place. The grandmothers of the fierce-eyed girls who still lurk in the dark doorways of the area would be all round us with their significant gestures, mouthing invitations laced with contempt. 'If you've a moment to spare,' one of my passengers said, 'would you feel like walking down to the shop with me?' We went down the street together and he stocked up with his archaic and inefficient hooks. After that I had business of my own to attend to. He agreed to wait for me in the car and I showed him how the door-locks worked. 'As a foreigner,' he said, 'you'd have no way of knowing, but half these people are sick. It's something you pick up in the air. Among other things it makes you piss blood.' 'Let's go and have a drink,' I suggested. 'No,' he said. 'I don't want to do that. You never know what they put in it. There was a man from the village who was down here last year and they slipped something into his *hierbas*. When he woke up even the gold fillings in his teeth had gone.'

This man has vanished from the earth, and not only he, but all his kind, his village, and the dramatic landscape in which it was set. The little patch of sea he so miserably explored with his antiquated gear is empty of fish, although, reduced to a tourist amenity, it contributes handsomely in other ways to the revenues of those who have developed the coast. Barcelona itself, nevertheless, remains in its central parts remarkably undisturbed. All the landmarks of the old town remain. Gaudí's fantastic cathedral is as far from completion as it was forty years ago. The innumerable nightspots of old are still in business. The chickens still turn nightly on the spits in the wall outside the Caracoles restaurant (last year the management announced that 1,850,000 had been readied for consumption in this way in the 100-year history of the business). A hundred thousand citizens each day still complete most of the mile's walk in each direction up and down the Ramblas between the Plaza de Cataluña and the port, moved to do this in the interests of social interchange, for the benefit of their health, and, above all, out of custom.

The Ramblas remains the heart and soul of the city; once a watercourse, now a tree-shaded promenade, copied in all the towns of the Hispanic world, local geography permitting. It provides traditional distractions all along its length. Flower-sellers and dealers in pets with their animals and birds occupy the higher reaches at the entrance from the plaza. There is no more touching sight than that of tiny pinafored children from the local infants' school, clinging at exact intervals to the long rope by which they are led, a teacher at each end, past the cagefuls of puppies and rabbits to top up their morning happiness before lessons begin.

Barcelona is exuberant, enterprising and prosperous, with a population comparable to that of Madrid. With the country's highest standard of living and plenty of money to throw away on whimsical fancies, its citizens can afford unusual and expensive animals, often transported here to an unsuitable environment. Baby chimpanzees are in fashion. You can buy a piranha that requires to be fed on meat, a small Galapagos turtle, or an Amazonian parrot, bilingual to the extent that it can swear in Spanish or Portuguese. Nothing must be *ordinary*. Sellers of dogs concentrate on unusual breeds. Those with long hair (inappropriate to the climate) are in demand. Old English sheepdogs are a current favourite, but woolly versions of the Alsatian are also on offer.

A taste for the bizarre, typified by Gaudí's occasionally nightmarish architecture and always present here, finds expression even in small ways. Half-way down to the port, the principal market opens its grandiose portals on to the Ramblas like those of a baroque church. The visitor may be confronted with a stallful of fungi, some sinister, some startling, all curious. There is an element of freakishness, even in fish-market displays, where you might find a deep-sea monster, armoured like a Dalek, parading jerkily with an occasional flicker of internally generated light among a mixed exhibit of live crustacians. The more grotesque the fish, the greater the admiration aroused.

The meat market also sets out to impress. My visit there followed a *corrida* in the Plaza Monumental in which six bulls had been killed, and here were their bodily parts arranged in ingenious and arresting ways, the whole show overlooked by the heads of the animals themselves staring down with misted, reproachful eyes upon the throng of excited buyers. These were prepared to pay 25 per cent more for the flesh of bulls killed in the ring than for that of those who had encountered death in the ordinary way.

The Ramblas slopes gently down to the port. On the right it skirts the Barrio Chino, an area that still retains a sinister waterfront vitality, only comparable to that of the Vieux Port of Marseilles in its seedy prime, now long past. Perhaps under the Barrio's influence a certain profligacy is in the air; the ranks of bourgeois promenaders thin, and some turn back. The last of the bookstands with their lavishly produced special editions and rich offerings of soft pornography are left behind as the performers, the buffoons, the illusionists and the cheats come into their own. They are drawn from many countries: Venetian tumblers in their bird masks; Indian flute-players from icebound Andean villages; a Hindu ascetic on his bed of nails; fire and sword swallowers; tellers of Tarot card futures; a Bolivian peddling llama foetuses from the witches' market in La Paz; a man who throws all his limbs out joint; nimble, confiding pimps on the watch for elderly loiterers.

Barcelona, infinitely indulgent, tolerates them all. It is now said to have been 'discovered' only in the last few years. If this is true, it is hard to imagine how it could have been overlooked because, in reality, it has always been like this – a good-natured and permissive city, even in the darkest days of the Franco régime. An English boy of 17 who had gone abroad with his guitar to join forces with a group of Franco-Italian strolling players said of it: 'This kind of scene doesn't happen anywhere else in Europe. The Spanish people are nice and the police don't give you hassle. The worst place to work in is England; this is the best. We're always sorry to pull out of Barcelona, and glad to be back.'

Barcelona stands on the frontier between the familiar, sun-cured Spanish landscape to the south and, to the north, the most densely wooded countryside of the Mediterranean, stretching to the Pyrenees and the French border. This area, nearly 150 miles across, contains forests of almost Amazonian density of cork-oak and pine and – with a curiously oriental touch – even thickets of bamboo. The woods are full of flowers in spring, some of great rarity. Empordà, to give the north-east corner of Spain its ancient name – still in use – is an Arcadia to be explored with all possible speed for, like all Arcadias that have come within reach of affluent and expansive cities, it must inevitably disappear.

Owing to its distance from the coast, the times have passed Empordà by, which is why many of the gracious customs of the past have survived here and why the cuisine is the best in Spain – and therefore among the best anywhere. It is a terrific fallacy among English travellers who have been subjected to Spanish food in the hotels and restaurants in holiday resorts to judge it as second-rate. Those who take to the byroads of Empordà will encounter a cuisine of an ingenuity, variety and charm hard to equal in similar circumstances in, say, Italy, or even France.

A car is essential for the exploration of these low mountain ranges and forests. The general strategy is: never leave a third-class road unless it cannot be avoided. Here, as elsewhere throughout the Peninsula, they conduct the traveller into those nooks and crannies of the countryside where the past makes its last stand. Behind the scenes in Empordà nothing has changed visually since the Middle Ages. Cows still carry horns, farm-carts are drawn by horses, fields mown with scythes. Great porticoed and colonnaded farmhouses dominate the fields, their architectural form inherited from Roman predecessors. Their large numbers reflect the richness of the soil and the prosperity of the rural past. Inevitably, these masterpieces have attracted the attention of city-dwellers in search of a country house of noble proportions for weekend use. For those prepared to drink well-water and generate their own electricity, such a building in grand mediaeval style can be picked up cheaply enough. Agents in nearby towns such as La Bisbal specialise in unusual country properties and will even increase the feudal atmosphere of the purchase, if desired, by the addition of a defence tower, built with authentic materials, at an additional cost of about £10,000. An agent in San Feliù de Guixols will undertake to demolish three substantial farm-houses and rebuild them in the form of a pigmy castle, authentic in every detail, for about half a million. Where new stonework has to be patched in, the patina of age can now be sprayed on.

The penetration of the rich into such regions, whose charm depends upon simplicity and the restraints imposed by sparse incomes, can have a curiously deadening effect. There are four mediaeval villages immediately east of Gerona; Pals, Peretal-lada, Villastret and Gruilles (which has a 150-foot tower with a tree growing out of its top). All are of great interest, and not to be missed, for until now they have withstood intrusion by our times, remaining productive living communities of their own. Now the eyes of affluent city-folk have fallen upon them, and it is hard for a peasant owner to resist an offer of a level swap for his small, dark gem of twelfth-century architecture for a comfortable and well fitted modern flat in the nearest town.

In due course the new owner from Barcelona or Gerona moves in. Usually he is a man of education and taste and a sympathetic restoration begins under the watchful eye of the planning authority, determined to ensure that none of the harmonies of the ancient village are disturbed. At most, the new man will get away with the addition of a discreet picture-window. To take the case of Pals, whatever has been done has been with huge respect for the past. Yet, this small town is fossilising into a museum piece. Two thirds of its original people have sold out. There are no children or animals, and in its over-clean streets the only sound apart from that of a Mercedes sneaking past to the place where it will be parked out of sight, is likely to be Handel's choral music piped from the church.

The story of Catalonia's coastal development is a sad one. The once stupendous coastline between Blanes and the French frontier – much of it unchanged since the voyages of

Odysseus until forty years ago – has been buried under concrete so that many entrancing small towns such as Tossa, Lloret and Estartit are hardly now to be identified. The few exceptions are Cadaquès in the far north and a string of villages, probably saved by difficulty of access – Aigua Fredda, Sa Tuna, and Aigua Blava – the most impressive in its location, with rufous cliffs stacked at the entrance to a tiny bay and a few houses wedged among rocks and pines. The water is of unexampled transparency, provoking a sensation of vertigo in the mask-wearer when swimming over great depths. Mysteriously, it is quite free of pollution, now afflicting so much of the Mediterranean.

Ugliness is encountered elsewhere, surging up from the coast. Grey, fortress-like hypermarkets, car cemeteries, pretentious restaurants, sport-cabin villages and parking lots intrude upon the natural order of the landscape. The ancient honey-coloured sandstone buildings of Empordà are perfectly proportioned and in total sympathy with the sombre green foliage of oaks and pines, and russet earth. Here the monotonous white cubes of Mediterranean coastal villas are offensively out of place.

Fortunately, ugliness on the Costa Brava is easily escaped by a quick retreat into the interior. In the north, where the country is flat, the no-man's-land of eyesores may extend for five miles. South of Palamós along the remaining 30 miles of the coast the undefiled woods come right down to the sea, offering instant retreat into delight.

WINTER IN
SEVILLE

'MY NAME IS Elena Valleverde,' the Sevillian lady said, 'but I am more familiarly known as "Elena of the cats".'

I found her on my way to the city's centre on the once gracious promenade, now fallen into decay, known as the Alameda of Hercules. She had just unpadlocked the garden gates of an abandoned great house and was about to feed some of the several thousand cats that have taken up residence in such pacific surroundings in Seville. She was fiftyish with the figure of a young girl, an expression of maternal sweetness, an old-fashioned frilled dress and a high Spanish comb. She had arrived with a boy assistant carrying a case neatly packed with the remains of meals collected in neighbouring restaurants. Today's menu for the cats, which were exceptionally large, sleek and calm, was paella.

'I look after about 500 in my daily round of the district,' Elena said. 'In addition to food a number of residents contribute small sums of money for their upkeep. I am one of several volunteers who undertake this work. We Sevillians admire cats for their dignity and restraint, and regard them as an ornament to the city. Friends of mine also take care of the birds.'

Beyond and above the splendid decrepitude of the street, with its tousled palms, its Roman columns and its windfalls of oranges, the belfries of great baroque churches floated like the poops of galleons in a sparkling winter sky. It was one o'clock and the children came pouring out of the nearby school and went dancing past. Elena and her assistant moved on to the next vast Amazonian garden, unpadlocked the gates and went in. This was the peak of the Sevillian day, with every bar crowded, and the lottery-sellers going with the voices of heralds through every street. Even in winter, Seville lives out of doors.

For this reason, all business deals are conducted not in boardrooms but bars, and preferably in one of the hundred or so in and around the Calle Sierpes. This is the home ground of all that is essentially Sevillian and the showcase of wonderful survivals. A patisserie at its entrance on the corner of the Plaza Campana is embellished with Art Nouveau panels, almost certainly overlooked by its clientèle who flock in to buy its ingenious and somewhat oriental cakes. Many advertisements have been executed in charming but imperishable azulejo tiles and urge the purchase of such things as early Kodaks, gramophones with horns, mustard plasters and treadle-operated sewing-machines, most of them obsolete for at least half a century. The finest example of lost promotional effort is in the parallel Calle Velasquez, which still devotes 60 square feet of wall space to the 1926 Studebaker, showing five ladies of the day in their first ecstatic outing. Back in the Calle Sierpes a vintage hatter displays typical Sevillian headgear in several colours, a clock maker's features an example of their craft that chants the hours in plainsong; and a nearby chemist sells asafoedita, gum Senegal, snake bite, leeches, blue unction, and a range of glass eyes. The Calle Velasquez offers nothing better in the way of clubs than the Tertulia Culturál Bética, which seats six members in two rows to face the street in an environment hardly more cheerful than that of a dentist's waiting-room. By comparison, accommodation at the Sierpes's

Círculo Mercantíl y Industriál is luxurious, as well as immensely discreet. Here, when night falls, members settle behind tinted glass in almost complete darkness to entertain themselves with the gay and melancholy flux of life surging through the street within feet of where they sit.

The secretary was away, so information about membership qualifications somewhat vague.

'It helps to own 10 caballerías of land,' the employee suggested.

'How much is a caballería?'

'Do you ride?'

'More or less.'

'It is the area you can ride round in 15 minutes at a steady trot . . . There is a waiting list of about fifty years.'

The Sierpes saw the origin of that inspired and revolutionary snack, the tapa, meaning cover, thus named because it started life as a slice of ham covering the glasses of wine sent out for to the nearest cellar, in the days when dust swirled in Seville's unpaved streets. Since then it has evolved to a point when all dishes, however elaborate, can be sampled in this miniature form. Leading bars offer up to fifty varieties of the tapa, and for many Sevillians a selection of a half-dozen eaten at the counter constitutes an imaginative midday meal.

Beyond the narrow Calle Sierpes the city spreads its wide streets and squares in which stand those great islands of mediaevalism, the Cathedral (the world's third-largest church), and the Moorish fortress of the Alcázar. The Christian faith of its day advertised itself in the sheer size of its undertakings. 'Let us build a church so big that we shall be held to be insane,' a member of the Chapter urged, as soon as the great mosque had been levelled and the building of the cathedral began. The Emperor Charles V broke in upon the scene a few tragic years too late. Most likeable of the Spanish monarchs, who collected parrots, enjoyed gardening, and had done his best to impress his subjects by taking on an enfeebled bull in the arena of Madrid, he had been in time to prevent the destruction of the Mosque of Córdoba. To the Sevillians he said, 'You have built here what you or anyone might have built anywhere, but you have destroyed what was unique in the world.'

The Cathedral of Seville is indeed vast and very dark, and wandering in its perpetual twilight one has sometimes the feeling of being lost in some huge railway station in a foreign land. Nevertheless, seen from the exterior at night, its icy gothic traceries lit against the sky, it produces a stunning impression. It is set in surroundings of outstanding charm. Beyond its bustling central streets, Seville is a quiet city. All this historical area, patched with small plazas and dominated by ancient buildings, fosters its own brand of tranquillity; where elsewhere the mediaeval background may be remote and often lifeless, here it is close and familiar. An aesthetic experience of the first order is within reach of anyone prepared to arm themselves with a map and approach this enchanted area not through the city streets but along the ancient lanes skirting the walls of the Alcázar – which to some minds is a more impressive building than the better-known Alhambra of Grenada. The quarter is entered by Alfaro de Murillo, leading from the Calzado de Ribera gardens. The first turning to the left, into a lane called Aguas, is followed by one to the right into Judería, which opens after a few yards into the Patio de Banderas. Orange trees have been planted all the way, and the memorable Patio de Banderas is virtually a grove in the heart of the city. Fallen oranges littering the square by night are picked up at first light and piled in a central fountain awaiting collection. It is better to undertake this ten-minute excursion at about nightfall, best of all in the mild Sevillian winter, in the hope of finding the patio misted with rain through which fruit by the thousand glisten under the lamps. From this small, ancient, and virtually deserted square a Moorish gateway opens upon a theatrical presentation of the Cathedral and the Giralda tower. It is a scene to which one returns repeatedly.

The Calle Dos de Mayo remains my favourite Sevillian

street, with its entrance just across the road from the Cathedral. It widens immediately into a tiny plaza called Almirantazgo, then squeezes through a narrow arch in the Sevillian baroque manner – the original toll-gate of the city. A wall-panel in ceramic tiles put up by a forgotten soap-manufacturer nearly a century ago depicts this spot as it was then, and hardly anything has changed. This remains almost a countryside byway, with sparse traffic and a few elegant horse-drawn carriages mixed in with the cars. All the windows in the high white walls are draped with sumptuous folds of baroque plaster picked out in chrome yellow. The colour is exclusive to Seville, the paint being produced by some millenial process from the richly coloured soil of the nearby Alcalá de Guadaïra, which otherwise lays claim to local fame with its bullfighting school.

A turning to the left 100 yards up the Dos de Mayo leads past the house of the legendary Don Juan, who, persuaded to repentance by a dream in which he found himself attending his own funeral, turned the magnificent building over as a charity hospital for the use of the poor.

Immediately ahead in the rundown but atmospheric Calle Santander, a badly tended wall shrine has attracted much veneration since the intervention of the Virgin it contains, in a nocturnal duel, extinguishing the light of her lamp whenever the opponents lunged at each other with their swords.

The same building houses the Bodegón de la Torre d'Oro. This restaurant is a local institution that in some miraculous way has been able to resist the standardisation imposed by our times. Strangely, Sevillians who prefer to eat in small, crowded, intimate places are apt to object that it is too large. Nevertheless, they are drawn there by its unbeatable value. What marks it as different in the experience of a foreigner is the bearing that one's distance from the serving counter has upon the price of food. There are three tariffs, and the nearer the customer stations himself, whether standing or crouched at an exceedingly small table, to the anarchy at the bar, the less he pays. At about 7 p.m. neighbourhood families with many children drop in for beer and snacks, vacating their tables to more affluent-looking diners by 9. After that customers under no compulsion to rise early begin to drift in, and may stay on until midnight. About a third of the Bodega's cavernous interior is screened off to provide a restaurant of the conventional kind, patronised by the occasional Japanese in search of local colour. Sevillians breakfast here at about 11 a.m., often on *picatosta* – a slice of fried bread sprinkled with sugar – usually accompanied by a glass of manzanilla, sipped slowly and in a reflective manner. Otherwise the Bodega specialises in potato omelettes, cooked until quite dry, and eaten with the fingers, and fried fish, the latter offering a prime culinary experience that bears absolutely no relationship to the English version.

The River Guadalquivir flows quietly at the end of the street, overlooked by the chrome-yellow and white bull-ring – the most elegant in Spain. From across the road a statue of Carmen keeps an apprehensive watch on its principal gate, opened only for the departure of a bullfighter who has been accorded a triumph in imperial Roman style, or for the removal in state of one whose life has ended in the ring. On the last occasion (in 1985) when it opened for the second reason, the circumstances were extraordinary. The bull was already down, regarded technically as dead, and the matador had turned away to acknowledge the plaudits of the crowd, when with a last convulsive effort the bull righted itself to kill him with a horn thrust through the heart.

Such a death still provides immortality of a kind, even in the days when the goal-shooting stars of FC Sevilla have become the idols of youth. Bullfighting, as its aficionados insist, is an art, not a sport, and there is even a touch of the old pagan religion about it. Those who sacrifice themselves to it are never forgotten. The great figures of the past, such as Joselito, drew more crowds to Seville than the reigning king on one of his visits. Joselito spent half his fortune on the purchase of four emeralds for the Virgin of Macarena, patroness of bullfighters (and originally smugglers) and when at the age of 23 he died in exemplary fashion in the ring, the Virgin was dressed by her attendants in widow's weeds, in which she remained for a month.

Belmonte, considered the greatest bullfighter of the century, was a depressive, who committed suicide, having failed to die, as he would clearly have wished to do, by the horns of a bull. An attempt by the Church to deny him burial in sacred ground collapsed in the face of public outcry, and permission was given for interment in the Seville cemetery, provided that the tomb was black and devoid of any normal religious ornamentation. Juan Belmonte, who lies under the model of a black marble piano, continues to live in the popular memory. Seville, always on the look-out for an excuse for a fiesta, decided this January to revive the traditional procession known as the Cavalcade of the Three Kings. There were to be many children robed in white, an assortment of bands, and camels if they could be found. Inevitably, on such occasions the name of Belmonte springs to mind, for the leader of the three Kings was to be dressed in the very same attire worn by this folk hero when he had led the cavalcade so many years before.

It was the first procession of the Sevillian year, to be followed by many others in a city where the mere act of pacing the streets in the company of those who share the same spiritual tradition establishes a bond with religious overtones. The ceremonial year would reach its peak with the church parading its magnificence, and its incomparable sense of theatre in the festivities of the Semana Santa. Seville possesses 70 confraternities, dedicated, as they have been for 600 years, to the sombre pomp of Easter. This year once again the hooded penitents of each cofradía would form the many nocturnal processions (the longest itinerary takes twelve hours to complete) to carry their images to every corner of the city. Every street and square would resound throughout the night with drum beats and trumpets, and the strident outcry of flamenco singers from balconies and roof-tops, saluting the passing of a succession of virgins beneath. Only Seville has the history, the traditions, and the passion to stage such a pageant.

BURNING THE
TREES

THE AMAZON FOREST leaves its mark on the imagination of all who see it. It is one of nature's exaggerations, matching the great river, which viewed across white beaches, the further bank out of sight, could be an ocean drifting eastwards.

One third of the world's trees grow in the forest's five million square kilometres – an area larger than Europe. It extends its umbrella of shade over half Brazil; the cool, damp, crepuscular corner of a continent. It is shown as blanks on the map between the veining of rivers and has little legend and no history.

Romantic explorers and holy madmen like the celebrated Colonel Fawcett paddled their canoes up creeks, and hacked brief trails in the jungle in search of hidden cities, but there was never anything there but trees and painted, feathered Indians, almost as much a part of the jungle as the trees themselves. The first satellite photographs revealed more of the details of the forest than had three centuries of exploration. The trees provided the final refuge of 100-odd Indian tribes, numbering perhaps 40,000 people. It is believed that almost as many have disappeared since the turn of the century – many as the result of outright murder, more through the white man's diseases, against which the Indian has no immunity. Occasionally a new Indian group is found – flushed out of the trees by pioneers who cut the trails ahead of the road-building gangs – and when this happens about a quarter of those 'contacted' can be expected to die of one commonplace Western ailment or another within the year. Indians are entirely dependent upon the forest. They cannot survive outside it.

Theodore Roosevelt, spokesman and clairvoyant of the world of quick profits, pondered over the Amazonian vacuum and predicted what was to come. He had written a book about the pleasures of ranching, but had little use for trees. 'The country along this river', he wrote in 1914, 'is fine natural cattle country, and one day it will see a great development.' His judgment as to the suitability of the land for cattle ranching was abysmally wrong; his prediction at least half correct. The ranchers arrived and the great attack on the trees began.

Sixty years later the Brazilian people were to learn that about a quarter of the forests of the Amazon Basin and Mato Grosso had already been destroyed. Eleven million hectares of trees had been cleared in the preceding decade alone, and it became a matter of simple arithmetic, if this were allowed to go on, to forecast a date when the forest would cease to exist altogether.

Most of the clearing was done by foreign enterprises such as Daniel Keith Ludwig's Jari Forestry and Ranching Company, the Italian firm Liquigas, Volkswagen do Brasil, and King Ranch of Texas. These and many more had been encouraged in their attack on the forest by financial incentives offered by the Brazilian Government. Great fires – some of them ignited by napalm bombing – raged all over Amazonia, consuming trees by the hundred million, and for months on end travellers on planes on their way from Belém to Manaus or Brazilia saw little of the landscape beneath them through the smoke.

There were few parts of the world left in this century where uninhibited commercial adventures of this kind were still possible, where land could be picked up for next to nothing. Wages were about a tenth of those paid in Europe or the US, and a modest investment in stock and equipment offered the prospect of spectacular profits. The Government's early enthusiasm for giant ranches began to falter when it was found that, like the trees they replaced, they seemed to live on themselves, and produced little surplus to help with the balance of payments. Nor did they relieve unemployment, because when a ranch became a going concern it took only one man to look after 1,000 head of cattle.

With the growing suspicion that the multinationals were little concerned with the long-term problems of the nation, voices were raised to inquire whether this rape of the forest, so apparently devoid of economic reward, might not in the long run have some undesirable effect on the climate. The mild obsession, familiar in northern latitudes, over the possibility of the return of the Ice Age is replaced in the tropics with a conviction that the reverse is likely to happen. In Peru a loss of permanent snow has been recorded from the Andean ice-peaks. Bolivia has suffered from declining rainfall and searing winds, while in Brazil itself parts of the north-east in the area of Ceará have been reduced to near-desert.

These misgivings were given alarming substance by the publication of figures based on 17 years' field-studies in Amazonia. This research was done by Harald Sioli, Director of the Max Planck Institute of Limnology, in West Germany, and his calculations argued that the Amazon forest contributed through photosynthesis 50 per cent of the world's annual production of oxygen. He claimed that it could not be sacrificed without a dramatic, if not fully predictable, deterioration in world climate. He calculated that the forest contained about 300 tons of carbon per hectare, and that its total extension of 280 million hectares, if burnt down, would allow sufficient carbon dioxide to be released into the atmosphere to cause a 10 per cent increase of the gas. The threat was two-fold: the loss of the forest's important contribution of oxygen, and of its capacity to absorb carbon dioxide. Sioli noted that the burning of fossil-fuels had already caused a 15 per cent increase in carbon dioxide over the past century, and that the forests were failing to contain the increase. He concluded that destroying the Amazon forest would be like getting rid of one of the world's major oceans – environmentally suicidal.

There has been some scientific bandying of arguments over these figures, which have been wholeheartedly endorsed by some experts and received with caution by others. One climatologist, for example, has argued that one-third of the carbon dioxide released by burning fossil-fuels remains in the air, while another believes that the proportion is two-thirds. These are matters for discussion by the *illuminati*. On the danger represented by oxygen reduction, Dr Mary McNeil, an American specialist in laterite soils, says that were all tropical forests – of which the Amazon forest is a major component – to go, the earth's atmosphere would soon be denuded of oxygen.

To turn to the other problem of the excess of carbon dioxide, Norman Myers, a consultant in environmental conservation, wrote in *New Scientist*, in December 1978, 'Widespread deforestation in the tropics could lead to increased reflectivity of sunlight in the equatorial zone (the "albedo effect") and to a build-up of carbon dioxide in the earth's atmosphere. Both these processes could upset global climatic patterns . . .'

Enear Salati, professor of physics and researcher in agriculture at the University of São Paulo, was quoted in *Critica* of Manaus as saying that the destruction by burning of the Amazon forest, and consequent increase in the carbon dioxide content of the atmosphere, could result in heightened world temperature, the melting of the polar ice-caps, and a sufficient rise in ocean levels to bring about the inundation of hundreds of coastal cities throughout the world.

The predictions of all these experts are deeply worrying in their various ways. It seems clear that the least we have to fear from the loss of the Amazon forest is undesirable meteorological changes, and the worst the catastrophe promised by Sioli and Salati.

The threatened forest offers the paradox of an area into which is crammed the greatest abundance and diversity of living things to be found anywhere on earth, yet is potentially a desert. Only the thinnest skin of humus covers the laterite floor. Apart from what is derived through photosynthesis, the trees live almost by what can be described as self-cannibalisation, upon nutrients furnished by the litter they themselves provide, made rapidly available through the action of insects, worms and fungi. The forest recycles 51 per cent of the rain that falls on it, and produces little more energy than it consumes. It lives then, almost independent of the soil, in a state of equilibrium.

Remove the trees and the average temperature of the area where they once stood increases by 30°F, rainfall declines sharply (by five per cent per year over the last 10 years in some areas recently deforested in neighbouring Bolivia), yet flooding becomes a recurrent hazard, because with the loss of the 'sponge effect' of the forest's root-mat, the soil can no longer contain the excess of water. With the rains, such nutrients as the forest floor contained are instantly washed away, and the laterite, laid bare to the sun, oxidises and loses every trace of fertility. This is no equatorial replay of the slow process of the formation of dustbowls in ruined US prairies: this is instant desert unless immediate and costly counter-measures are taken.

From the time of its discovery until now, as it faces the threat of obliteration, the Amazon jungle has remained a scientific void. Those who have penetrated it – in the main rubber tappers and diamond prospectors – have been acquisitive rather than curious. Rough counts of its fauna have been made. Bates, the Victorian naturalist and contemporary of Darwin, collected 17,000 different insects before giving up, and it has been estimated that there may be 2,000 species of birds.

All the figures attempting to define this vanishing abundance are vague. Forest ecologists at INPA (the National Institute for Amazonian Research) had counted about 400 species of tress growing in a single hectare. New plants and trees were being discovered with almost every week that went by. Even to the scientists it was beginning to appear pointless to continue with the labour of classifying and cataloguing all these living things so soon to vanish.

Where the destruction of trees threatens a commercial resource, the government is sometimes moved to act. In the province of Acre, where the worst deforestation took place, 10,000 Brazil nut-gatherers had lost their livelihood and only a handful of them could find work on the new ranches. A law was therefore passed prohibiting the cutting down of the *castanheiras*. But forest fires are not selective, and as before, the nut trees went with the rest. Where it was possible to leave one standing in isolation it was soon found that such solitary survivors failed to produce nuts. It was discovered that without the presence of certain insects the pollination of their flowers could not take place, and the pollinators had gone with the rest of the forest. Even had nuts been produced, such trees could not have increased their numbers, because this called for the co-operation of a species of rodent, also defunct, which had been programmed by evolution to chew the hard coating off the nuts, and distribute them in places suited to their germination.

These recently discovered mechanisms responsible for the production of the Brazil nut provide a clue to the dimensions of our ignorance of the workings of the forest. Some trees will not fruit without the aid of a single specific bird, others are fertilised by bats, yet others by moths, and a number of seeds receive their germinative impulse in some selected animal's digestive tract. The macaw, an agent of this kind, is relentlessly hunted for supply to the pet trade, and its disappearance from any area eventually damages that area's ecology. There is a tree producing pseudo-fruit, with no biological function other than the reward of its private army of insects, kept to ward off the attack of such predators as leaf-cutter ants. Strangest of such arrangements is the case of the *inga edulis*, a gigantic runner-bean, dangling from the tree that bears it in the waters of a creek; the bean can only germinate after a spell in the gut of a fish, which eventually defecates it into propitious mud.

Such are the marvels of these vegetable-animal alliances for survival: the tree providing shelter and food, the animal offering those complex biological services without which the tree could not reproduce. INPA's Department of Forest Ecology was involved in an experiment to establish plantations of certain valuable trees, such as the rosewood, source of an oil used in the manufacture of perfumes, and exploited to the verge of extinction in its forest habitat. The rosewood project promised success, but seedlings wilted and flagged when transferred to INPA's facsimile jungle. One of the many defence mechanisms developed by the Amazon jungle is the dispersal of its species, which grow in isolation, sometimes only one to a hectare.

There may exist in these particular trees an inbuilt dislike for the proximity of others of their own kind, causing them to frustrate all attempts to grow them in the nurseryman's row. So extraordinary is their sensitivity that no more than four trees per acre can be cut down without causing environmental trauma, and when disturbed a tree may suspend its growth – no one knows how – for up to 20 years. 'The fact is that we don't really know how to plant forest trees,' said an INPA scientist. 'There just isn't enough money for research.' INPA employs at present 43 such specialists, although according to Dr Warwick Kerr, its director, a mimimum of 1,500 would be required to solve the problem of the forest's economic development without destroying it.

Above all there was an urgent need for research into the therapeutic utilisation of the many types of chemical defences developed by tropical trees against insect or virus attack. Very few species had as yet been studied, but they had provided quinine, cortisone, new types of oral contraceptives, and what was hoped would prove to be effective anti-cancer drugs. In all such discoveries, the drugs had been found to be in use by the Indians who, it might be supposed, were the possessors of other valuable therapeutic secrets yet to be communicated. To quote Dr Paulo de Almeida Machado, the previous director of INPA, 'Whatever science can learn before the forest is destroyed will mean the difference between short-term prosperity and sound economic development.' He added that although Indians might survive, their culture will not.

The approach of Doomsday for the Amazon forest was signalled by the launching of the great road-building programme of the early 1970s intended to slice it into easily accessible segments. This enterprise, undertaken in haste and with small forethought, followed a visit in 1970 by President Medici to the chronically distressed north-east, at that time proclaimed a disaster area after one of the worst droughts in its calamitous history. The President spoke movingly to the large crowds who had flocked into the town of Recife to hear him. By chance he was standing within a few miles of that once enchanted spot in Pernambuco of which Darwin had written in 1832, 'Forests and flowers and birds I saw in great perfection, and the pleasure of beholding them is infinite.' Of these Arcadian delights nothing remained, replaced as they were by treeless wastelands, ruined smallholdings among the thorny scrub, and the shanty villages of peasants who had to live on an average of 50 American cents a day.

The President promised, in effect, to spirit these wretched people away from their dour surroundings and deposit them in sylvan glades of Amazonia, where they would receive 100 hectares of land apiece. Along the new highways he proposed to build low-cost but cheerful housing, and supply credits and facilities of all kinds, and thus they would be encouraged to lay the foundations of new and fruitful lives.

As a safety-valve for the chronic poverty of the north-east the project was a failure. The intention had been to settle five million peasants in Amazonia by 1980, but after two years, only 100,000 had come and many of them were already beginning to slip away back to the badlands they had left.

Like poor city-dwellers induced to leave the companionable slums for the aseptic planning of a garden suburb, they soon yearned for the familiar squalor they had left. They lacked the energy and the improvising genius necessary to come to terms with soil that produced two crops – three at most – before giving up the ghost. Rain, the greatest of all blessings in the north-east, was now the enemy. Life had to be shared with a multitude of stinging insects; new sicknesses defied the familiar remedies, and there were snakes in the back garden. Thus the planning floundered and collapsed, leaving Amazonia littered with destitute homesteaders.

The new highways – the desert-makers as they have been called – did nothing to improve the lot of Brazilian subsistence farmers, but they fulfilled the wildest hopes not only of the multinationals, but of a new breed of predators who knew the true facts of the expendability of Amazonian soil and made it clear that they were not there to stay. As one American rancher put it to Robin Hanbury-Tenison, Chairman of Survival International: 'You can buy the land out there now for the same price as a couple of bottles of beer an acre. When you've got half a million acres and 20,000 head of cattle, you can leave the lousy place and go live in Paris, Hawaii, Switzerland, or anywhere you choose.'

Inevitably, these roads open the way to the destroyers not only of trees but of men, for they pass through a number of Indian reserves, promoting the contacts that are so often fatal. Where thought necessary the Indians have simply been picked up and put down elsewhere, despite the fact that the new environment may not provide a living.

Brazil abounds with vigorous and articulate conservation groups, but they are powerless in the presence of one crushing fact: the desperate need of the country's many poor. In January 1979 *O Journal do Brasil* published figures showing that in Rio de Janeiro alone 918,000 people were living in 'absolute poverty', and in the city's total population of nine millions, 27 per cent lived in 'relative poverty'. These are the statistics that blunt conservationist scruples. There is a constant pressure to develop more sources of food, joined to an irrepressible belief that sooner or later a way will be found to turn the relatively unproductive five million square kilometres of the Amazon Basin into a bottomless larder.

The Government seeks to put a brake on the excesses of 'developers' by measures that are too often evaded or ignored. Official approval must be obtained for large-scale forest clearances, but nobody seems to bother. Regulations exist prohibiting the burning-off of forest close to river banks where animals tend to congregate. These go unheeded. Slopes are not allowed to be cleared, because to do so is to guarantee immediate erosion, but in our experience landowners give priority to clearing the slopes on their estates. They do so because it is easier to drag or roll the treetrunks down the slopes and leave them to rot at the bottom, than to go to the trouble of extracting them. A promising law forbade the clearing of more than 50 per cent of any concession, but many methods exist by which it is dodged. A common one is to clear half one's land in compliance with the regulation, and then sell the forested remainder, a half of which will be cleared by the buyer in his turn – and so on.

Implementation of these laws is left to IBDF, the Brazilian Institute for Forestry Development, but this body is said to possess less than a hundred inspectors to police an area in which 20,000 might be too few. It has been announced that its hand will be strengthened by the end of the year by Brazil's new independent space satellite, which will report back on violations of the forest code. Here it might be argued that by the time photographic proof of such violations is supplied, the damage will have been done. But how, it may be asked is the feeble David of the IBDF to stand up, if needs be, to such Goliaths as Daniel Keith Ludwig, absolute ruler of an area somewhat larger than Belgium (referred to sarcastically as

'The Kingdom' in the Brazilian Press) from which, incidentally, observers are debarred?

IBDF's one semi-success was with Volkswagen do Brasil, a pigmy by comparison, with a ranch no bigger than Luxembourg. The US Skylab satellite photographed a huge unapproved fire that had been started here, and it was reported that a million adjacent hectares of the forest were alight. Reprimanded for carelessness or wilfulness by the head of SUDAM, the Superintendency for Amazonian Development, Volkswagen's director is reported to have replied that burning was the cheapest way of clearing land.

Of course it is the cheapest for those who are not there to stay, but the short-term yields they derive are paid for by a huge and irreversible loss suffered by Brazilians who have to live with the results. Ninety per cent of the soil of the Amazon Basin is so poor that it cannot be converted into adequate pasture without the addition of costly fertilisers, and as soon as these fertilisers are no longer forthcoming, the coarse African grass it supports will go. For a multitude of small-scale ranchers three acres of land can hardly feed a single cow, and after two or three years, when the rains have washed the nutrients from the soil, over-grazing and over-trampling take effect and the dust-bowl process begins.

Wild animals are of less than secondary importance in developing countries, and little is said in newspaper polemics on the fate of the animals in the path of the fires. Their lot is death on a hardly imaginable scale. Birds, monkeys, jaguar and deer may escape the racing flames, but most of the Amazon animals, armadillos, anteaters, porcupines, sloths and frogs, are slow-moving and are doomed to incineration. Innumerable bats, whose beneficent function it is to keep insect populations in check, are disorientated by smoke, and fall into the flames. A great variety of small mammals, rabbits, agoutis, pacas, and rodents of all kinds are moved by instinct to take refuge in burrows or in holes quickly scuffled out in the forest litter, and in these they are roasted. Animals that live by, and in the water, otters, water-opossums and fish are doomed, too, not always directly by the fire, but the loss of forest cover, causing streams to overheat and become clogged with algae and silt; devoid therefore of both oxygen and food. An INPA scientist said: 'We are threatened with possibly the greatest ecological disaster in world history.' He had calculated that between 5,000 and 20,000 vertebrate animals were killed per square kilometre when the forest burnt down. But the burning goes on.

In only one year, 1975, Amazonia lost four per cent of its trees, and scientist Harald Sioli said that if the rate of destruction was not slowed down, nothing would remain of the forest by 2005. It was a sum that people could do in their heads, but the conclusion was one that few could bring themselves to accept, on the grounds that 'the authorities' – that disembodied but relatively intelligent force set between them and God – would never be stupid enough to allow this to happen.

But in January 1979, coinciding almost with our arrival in Brazil, the deadline of conclusive destruction seemed to have come even nearer. Speakers at the Third World Forestry Congress at Manaus had hardly risen to their feet to congratulate themselves and the audience on the beneficent change in the official attitude towards problems of conservation, when a sensational story broke in the newspapers. This revealed details of a secret deal in which huge tracts of Amazonia were to be sold off in lots to acquire the foreign currency required to liquidate Brazil's current balance of payments crisis. The newspaper *Folho do São Paulo* valued the concessions it alleged the Government was proposing to grant at 20 billion US dollars, and saw that 40 per cent of the forest would have to be sold to foreign concessionaires to produce this figure.

In Brazil, as elsewhere, governmental right hands often do not know what left hands are doing and these revelations set off a flux of outraged denials, sometimes published in the Press side by side with astonishing admissions. 'Such a proposal would be political madness,' said the Ministry of Agriculture, and a spokesman for the President agreed. 'The thing is absurd. Anyone who tries to put such stories about must have an ulterior motive.' SUDAM, the Superintendency for Amazonian Development, seemed oblivious of these high-level denials, and burbled on endlessly as to what was intended. SUDAM had always seemed to prefer ranches to trees, and had licensed and partially financed the deforestation of 3½ million hectares in 1976. In this instance it was happy to indicate the rough location and size of the areas to be opened up to foreign investment.

Worse was to come. Paulo Berutti, Director of the IBDF, the very instrument created to preserve the forests, let it be known that he had gone to the United Nations' Food and Agriculture Organisation in person, and persuaded them to supply a team of 22 technicians to carry out a study of the Amazonian forest and present a plan for its 'economic development'. He agreed with SUDAM that 40 per cent of what was left of the original 280 million hectares might be involved.

This admission turned Berutti overnight into the most detested man in North Brazil. A meeting of the Legislative Assembly of the State of Amazonas demanded his banishment from the country, while a civic march in protest organised by various academics, conservationists and members of Berutti's own staff was promptly suppressed by the police. The new proposals made Sioli's predictions look optimistic. Berutti's assurances that future exploitation of the Amazon would be based upon the principle of recycling forest reserves failed to convince. Too many people remembered the holocausts caused by Volkswagen do Brasil and others. Paulo Nogueira Neto, Special Secretary for the Environment, said, 'This amounts to handing over our forests to the tender mercies of the multinationals. You might as well put a goat in charge of a garden.'

★

In Manaus, capital of Amazonia, the weather provided evidence of secondary inconveniences to be expected as deforestation progressed. It had been raining torrentially off and on for some weeks, and could be expected to go on doing so for at least a couple of months. The Rio Negro, on the banks of which the city is built, was rising at the highest rate ever recorded: 7.5 centimetres a day. The Hydrographic Service was able to predict at this stage the strong possibility of a repetition, by the middle of February, of the floodings of the past three years, when the city's centre had been under water. The news from the Manaus-Cuiabá highway was that 600 lorries were stuck in the mud without hope of immediate rescue, filling the air with the stench of their decaying cargoes of food. The passengers from a stranded bus had taken refuge in an Indian village. Such floods, occurring at rare intervals in the past as a result of freak weather, are now coming to be accepted as a normal feature of the rainy season, lending weight to the theory that they are caused by the forest's loss of capacity to absorb water.

We took advantage of a break in the weather to hire a plane and in this we flew northwards from Manaus, keeping in sight the new BR174 Highway.

It was a good time to see the forest from the air, because by January the dry season's smoke has cleared away. A little late burning-off and tidying-up goes on, as the weather allows, but all the essential details of the landscape below are visible in the clear, rain-freshened air.

We flew at about 1,000 feet over the limitless spread of trees, having from this height the appearance of sparkling moss. Across this the BR174 was a red line, ruled to the horizon. Immediately beneath, the road was close enough for the erosion to be visible, biting into its margins, and there were swamps created in its making, bristling with dead trees and gaudy with stagnation. Fires appeared as blue smudges here and there, and there were never less than a half-dozen in sight, and many charcoal scrawls and flourishes showed on the green pages of the jungle where others had burnt out. Such clearances were often the work of rich businessmen running plantations as a side-line, or hobby-farmers from the city. Land here costs too much to attract ranchers thinking in terms of 20,000 to 30,000 hectares, whose operations would show up on a satellite photograph. Close to Manaus it was a matter of 100 hectares here and 200 there, but it was sad to think just how many small fires must have been alight all over the Amazon Basin on a fine day like this.

What our bird's-eye view made so startlingly clear was that the process the scientists called 'desertification' was even more rapid than we had been led to expect. In many places where patches of forest had been left, strewn with ash to await replanting or cultivation, the arid ochre of the sub-soil already showed through. There were old, abandoned fields, too, now totally eroded, and from them the new desert spread like a creeping tide in all directions.

Later, accompanied by an INPA scientist, we drove along the BR174 with the object of studying the close-quarter effects of what we had seen from the air. An hour's drive brought us to the scene of a recognisable fire on the 100-hectare estate of a successful Manaus shopkeeper. We had passed several estates like it along the road, often bearing romantic names (in one case 'My Blue Heaven'), and sometimes furnished with a swimming pool by which the *fazendeiro* and his friends could have sat to enjoy the view across a wasteland resembling the aftermath of the Battle of the Somme.

The estate we visited would be largely for the owner's weekend use, but a manager had been put in charge to make sure of a reasonable return on investment, too, and when cleared of forest the estate would be planted with profit trees.

The manager had no objection to describing and even demonstrating his methods. Clearing the forest with machete, saw and axe, he said, was a slow and laborious business. You could do it with a tenth of the effort by getting a big fire going, and to do this all that was needed was a good supply of combustibles. His own method was to buy up all the old lorry tyres he could find. Having cut down the big trees and left them to dry for a few weeks, the lorry tyres would be stacked at intervals through the dry foliage, doused in petrol, and then set alight. The heat generated by this kind of fire took care of all the small standing trees and the undergrowth, and all that anybody had to do after that was to go round and saw down a few stumps that might have been left.

A final hectare or two was about to be cleared, and we looked on while this was done. It was a sad but spectacular business, with small risks to be taken if one were so inclined, and these were clearly enjoyed by the young fire-raisers who went in to the attack, cans of petrol in hands. As fire roared up from the underbrush a whole panorama of foliage shrivelled, leaving the bone-structure of the trees sheeted in flame. We were startled by the speed of the fire's advance, dodging and leaping into the branches, clinging to lianas, turning into small bonfires among the bundles of orchids and ferns lodged in the forks and axils. The noise, as wood exploded everywhere under pressure of boiling sap, was terrific.

If there were a real danger here, it lay in the chance of getting in the way of a frantic snake as it came twisting out of the flames. One or two of these were quickly despatched by the club-armed workers. This was the moment providing the manager's children with the opportunity to capture an occasional baby boa-constrictor, much in demand as a pet. They had managed to cut one off a week before, and it was already quite tame; an engaging and endlessly curious creature, which slithered away to inspect any new arrival at the farmhouse, and was overfed on live lizards by its admirers. But few animals were as lucky as this, and a short walk into the most recently burnt-off area revealed a number of small charred skeletons.

The estate was to be planted with fruit, rubber and avocado pear trees, and the soil here was so poor that an inch or two of humus and ash could be scuffled away with the boot to expose subsoil like yellow concrete. Several hundred seedling trees waited in containers. To give them as good a start as possible the manager had dug holes by the hundred and replaced the arid subsoil with good earth, and in this the young trees would be planted. Not a single forest tree was to be left. Asked if he had not heard of the Forest Code, and the 50 per cent rule by which no more than one half of the forest cover could be removed on any property, the manager agreed that he had. In a case like this, he said, it did not apply. It was not as if he had cleared the land for pasture or for agricultural use. Trees had been cleared, but others would be planted in their stead. Where was the difference?

There is no country where the problems of conservation are so earnestly and endlessly discussed as in Brazil, no country where intentions are better and the determination stronger to protect a national heritage – in this case above all the Amazon forest, and all the life it shelters. The furious outcry provoked by the alleged proposal to hand over a huge proportion of the forest to foreign companies makes it seem unlikely that this will be allowed to happen. What is more probable is that after the clamour subsides things will be found to be drifting along much as before, with a million acres of forest quietly snipped away here and there, worse flooding year by year, yet another increase in such diseases as malaria (known to be aggravated by forest disturbance), more Indians dying of disease.

Meanwhile a new threat to the existence of the forest is about to develop – this time one that is far more likely to bring about the final solution. The appetites of the big ranching concerns have been to some extent held in check by the pressure of Brazilian opinion, but the assault on the forest to come is likely to engender less opposition, as reflecting an urgent national need.

Two barrels of petroleum substitute can be made from a ton of wood, and the Amazon forest is estimated to contain 415 billion cubic feet of timber. The Brazilian Press – already punch-drunk from the battle over the proposed surrender of 40 per cent of the forest to foreign concessionaries – signalled the opening of a new battle front by quotations from an article in *Data Shell*. Ethyl alcohol and methane, commonly substituting for petrol in the last war, said the article, were now easily and cheaply produced from vegetable matter. Technical difficulties hampering Amazonian production in the past had been overcome, and with the decrease in reserves and constant increase in petroleum prices, substitutes were about to come into their own. *Data Shell* mentioned an expectation of increased production in the Amazon region.

These are all the facts one really needs to know in deciding for oneself whether or not the trees will still be there in the year 2000.

IN THE
SIERRA

S OUTH FROM MADRID the Estremadura highway unwinds
through the sun-devoured plains. A tide of affluence flowing from the capital has rolled over this part of the land. The
horizons are smudged by factories, there is neon in the villages,
and once in a while a little pyramid of wrecked or exhausted
cars has been piled up by the roadside, like the burial cairn of a
chieftain of our days. After Talavera, which supplies the world
with bathroom tiles, the pencilled outline of the Sierra de
Gredos shows to the west at the bottom of the sky. It is less
than an hour away, but entering it the traveller is transported
instantly to a different world where the traditional Spain
makes a last stand.

Oropesa, which crowns the summit of a hill a few miles
south of Talavera, is the ancient capital of the region. It is a
place where nothing much happens, and apart from the plea-
santness of an old-fashioned town and the spectacle of people
living quiet lives in traditional fashion, there is nothing to
attract visitors but the fifteenth-century castle-cum-palace,
now a State parador. The setting is impressive and one questions whether the builders of these battlements, walls, and
towers were inspired purely by military considerations, or
whether romantic notions could not have entered into it, so

fanciful is the final result. The castle illustrates the appetite of mediaeval Spain for silence and a dignified gloom, for, on passing through the hotel's doors, one is instantly swaddled in a twilight scented with the faint, dark odour of antiquity. Details of battle tapestries decorating the walls of vast halls and chambers are made out with difficulty. Voices are hushed in space.

By contrast the bedrooms are small and austere – a manifestation of the Spanish spirit which strives to counterbalance grandeur with simplicity. The view is over the roofs of the town, descending layer by layer in pink and grey striations, the oldest of them curving gently like those of pagodas at their edges. Beautiful roofs advertise poverty, and outside the palace-castle complex there has never been any money in Oropesa to finance innovation and ugliness. The town, like the castle, is silent in the Spanish way, with all its window shutters closed and no one in the streets outside the social hours of the evening. The sky is full of swifts and circling storks, and these, with their breeding season now past, have left their nests everywhere, like huge discarded hats on all the high places of the town.

To the west the view from the castle is of the Sierra, rising like an enormous wave from the 15-mile-wide featureless plain. Fifty miles of it are on view although seen no more than as an outline in mist, sometimes momentarily obscured by the storks as in the evening they come up by the hundred from the plains to roost in the towers and pinnacles of Oropesa. After the Pyrenees the Sierra de Gredos, 150 kilometres in length, is the largest mountain range in Spain. It is also the least known and therefore the most interesting. Although there are no towns, and hardly any villages in the sierra itself, a string of villages in the foothills are a living museum of the Spain of the past. It seems incredible that these mountains should have waited until 1834 to be explored. The expedition sent reported on the presence of innumerable wild goats – about 4,000 of which remain – ancient burial-sites and dolmens, and wild men dressed in skins. These early hunters lived in *chozos*; tiny, circular stone-walled huts of the kind built by their Celtic ancestors, and still occupied by their descendants, the shepherds of today. Since then, only botanical expeditions are likely to have investigated the sierra with any thoroughness.

There was no wealth of any kind to be exploited in Gredos, therefore little incentive to build roads. A single highway linking the towns of Avila and Toledo crosses the range at its narrowest point. It is narrow, winding and dangerous. Two secondary roads run parallel to the chain of peaks, north and south of the range. They are of the kind that discourage modern traffic and are devoid of side-roads leading into the mountains themselves.

In an attempt to attract tourism, a single track about 15 kilometres in length has been built, leading into the central massif from a point in the road near the somewhat gloomy parador of Gredos. Colossal rocks – often balanced two and three on top of each other in an eccentric and precarious fashion – are strewn about this amphitheatre, and glinting lizards of several colours scuttle over their surfaces. A wide spread of water, the Laguna Grande, appears at a distance to be veiled in gauze, an impression given by the innumerable dragonflies exploring its surface. Once in a while the water fountains up as a fishing eagle plunges after a trout. There are roe-deer and ibex under the peaks through which in mid-summer the old snow still curls like a white river. In the holidays a few children trudge up here to camp by the banks of the many trout streams, but, their brief occupation at an end, Gredos reverts to the primaeval wilderness.

Isolation is the keynote, not only of these mountains, but of the swell of foothills and the plains among which they are set. Only a handful of shepherds inhabit the Sierra itself but the approach to it is through areas among the least populated in Spain. A history of Oropesa offered for sale at the parador explains why this should be. It was the custom of Spain over the centuries to spend up to a third of its income on foreign wars, and in 1635, with the nation reduced almost to bank-ruptcy by the wars in Portugal and France, Philip IV applied to the Count of Oropesa for a contribution of 60,000 ducats to the public treasury. In return, a royal decree granted the Count the right to enclose the common-lands in the Gredos region and convert them into pastures for sheep. 'The consequences of this action are with us today,' the historian writes, and he provides a long list of communities of which no trace remains. Mysteriously half a dozen villages, favoured by their position in the flanks of the mountains, were able to hold out. They drove off the attackers, including those sent by the Count, fed themselves, did a little trade, built up a little prosperity. The isolation that defended them, held them back, so that medi-aeval practices, long abandoned elsewhere, have survived into our times. For this reason they are among the most interesting communities in Spain.

There is no better way to make an approach to the Sierra than across the straight and narrow road leading to it from Oropesa. This is without motor traffic, and the absence of almost all signs of human life along its length of 25 kilometres has encouraged the presence of spectacular birds. The River Tiétar spreads its tributaries through the oak woods, in which enormous boulders that might have been designed by Henry Moore have been scattered among tall flowers, branching like yellow candelabras. Sheep pass through in vast herds, moving at considerable speed and apparently unattended. Where there are pockets of good grass by the water, black fighting-bulls, looking outstandingly pacific, graze behind flimsy wire. There are here storks by the thousand, sometimes placed in contem-plative ranks by the banks of a stream. A splendid crow, the azure-winged magpie, flocks in the oaks; but above all, the Egyptian Vulture, which apart from its black wing-tips is white and immaculate, spirals above the tree-tops in a brisk territorial survey, covering 10 square miles in an hour. In the background the Sierra takes shape on closer approach, its green sheen breaking through the vapour, gently rucked and folded here and there like a carpet lifted by the wind.

This is a landscape of antiquity restored by the banishment of human presence. The boundary containing it is the Toledo-Avila highway, packed with transient traffic. Mombeltrán is built where the mountains close in to defend the pass and cut the lines of communication of marauding soldiery in the endless wars. It had been taken by surprise by the widening of the road and the arrival of trippers from Talavera (who are sometimes rebuked for their failure to maintain decorum in the matter of dress), otherwise it sleeps fairly comfortably in the past. The town is overlooked by a massive castle with no romantic nonsense about it, being provided with enough dungeons to hold an army; everything has been sacrificed to the necessities of defence. Narrow crooked alleys, taking the place of streets, run up and down the mountainside, and the tall half-timbered houses that lurch into each other are honey-combed with secret chambers and passages. The Gothic church served when necessary as a fortress with a construction like a stone igloo built into its side into which the defenders of the hill upon which it is built could crawl for a last stand.

At one point in Spanish history a royal decree commanded subjects with incomes too low to be subjected to tax, to seat themselves on chairs no more than a hand's span in height. Many still do, and it is a strange sight in the cool of the evening to see little circles of old people who have carried their chairs out of the cellar-like darkness of their houses to sit facing inwardly, hardly a word passing between them, in the other-wise empty squares. The typical dishes of the Gredos area are not to be found in hotels and most restaurants, but are served in a bar here called *La Ilusión del Cazador* (The Hunter's Illusion), including pigs' ears in sauce, and *migas*, bread fried in garlic with ham and onions, topped with black grapes, lightly boiled. Seating, influenced by ancient custom, is uncomfort-able even in this public place, with the plates on the table hardly accessible to knife and fork.

It is in this cramped, secret and defensive style that Valverde de la Vera, on the southern flanks of the Sierra, is built. It is clean, austere and silent, scented with the clear mountain water that runs in shallow conduits down the middle of each street. There are no dogs or cats to be seen; not even the usual caged canaries on the walls. Most of its wooden houses were built in the far past, by the families who were to live in them. Some are very beautiful with carved balconies supported by wooden columns, a few of which retain their ancient carved capitals. Occasionally, the upper stories of houses facing each other across a street have been extended to touch or even fuse with each other, thus creating a tunnel for the passage of pedestrians beneath. The Plaza de España, presenting this architectural theme as an uninterrupted unity, is unique of its kind.

Valverde's income is derived from tobacco, of which it grows less and less. Apart therefore from its innate conservatism, determined to leave everything 'as it has always been', there is no money here to pay for change. Thus an ancient stone phallus still crowns the well at which women gather throughout the day to draw water, and a sinister-looking pillar – a chain hanging from it – stands at the village's entrance, to which, in the absence of a prison, malefactors were once shackled and left.

Against this background of self-sufficiency and isolation, it is not surprising that Valverde's Easter Week celebrations should be purely mediaeval. There is proof that the somewhat macabre ritual of the Thursday of Holy Week has remained unchanged for centuries, for in 1556 a Flemish painter in the suite of the Emperor Charles V visited the village and recorded on canvas the scene as it is to be witnessed today. The Emperor himself was almost certainly there, watching from his litter, for he had just formally renounced his kingdoms, and chosen the area of La Vera, seen as the back of beyond, for his retirement from the world.

The unique feature of Easter Week at Valverde is the representation in its procession of the suffering of Christ, dragging himself under the weight of his cross along the Via Crucis on his way to Golgotha. In such manifestations elsewhere in Europe the custom is for a man to be selected for the part on the basis of his high moral standing. In Valverde on the contrary, it falls to a *penitente* (a confessed sinner) who commits himself to the agonising experience as a result of a *promesa* (vow). What is more extraordinary about the procedure is that there is no limit to the number of *penitentes* – as many as ten or fifteen are usual – who are permitted to adopt the sacred role. 'There's nothing exclusive about this,' the mayor's secretary said. 'Say the word and we'll put you down for next year. It's purely a matter of whether or not you think you can stay the course. All we expect of you is to learn the verses to be repeated at the various stations.'

As the secretary made clear, this is an ordeal. The penitent sinner, referred to as the *empalao* (the man fixed to a pole) walks barefoot through every street of the village, his arms extended and bound with esparto rope to the beam of a plough carried on his shoulders, which may weigh up to 100 lb. The same esparto rope is wound so tightly round the torso that it would appear to restrict the breathing. The *empalao* wears only a woman's white skirt, and a veil serving to conceal grimaces of pain, and the blood trickling from wounds caused by the crown of thorns clamped down over his head. Two crossed swords, pointing upwards, fastened to his back, compel him to walk with head bowed. He is accompanied throughout the dark streets by a 'second', draped from head to foot in a dark cloak, whose task is to light the way with an oil lamp and give what aid he can in the case of the *empalao*'s collapse. This scene was also painted by Goya, who has encircled the *empalao* with the night-gowned and hooded figures of an *auto-da-fé*, capturing thus the slightly nightmarish quality of the scene in the way only he could have done.

Villanueva de la Vera, four miles down the road, devotes itself to its annual carnival in a spirit of what at first appears no more than innocent merriment. At the height of the jollifications a man-sized doll – Pero Palo – dressed in seventeenth-century clothing, is delivered to the crowd to be torn to pieces. At one period this act of light-hearted destruction was preceded by a semblance of castration, now omitted from the festivities, but there is still fierce competition for the possession of the carved, wooden head. Differences of opinion exist in Villanueva as to who the effigy represents, a common view being that in real life Pero Palo was an inquisitor, finally lynched by the populace in retribution for intolerable abuses. However, the fact is that the ritual is known to have been performed long before the establishment in La Vera of the Holy Office.

A clue to the possible origin of the custom is afforded by the fact that a year is spent in the preparation of the doll *in secret* – each year in a different house, the location of which is known only to the adepts of what amounts to a village secret society. Various stages of the manufacture and dressing of the effigy are accompanied by dancing and drumming, and *coplas* are sung, which, since they relate to the events and topics of the far past, are now largely devoid of significance.

At the end of the Civil War an attempt was made by the Franco régime to suppress the Pero Palo ritual along with folk custom elsewhere possessing an element of secrecy which the government could not approve. The people of Villanueva were able to avoid the ban with a modified version in which the effigy's name was changed and it was 'drowned' in the village fountain instead of being torn to pieces. Since then Pero Palo is back in its original form and a scientific work has appeared to deal with its origins. The author's verdict is that this is an example of the survival on the Peninsula of a Bronze Age fertility sacrifice, bearing in this case a strong resemblance to those practised in Ancient Greece. He has also unearthed the details of a trial conducted by the Inquisition in 1581 in which a number of villagers were charged with membership of a sect involved in the annual sacrifice of a human victim. Amazingly, they were discharged on the grounds of insufficient evidence.

Pero Palo at Villanueva, rooted in the magic practices of pre-history, may be the most anciently established of the springtide celebrations of the Sierra, but almost every village dismisses winter, and hails the coming of spring in its own special fashion. In Easter week the streets everywhere are full of hooded and barefoot penitents dragging their chains. In Fuenlabrada and Hichosa, the masked and horned devils of winter are chased away by the children. Elsewhere, *vaquillas* – young and aggressive cows – are released in the streets, and their domination provides the symbolism required by the season. Sometimes, as in Mogarraz, fighting bulls are included, to be put to death in the village square, adding to the theme of triumph over evil that of the fertilisation of the earth through the effusion of blood.

Jarandilla is the last of the Gredos villages before the Sierra sinks into the plains beyond Barco de Avila. It was once a place of some note and, under the protection of its own castle, could afford the luxury of living space and wide streets. Its principal building is an enormous church, once a Moorish fortress, built on an outcrop of rock, which from its battlemented exterior gives no indication of ever having been put to religious use.

Such appearances of affluence as Jarandilla retains are linked to a vanished past. The life of today – certainly at night – is concentrated in 100 yards of brilliantly lit street forming part of the road to Plasencia. Here half a dozen cafés are filled with patrons nostalgically watching the lively flux of main-road traffic. Behind them, Jarandilla is turning into a ghost town of enormous old houses with fallen-in roofs, like delapidated barns. The impression of desolation seems to be heightened rather than relieved by the occasional circle of old people, huddled in silence like mourners on their tiny chairs, in an otherwise empty and shuttered street. Jarandilla's annual fiesta is a relatively low-key affair, occupying only four days instead of the nine devoted to festivities in up-and-coming towns. Giants and big-headed dwarves parade the streets, there is a modest firework display, a poetry competition, a woman's football match, a folkloric entertainment including an ancient version of the *jota* in which girls dance with brooms, and a contest for the biggest tobacco leaf. The villagers would like to be chased by infuriated heifers, or even to release a bull with fireworks attached to its horns – the most popular of such diversions – but they cannot run to the expense, so make do with what they can get.

The Emperor Charles V spent two of his last years in Jarandilla's castle, and just as largely apocryphal stories of royal doings of old still circulate in villages of the home counties exposed to the occasional excursions of the Tudor or Stewart monarchs, the presence of the Emperor is still felt here. By this time, at the age of 56, he was already a bespec-tacled old man, unable to stand and having to be carried in a litter like an oversized pram through the village on his occasional sorties to watch his subjects at work or play. He was simple and genial; the most human ruler of his day, who kept parrots, and had once liked to garden, his health fatally undermined by an addiction to spiced Spanish food which had left him crippled by gout. The Emperor loved to commune with nature and, as revealed in his letters, to listen to the song of the nightingale. He chose Gredos because it offered him these things and also because he believed that in the high mountains a man was nearer to God.

As soon as it could be done, a monastery was got ready for his retirement at Yuste, 12 kilometres away, and to this he withdrew to end his days. His apartments are dark and austere, furnished in the lugubrious style associated with piety in the minds of the Spanish of those days. A chair of a rustic kind with iron leg supports was made for him locally, and in this he spent most of the day on his veranda. He was seated here when overcome by his fatal stroke, and his last view, according to the position in which he had been placed, would have been of the peaks he so much admired, or perhaps of the lush valley of La Vera with its strange villages, which, as painted by the Flemish artist, would have appeared very much as they do now.

THE NIGHT HUNT FOR
THE NEW YEAR

IN THAILAND PEOPLE set out with the determination that everything should go well on New Year's Day, which establishes the pattern and style of the twelve months to come. The average active and hopefully minded citizen bounds out of bed at dawn, puts on a new suit with nothing less than 1000-baht notes in its pockets, resolves to renew failing friendships and to forgive his enemies. Next he collects the up-market car, such as a convertible Mercedes, that he has hired for the day and drives over to the nearest temple to join in the pleasant ceremony of washing the Buddha image. On this day, men of cool-headed decision, like bankers and stock-market manipulators, discover untapped reserves of superstition in their personalities. For once all their endeavours are tempered with caution. Above all they must be sure not to put a foot wrong until the sun rises again, twenty-four hours later.

Amorin Surin, who lived by selling beautiful and often rare butterflies to tourists in the night market of Chiang Mai, took me in his mini-van to the renowned temple festival at Wat Prathat Haripoonchai in Lumphan, a town profoundly asleep in the past as a result of being by-passed by the main Bangkok highway 16 miles below the northern capital. Surin was a dedicated hunter and therefore in the top category of those addicted to superstition of every kind. All the hunters in the area made a point of a New Year's visit to the Wat, favoured by them for its proximity to Doi Khun Tan National Park. Although debarred by zealous wardens from entry into the park itself in pursuit of the splendid game harboured in its forests, there was no law to prevent them lying in ambush along the perimeter for animals crossing the frontier between relative security and danger. Even on less auspicious days, many of them made a point of calling in at the Wat to ask the Buddha's blessing when any such enterprise was contemplated.

Wat Hari Poonchai is one of the most venerable temples of the kingdom. It houses innumerable Buddha images and holy relics, possesses a 50 metres' high spire, and a number of buildings over 1,000 years old. To the average, uninstructed and only moderately devout visitor, its principal feature is the two colossal lions that guard the entrance. The mere sight of these animals, resembling enormous chocolate dogs, puts a Thai in a good humour. The ferocious snarl intended by the sculptor of old has turned out to be hardly more alarming than a Disneyland grin. It is all very relaxed. The visitors come here to worship but also to have a good time.

By the time we arrived, the festival was in full swing with yellow-robed monks bustling among the well-dressed visitors whom they were helping to park their cars. Two trestle tables had been set up under the benevolent scrutiny of the lions outside the compound. Merriment in Thailand is interwoven with formality. This was an occasion when ladies were expected to wear hats. One table bore a selection offered for hire, and the ladies were trying them on. At the other, their husbands were lined up to be served with half-tumblers of hot *mekong* whisky, downed in a couple of gulps before entering the sacred precincts.

Hot whisky drinking, introduced as part of the modernisation campaign in the early fifties, has remained in the eyes of the Thais a cultural exercise borrowed from the West, and its occasional effects on the drinker's conduct in no way exposes him to censure. As ever on such occasions, the scene within the compound was a lively one. The Army, taking a willing hand in the arrangements, had proposed to entertain the visitors by setting up a battlefield in miniature. The menfolk, some of them a little unsteady by now, were genially urged to try their hand with machine-guns and half-charge grenades in an attack on remote-controlled miniature tanks careering about at the bottom of a shooting-range. Many of them did so. Grenades exploded with a stunning crack, and ricocheting bullets whined away like bees. One tank, successfully blasted, went out of control and came in a zigzagging rush at the crowd who stampeded away with cries of pretended fear. An ambulance had been parked at the entrance to the orchid display, and by it immaculately uniformed nurses stood to attention to await casualties. On a background dais a dancing couple capered round each other, twirling their arms. Everyone smiled; the dancers, the smartly turned-out overseers correcting the ragged aim of the men at the machine-guns, the wives adjusting the angle of rented hats, the well-starched nurses. The scene was scented by cordite mixed with the odour of the fleshy white blooms on the compound tress. Rock music came across in disconnected blasts, only momentarily stifling the nasal outcry of a monk locked in a cage to preach in incomprehensible Pali against the pleasures of the flesh.

It was all good fun, but not what the serious-minded Surin was here for. Dominating this earthly confusion the great golden spire of the Wat soared up to spread its faint sheen into sallow summer sky. This was Surin's objective. Elsewhere, the Buddha images were washed in person on this day, but so great is the veneration in which the Buddha of Hari Poonchai is held that in this case it is enough simply to wash the temple spire. We turned our backs on the pious jollifications, made our way round the back of the crowd to the spire and took our place in the queue waiting to gain merit in this act of devotion.

Surin's turn came. A monk passed him a bucket attached to a rope containing a jugful of water blessed by the abbot. Surin hauled on the rope to hoist the bucket to the top of the spire, then jerked a second rope to splash its contents down the golden slope. Next, to nudge the celebrant forward a pace or two along the path to Nirvana, birds had to be released from captivity. A hundred or two, having been netted overnight, and now confined in pairs in tiny wicker cages, awaited release. We bought a pair apiece, and set them free from their wicker prisons, thus completing the ritual. For Surin, this was a moment of tension. If in subsequent flight the birds kept close together – which they usually did – it was a good omen. If they separated, each going its own way, there was nothing much to be hoped for in the coming year. Our birds could hardly have been closer. Surin clasped his hands together in prayerful relief. The first hurdle had been cleared. Now the encounter with Khun Tan had to be faced.

Khun Tan was a powerful spirit, overlord of the region he ruled from the 4,000-foot mountain peak rising from the Doi Khun Tan Park to the east of the Chiang Mai–Bangkok road some 10 miles before reaching the town of Lampang. In theory, Surin admitted, Buddha, who was not a god, had nothing to do with good or bad luck. People washed his image as part of the New Year celebrations to show their respect for his revelation of the five-fold way to enlightenment and release from the bondage of desire. Nevertheless, there was nothing to be lost in praying to him as to any other god. And who knew? – it might help. With Khun Tan the case was different. He was a powerful spirit who had once been a man, and assumed to have retained a fair share of human weakness. Although invisible, he remained within reach, bribable, susceptible to flattery, frequently sympathetic to a supplicant's prayer – in this instance, able and willing if approached in the right way to steer game within gunshot. Like so many of the national spirits he had ended his spell on earth in a tragic fashion. He had led, as Surin thought, a revolt against the

Burmese who had overrun the area, been captured and torn apart by elephants. Thus here as elsewhere the memory of the Robin Hood persists while the name of the king is forgotten.

We drove down the Bangkok road to the crest of a low hill where the peak of Doi Khun Tan came into view among the distant trees. Here along the verge was ranged one of the greatest collections of spirit-shrines in South East Asia: possibly a thousand of them in ten to fifteen ranks, each shrine about one yard from the next along a hundred yards of the road. They were like bird-tables of an elaborate kind having tiny spirit-houses on their platforms. Some of the newer shrines were of the sort on offer in supermarkets, put together cheaply from low-quality materials; but the older shrines in the back ranks were often of well carved teak. Every one of these contained offerings to the potent spirit of Khun Tan, an assortment of vitamin tablets, cough syrup, slimming remedies, amphetamines, miniature liquor bottles, sun-specs, and playing-cards, mixed in with spurious jewellery and toys of every kind – all of those things of which in their spiritual essence a powerful Thai spirit might stand in need. Surin deposited his contribution – a packet of Camels – and we made to leave.

Here we ran into difficulty. Hundreds of truck-drivers passed this way each day on the country's main north–south run. It was their normal custom to salute the invisible, though watchful, presence of Khun Tan in passing by a toot on the horn. On this occasion many had thought fit to stop, and to elbow their way through a steadily thickening crowd for a prayer at the nearest shrine. In the minutes since our arrival a traffic-jam had built up. We were badly parked, and Surin's efforts to extricate the mini-van provoked cries of protest from nearby drivers.

The incident left him momentarily depressed. He had hoped that the promising behaviour of the birds at Hari Poonchai would be capped by a good omen at the Khun Tan shrine. It was well known that sometimes at the moment of making an offering the spirit would appear in a vision to the supplicant, traditionally on a white horse, but in recent years at the wheel of a German car. Surin had never experienced this sign of Khun Tan's favour, granted to several of his friends, and now he was alarmed less the trouble with the truck-drivers might have dimmed our prospects for the night hunt, and in consequence for the year itself.

We drove on down the slow descent to the animal market of Lampang, which takes the form of a temporary village of thatched huts build by the roadside about five miles short of the town itself. Hunters by the hundred use the market as a starting point for their night excursions into the forest, and bring back to it whatever surplus meat they may have for sale. It is a place to which non-hunting citizens take their families in pursuit of *Sanuk* which may be described as innocent fun – provided in this case by the inspection of unfamiliar animals in cages, or tied by a leg to a stake, awaiting those in search of an unusual pet or simply meat on the hoof. Families picnic here, let off fireworks, dance the *Ramwong* and dress up as ghosts. It is possible to find basic accommodation for the night, and a rough sort of country restaurant can throw a meal together on request. Depending as it does largely on exotic materials it can provide the bold with an outstanding culinary adventure.

The reality of the market disappointed. There was said to be no better place to study the wildlife of Thailand, albeit in captivity or death. Surin made frequent trips down from Chiang Mai to buy spiders the size of a child's fist, six-inch-long scorpions and monstrous stag beetles for arrangement with his butterflies in framed pictures for sale to foreign tourists. There was something about the climate of the moist, deciduous monsoon forest that attracted a huge variety of animals, luring them eventually to the nets and guns of the hunters who gathered here to await them.

The display of animal wares on this occasion was meagre largely because a horde of day-trippers had bought up everything worth having by the time we arrived. A hopeful quest for uncommon specimens led to dead ends. Snakes were brought in quantity to the market, where they were sold for their blood, accepted as a powerful tonic when mixed with an equal amount of whisky. Of these a single example hardly more impressive than a large worm remained. The 'tiger' we were summoned to view turned out to be the kitten of a jungle cat, that sat in its cage imperturbably grooming itself. The only wild boar to be found was small and unpleasantly blotched by skin disease. The last of the deer had been divided down the middle between two eager buyers an hour before our arrival. A selection of squirrels, rabbits and huge blunt-faced forest rats had found no takers. Any of them, said the crest-fallen merchant offering them, could be turned into a reason-able stew, but at holiday times people were on the look-out for something with more prestige.

We were at the market for a meeting with a local guide whose services had to be regarded as a luxury since he charged double the value of the game his customers were likely to bag. He guaranteed results, which was all that mattered at a time like this. The arrangement was that he would come up from Lampang to collect us shortly before nightfall, then drive us in his Land-Rover by side roads and jungle tracks to an area near Ban Tung where the frontiers of the park were ill-defined and, by common consent, little respected. We were to hunt with jack-lights. In most countries, including Thailand, this all too easy method of animal massacre is outlawed, but in the whole of the Far East hardly any other kind of hunting is commonly practised.

The evening wore on. The children were growing tired and began to quarrel; a fox escaped; an angry man drew a pistol and fired it into the air, was pacified and led away. Thais are encouraged to throw water at each other on this day, and a party of embarrassed, giggling girls, fearing that we might feel left out, presented themselves with a bowl to give us a wetting. A meal was served. This, too, was a matter of ritual and routine. Nobody wanted the ants' eggs but some pretence of eating them had to be made. Few diners in all probability enjoyed the baked honeycomb with young bees cooked in their waxen cells. Like our neighbours we helped ourselves to a token spoonful apiece, and like them we made hardly more than a polite effort with the earth-coloured, glutinous rice.

With the sun low in the sky, Surin was becoming nervous at the guide's non-appearance. Then the news came through that the Bangkok road was blocked following a multiple car-crash, with an ensuing tail-back all the way to Lampang. The belief was that mobile cranes would have to be brought down from Chiang Mai – a possibility that was accepted with huge philosophy. Among excited cries from the children, revived by the emergency, families prepared to settle in their cars for the night. Those free from family obligations called for more *mekong* to be brought, and about a hundred people were now dancing the *Ramwong*. Surin gave up all hope of the guide's arrival, but explained that there was too much at stake for him to abandon the night hunt, saying we would have to do the best we could without the guide. There was nothing for it but to agree.

The light was already failing by the time we disentangled the mini-van from the cars left at the roadside. A mile back in the direction of Chiang Mai we turned into a dirt track wandering through low hills in the direction – as Surin thought – of the National Park. After a while the peak of Doi Khun Tan appeared as a dark triangle separated from its base by a sash of mist, and afloat in the green aftermath of the vanished sun. The track branched and then branched again. This was a journey without maps and all we could do was to take the fork that appeared to lead towards the mountain. We stopped for directions at the village where the lamps were already out, and dogs raised a hideous clamour. Surin got a villager out of bed, who seemed not only annoyed at the disturbance but evasive. When questioned as to the precise lay-out of the park he replied in a threatening fashion that we were already in it and that a full-time warden lived just down the road. Villagers with lighted lamps were beginning to appear in doorways and, according to Surin, the man, turning his back, said, 'Go now, and leave us in peace.' We started off again and Surin said, 'They should offer water with their blessing for the New Year. This they did not do. They were not polite.'

The track narrowed. Surin switched on the headlights and the jungle turned to white plaster, the trees appearing very close. After a while, we reached a clearing. I thought of the angry villagers and the full-time warden with his gun some-where down the road, and told Surin we should turn round and go back. This he refused to do, shaking his head with furious vehemence. 'There are deer,' he said. 'Now, one hour after sunset is the best time. To shoot one deer is no risk. One only we shoot, then we go back. After that we will have a good year.'

The car creaked and crunched its way softly down into a tunnel among the trees. Leaves like a million small mirrors caught and held the glare of the headlights. Winged insects swam towards us like shoals of fish through the beams. Small, yellow lamps hung in the whitened branches above us. Surin whispered that they were the eyes of owls. Points of light pricking from the embowered shadows betrayed the presence of alerted animals; red light was flashed back by cats and rodents of many kinds; white light by boars and deer.

Surin pulled up. 'Now we shall walk,' he said. We climbed down and he went to the back of the van to reach in for the equipment; a battery haversack feeding the latest Japanese jack-light on a headband with a three-position switch giving a 5,000-candle-power maximum beam throw, effective at up to 150 metres. 'I have one for you, too,' he said. I shook my head. He fixed the haversack in position and slipped the padded headband over his forehead, and I helped with the straps. He had a small calibre rifle of the kind favoured by poachers in a rack behind his seat. 'Here is another gun,' he said. 'Why you don't try?'

I told him I couldn't shoot straight and didn't want to spoil his sport. He shook his head, disappointed, stuck a torch into my hand, and told me to walk behind him. I had to shake the torch to make it come on. 'Sometimes there are little snakes,' he explained. 'Not many.' We started out, Surin about 10 yards ahead, showing like a black cut-out against the light as he trudged towards the incandescent tree-trunks and under the lianas hanging like stalactites in a cave. There was nothing under my feet but blackness and the soft squelch of vegetable decay. The pin-point eyes of rodents shone back as before, and once an owl went over like a puff of white smoke. The repetition of night shapes, no more than a plaster effigy of the jungle by day, became monotonous, then soporific. I was half-asleep on my feet, when the light stopped jogging through the trees and I saw Surin raise his gun and take aim, then heard the small, coughing reports, instantly smothered in the leaves.

I was relieved that it had been such a quiet affair; an explosion hardly louder than a burst paper bag – unlikely to rouse the sleeping warden and bring him in hot pursuit, wherever he might be. Surin had dimmed the light and was hauling himself through the fronds and bamboo towards a twisting animal shape. He dragged it into view as I reached him and saw long thrashing legs and black blood dripping from fur. He let it drop and showed a sad face. 'Now I shall not hunt for this year,' he said. He had shot a hare. It was the biggest hare I had ever seen, bigger than the smallest deer, but still a hare. An animal, as Surin said, that carried no luck.

With an obvious effort he accepted the sentence of fortune and smiled again. 'When I do not hunt,' he said, 'slowly my luck will come back. This is like money left in a bank. You don't touch it and it becomes more. We have seen many animals in this place. Now we will go to the car. Next year I will come back here again.'

LOOKING AT
FISH

SEEN FROM THE air, Raiatea in its lagoon appears to be menaced by cavorting dragons. These are sprawls of underwater coral, contoured by the intense ultramarine of ocean currents. The island is packed tightly with trees, delicate at a distance as asparagus fern. From these project the pinnacles of two ancient volcanoes, each wearing a small turban of mist. A white thread of reef encircles the lagoon with its nucleus of land. Opposite the Te Ava Moa pass in the reef, and clearly visible, are the ruins by the shore of the great temple of Taputaputea, second only to the Easter Island figures as a monument to a forgotten Pacific civilisation.

Raiatea turned out to be a quiet, slow-moving place, charged with the aroma of the past, and resembling, according to old photographs, the Tahiti of 50 years ago. I was there to meet a Dr Collins, regarded, although eccentric, as the authority in all island matters, and I had ridden a bicycle with only roughly circular wheels and without brakes from the hotel down to Uturoa, the capital, for the encounter. The doctor was waiting for me, his huge bulk overflowing his chair, shirt open down to the navel, outside a café overlooking the sea. There was no money in Uturoa and therefore it was marvellously preserved with scenes from Gauguin on every side. Coats of paint flaked everywhere from its surfaces to reveal palimpsests of sublimely weary colour. Boats were unloading copra among half-buried anchors on the front, and a string of beachcombers mooched like explorers in a blizzard, through fallen blossom scuffled up by the breeze. This was Sunday, 10 a.m., and the Protestant church down the road was crammed for Tahitian a cappella singing: a roaring of hymns sounding like war chants (and that, said the doctor – apart from the substitution of Noah for the names of the Polynesian sea-raiders of old – was what they were). Once, quite carried away, and hoisting himself like a sumo wrestler to his feet, he added a melodious bellow to the distant chorus. We should have gone to church, he said, but it was so crowded you practically had to fight your way in.

A waitress with an introspective *Girl with a Fan* face brought Root Cola and a saucer of crudités among which a small starfish concealed itself with a discreet movement. Cats striped like tigers lay in wait near by ready to pounce on any land crabs that moved too far from one of their innumerable holes. The doctor explained the mystery of his name – which, in view of his unmistakably Polynesian appearance, had seemed puzzling at first. It was one of a dozen or so, he said, handed out by the missionaries at the beginning of the last century at the time of the island's incorporation into the kingdom of the London Missionary Society. 'I use the original name on what I call tribal occasions,' he said. 'In our language it means shark. It was a shark, as you know, that led our seafaring ancestors to Raiatea. Many of us have a totemic relationship with this fish. I am supposed to have inherited the power to summon one up from the depths – a feat which I once performed in public, although it was generally regarded as a coincidence.'

There was no argument, the doctor said, about his ability to tame sharks, which, if approached in the right way, were the friendliest and most co-operative of fish. He suggested that I might like to meet one, which followed him about like a dog and allowed its fins to be tweaked, and I readily agreed to subject myself to this experience. The shark, he said, frequented an area in the lagoon in which fishing had been debarred by an ancient taboo, and where many singular fish had taken refuge. The chieftains of old had placed taboos on certain rivers and lagoons at spawning times, and for one reason or another this taboo had never been lifted. He instanced the case of the stream on the neighbouring island of Huahine, full of monstrous, sluggish eels that survived only by the charity of the local villagers. Rare flowers were also under a taboo, and I remembered the newspaper story of a development company that had brought a prime coastal site, only to learn that its use was restricted to the grazing of pigs.

Behind its front of run-down normality, everything about Raiatea was extraordinary, including the specialised canoe in which our trip to the off-limits area was to be made. This craft, an outrigger of the local kind, was notable for its possession of *mana*, a kind of spiritual radiation infused by the insertion into its hull of a sliver of timber from a war-canoe excavated from one of the ancient sites. It was the common property of several families, and much in demand for Sunday outings, due to the belief that the *mana* flowed into the bodies of those whose rumps came into contact with the seats and so set them up for the week. It had been out for most of the morning, and as soon as it came back to the jetty, the doctor grabbed me up, we made a rush for it, and jumped in. It now turned out that in addition to the area of the lagoon where an absolute taboo on fishing was in force, there was at least one zone where a kind of semi-taboo persisted. Puttering towards the distant reef we passed a number of women, bedecked as usual with flowers and in dresses hitched up to the knees, who were fishing in the shallows. A few minuscule fish dangled from their waists. Women – seen as inefficient anglers – were permitted here, the doctor explained, but men were not.

Seagulls hung like white ideograms in the purplish haze over our target area. Dr Collins put down the anchor, fixed his mask in position, and lowered himself into the waves. I followed him, finding myself in 20 feet of water over a bed of shimmering coral sand, in which had been placed, as if with premeditation, a single enormous rock honeycombed with caves. From this base, the fish drifted to form slow interlacing processions and stunning weaves of colour. Individually they were magnificent, often strange, sometimes startling. What instantly caught the eye was abstract decoration; an Arabic scrawl, a mathematical sign, an inky blot. Transparent fish with a barely visible outline showed little more than eyes and a digestive tract. Enormous sea horses went bobbing by, pipe-fish unrolled from crevices, and lion-fish scowled through their poisoned plumes. There were fish that switched colour to match the garish sea anemones against which they nestled; fish like Disneyland parodies of fish; fish that spun or tumbled about us like demented birds. Occasionally one turned aside in passing to search my face with flat, dejected eyes, but on the whole they showed indifference to our presence. Big stingrays shuffled uneasily under their coverlet of sand as we dived to swim close to them. A single small shark took shape in the milky distance, but as soon as it spotted us it dodged out of view behind the rock.

The doctor broke surface and pulled back his mask to comment on the shark's strange behaviour. He was worried by the absence of the confiding ten-footer we had come to see. A rumour had reached him of the presence on the reef of a party of spear fishermen from the Club Méditerranée on nearby Bora Bora. Sharks were highly strung, instinctive, exceptionally nervous creatures, he said, and if the report were true he had no doubt that fear had spread its contagion among them.

Half an hour later we were back in the port café. The outcry of Pacific starlings flocking in the trees broke for a moment into the chorus of 'Soldiers of Christ Arise'. 'Bligh of the Bounty's gone into that one,' the doctor said. 'He's been turned into an honorary ancestor since they showed the film.'

The singing stopped, the church door burst open and the worshippers poured out, all the men in their stiff Sunday suits with sprigs of frangipani behind the ears; some of the women wearing leafy crowns. They made for the line-up of veteran taxis, crowding as many as nine people into one for the ritual Sunday ride of a couple of hundred yards before the mid-day meal. A dishevelled, time-whitened old man, the last to leave the church, limped into sight. 'That's our *tatuna*. Witch doctors I believe you call them,' the doctor said.

'What's a witch doctor doing in a church?'

'They're all staunch church-goers. They're very devout. We have four varieties in all. This man's a healer. He casts out devils.'

It seemed impossible in this calm sunlit place, within easy range of so many mild satisfactions, that devils could exist.

'Anybody can go crazy,' the doctor said. 'At least we know how to handle it here. All they do is take the man into hospital, get rid of any doctor on duty – which could be me – and smuggle our friend in. They hold the man down and force his mouth open. The old fellow cuts a big lemon in half, puts on a terrible face, then rushes into the ward and rams the half lemon into the patient's mouth. After that he can go. He's cured. The *tatuna* has as much *mana* as that canoe. When you shake hands with him you see visions. His second speciality is finding things people manage to lose.'

'How does he do that?'

'I don't know, but I'll give you my personal experience. I was sitting with him roughly where we are now. I'd been out fishing and I gave him a couple of snappers. "What's on your mind?" he said. He could see something was worrying me. "Someone took my car keys while I was out in the boat," I told him. "Shut your eyes," he said. He put the tip of his finger between them at the bottom of my forehead, and it felt like ice. I asked him what he was doing, and he said he was emptying my brain. After a minute he said, "Can you think of anything now?" and I told him I couldn't. "Get up then," he said, "and go for a walk."

'I got up, laughing, crossed over the street to the Chinese supermarket and then back again into Arthur Chung's café on the other side of the road. Two boys were sitting there. I didn't speak to them, but I could feel that they were from Papeete. I held out my hand, and one of the boys dropped my car keys into it. The old man was waiting by the car when I got back. He asked me if I could think now. I told him, "More or less," and he said, "Well, in that case, let's go."'

Something was puzzling the doctor. 'How can it be that a man with so much power can go hungry?' he wondered.

'Isn't he paid anything for his services?' I asked.

'That's not the way we do things here. You give for the pleasure of giving. Only shopkeepers ask you for money.' He shook his head. 'Pity,' he said. 'If I'd thought we were going to run into him I would at least have caught him a fish.'

LOKE'S MERC

Back in Italy in 1937 someone sold me an Alfa Romeo car, a recent winner of the 24 hours Le Mans race. Having collected it off the train in London I set off somewhat cautiously to find a suitable road to try out its paces. This turned out to be the A120 going northwards through Epping Forest and virtually empty. The car accelerated easily up a slight gradient to about 110 mph, with power clearly in hand, which seemed good enough at the time. The test at an end, I pulled in at the Wake's Arms at Loughton, and almost immediately another car drew up at my side. This was an astonishing Mercedes of a kind I had never seen before. Out of it stepped a smiling and immaculate young Chinese who introduced himself as Loke Wan Tho. Loke wanted a close look at the battle-worn Alfa. Encircling it, excitement leaked from him like an electric current. 'Oh, absolutely!' he said. 'How absolutely!' It was a form of commendation lifted from P. G. Wodehouse, then reaching the end of a long vogue. For fifteen years young men of the upper classes, foreigners in this country in particular, tried to talk like Bertie Wooster.

I invited him to try the Alfa; he was breathless with gratitude (jolly sporting of you) and returned entranced by its bleak functionalism, its lack of concession to driving comfort and the sheer noise generated by the combination of the regulation track silencer, supercharger and straight-cut gears. In the meanwhile I had floated up and down the road at the wheel of the Mercedes in a silence and smoothness so unnatural as to foster a moment of illusion in which the landscape appeared to slide away while the car stood still. Loke asked me if I liked the Mercedes, and when I told him that I did he suggested an exchange, there and then and without further ado.

It was a proposition that astounded me. This lustrous and extraordinary machine with its voluptuous display of exhaust-pipes and its leopard-skin upholstery would have been worth, as I saw it, two or three times as much as the battered Alfa which had never recovered, and probably never would, from 2,000 miles covered at an average of 87 mph. I had never met a Chinese before, and for a moment I suspected a conventional oriental courtesy by which admiration was expressed, but which was not to be taken seriously. I had no way of knowing that this was a very rich man indeed, prepared at this moment to indulge what to him was no more than a trivial whim. Loke took my hesitation to mean that he had not offered enough, and hastened to add a cash inducement. I explained that it was not a matter of relative values but the fact that I was half committed to a project to be undertaken in partnership with a friend. This was to convert the Alfa for racing on Brooklands. The explanation satisfied him and he gave me an address in Cambridge in case I changed my mind.

I was now presented to his companion, Miss Dovey, a neat and sparkling English girl, who had stood aside while these transactions were in progress. Miss Dovey thought we should have a drink. We went into the Wake's Arms where we sipped orange juice and nibbled sociably at potato crisps, which Loke, trying them for the first time, responded to with what struck me as no more than simulated pleasure. I picked up a few scraps of information. Loke was at Cambridge, reading English. Of Miss Dovey I learned little except that she collected shoes and had a hundred or so pairs. She made mention of Loke's interest in rubber plantations in Malaysia, and that he kept an apartment in a Park Lane hotel for his use when in London. This, she added, with a touch of proprietorial satisfaction, she had helped him refurbish according to his taste.

In the course of a further half-hour's amiable exchange of ideas Loke said that they were both interested in birdwatching and the visit to Epping Forest was to facilitate their study of the wren (Troglodytus troglodytus troglodytus), found in its woodlands and glades in exceptional concentration. He opened up the boot of the Mercedes to display a collapsible hide imported from Switzerland into which, when the occasion presented itself, he and Miss Dovey would creep to take photographs and record the bird's song. This, he agreed, most laymen would regard as an uninspiring twitter. It was none the less of great scientific interest since the troglodytus was believed to possess extraordinary ability to vary it according to the environment.

We parted company. The Mercedes stole away down the road, turned off into a track and embedded itself in a likely thicket. I made for Weybridge where an expert on the staff of the firm undertaking conversions of the kind I had in mind, took one look at the Alfa and shook his head. It would be cheaper to buy a car designed for track use than to convert one that was not. They had an ERA, and a Maserati in reasonable shape in their used stock, but both were far and away outside my price.

Faced with this verdict I decided to go ahead with Loke's proposed exchange if by this time he had not changed his mind, and thereafter sell the Mercedes to raise the cash required. I wrote to him but there was some delay before the reply came. He had been away touring in Germany and a photograph enclosed with the letter showed the wreck of his car. It had been hit by a train at an unguarded railway level-crossing and, while neither he nor Miss Dovey had been hurt, the impact had sliced away the Mercedes' rear wheels. It would have to be rebuilt, he wrote and this would take some months. It was clear that the matter of the exchange was not ruled out. Mentioning that a complete repaint would be required, he added, 'What colour do you prefer?'

Almost with that, it seemed, the Munich crisis was upon us, changing not only our plans but those of the world. Loke, obliged to drop everything, was called back to Singapore. Escaping subsequently from the Japanese invasion, he was on the *Nova Moller*, sunk in an air attack, and rescued from the water with severe burns and temporary loss of sight. In the meanwhile, I was in North Africa and Italy, and it was 1947 before we met again.

I was in Pembrokeshire, where I spent that summer rock-climbing, when a letter from Loke, forwarded from London, announced that he was back. When he heard where I was he wanted to come down. The cliffs of Pembrokeshire – although I had no idea that this was the case – were a famous venue for birdwatchers. He arrived overbrimming with enthusiasm and, apart from an area of pink new skin surrounding the eyes, little changed in appearance. The conditions in which I was living must have been among the most primitive in Europe; certainly far beyond anything Loke had ever experienced. The three-room cottage I had rented in a fishing village possessed no running water, no sanitary arrangements of any description, and no electric light. It was a scene into which he plunged with relish, although unable to believe his eyes at his first view of one of the mild and contemplative rats that were a feature of the place ascending the step-ladder that gave access to the bedrooms. The villagers seemed not to notice their presence and Loke, always on the lookout for virtue lurking beneath everyday attitudes, saw this as evidence of a latent, intrinsic Buddhism in the Welsh character. The truth was that due to a superstitious local aversion to cats, rats were tolerated in their place for the efficiency with which they cleared up the mess left on the quayside after the fishermen had boxed up their catch.

Loke was in his element. Littlehaven was brilliant with life, with seals in every cove, the morning fox on the beach in search of anything left over by the cats, a stream with an otter at the back of the hill and a bluster of wax-white gulls always in the sky. Ensconced in brambles and bracken Loke trained his 20-inch telephoto on a 1½-inch bird. Despite all the ravens and peregrines around him he was back to his first love, the common wren hunting its microscopic prey just out of reach of the spume. He informed me that three island sub-species of troglodytus were to be found on St Kilda, the Hebrides and the Shetlands, and his hope was to identify a fourth variation, based on the large and deserted island of Skomer, a few miles away. This, despite many days of field-work, he never did. When I made some mention of the Mercedes, he seemed momentarily puzzled. Then he remembered. 'I had to leave it behind,' he said. 'I expect my people will have dealt with it.'

He was now in control of his family empire, of its cinemas, rubber, tin and real estate, and had become one of the rich men of the world, yet he admitted that when the time came for his return to Singapore he would do so with reluctance. It evidenced a personal schism never to be repaired. He was committed by custom to a pursuit of wealth for which he had little true inclination, and removed from the convention of his background, his tastes were frugal, even austere. In the introduction to his book, *A Company of Birds*, published when he was seen as the best bird-photographer in Asia, he lays blame on destiny: 'I was destined to be a businessman.' Of his ornithology, he adds an explanation, 'Every man needs some invisible means of support.' How sad that the empty ritual of a man of affairs should have usurped so much of his life.

A year or two later he invited me to join him in an expedition to northern India, the proviso being that I must first learn to skin birds, but this it proved impossible to do in the time. We met again in 1954 in Singapore when I stopped off there to snatch a night's sleep on my way to North Vietnam. I phoned

Loke from the hotel and shortly afterwards an extraordinary cortège of cars drew up outside. It was impossible not to be reminded of a top mobster's funeral, minus the flowers. Loke had clearly arrived, but I found it hard to associate him with this arrogant display. The explanation was simple, and his smile apologetic. 'We're going to my sister's birthday party, dear boy,' he said. 'Black tie – white Cadillac. Hop in.'

The main feature of the open-air restaurant taken over for this event was a rotonda set in a garden of flowering trees among which birdcages were artfully concealed, some furnished with real songsters others with vociferous mechanical bulbuls used to encourage natural song. About 200 Chinese guests were seated at long tables forming a hollow square. Within the rotonda a pianist in tails seated at a grand piano worked his way with some panache through a repertoire of Sankey and Moody hymns. Loke explained that most of the guests were Christadelphians, members of an American fundamentalist sect that attempts to inculcate severe morality upon its adherents, including – despite the example of the marriage at Cana – an absolute ban upon alcohol. For this reason all believers present were invited to wash down the exquisite food placed before them with Dr Pepper, Coca Cola, or other such blameless refreshment. Nevertheless, discreet arrangements had been made for the 'unsaved', such as myself, to be provided with whisky contained in antique bowls of great beauty and doubtlessly of great worth.

It was a lively affair, the guests exchanged jokes, pulled funny faces, and punned in English – probably in Chinese too. They were easily amused; a feature of the ingenious and interminable banquet was a partridge served to each guest in which a simulated and edible bird's nest had been inserted. Someone stood up and said, 'Normally the bird is to be found in the nest. Now we are eating the nest that was discovered in the bird.' Everybody clapped.

The real and mechanical bulbuls warbled in their cages, the pianist charged for the third time into *Through The Night Of*

Doubt And Sorrow, played as if it had been a wedding march, and a pentatonic tittering arose from the guests, encouraged at this stage to indulge in horseplay of a decorous, almost formalised kind. A Chinese lady in a white robe upbraided us all in a brief sermon which appeared to fall on deaf ears. Towards dawn the scent of frangipani strengthened, and at sunrise Loke drove me in one of the white Cadillacs to the airport. At our parting I promised to take a crash course in taxidermy, and Loke agreed to include me in his next expedition. We continued a regular correspondence but were never to meet again, for a year or two later he was killed in a plane crash in Taiwan.

Last August a national newspaper published a piece about a 1936 Mercedes Grand Tourer – described as rusted all over, with mouse-gnawed seats, and full of holes – being sold at Christie's vintage car auction for an unprecedented £1,595,000. A. M. Davies, a butcher of Walsall, had been left the car by an uncle in 1956, since when it had slowly mouldered away in the garage at the back of his shop. It had gone to a Swedish financier, and the extraordinary price depended, the newspaper had ascertained, on the crucial fact of this car's possession of a right-hand drive, being one of only two models thus built out of a total production of 356. Loke's 500K, too, had been a right-hand drive version. Was this the self-same car? Possibly, and if not it could only have been the twin – equally valuable to a financier one supposed – if it had managed to escape the scrap heap.

THE LAST OF
OLD EUROPE

DON JUAN SERRA told us: 'We cope with our numerous wolves pretty well; largely because we refuse to provide them with food.' Don Juan is the parish priest of the almost inconceivably isolated village of Arbeyales, tucked into a wide ledge of the Cantabrian mountains in the National Reserve of Somiedo, which is roughly the size of the Isle of Wight. A census conducted about 10 years ago put the population of the zone at 20,000 inhabitants spread over 200 villages – an average 100 each. It is now certainly much less, and falling fast as the lure of the cities empties these peerless solitudes, and the wild animals return to the deserted fields.

This was the alpine redoubt of the few that remained of the European brown bears. From where we stood on our ledge at Arbeyales a mist-veiled cliff that was not quite a precipice was in sight about three miles away: the bears had actually learned to climb its almost vertical face to reach caves where they were beyond reach of their pursuers. Once the brown bear was to be found comfortably browsing or dozing in the woods of all parts of Spain, including those on the outskirts of Madrid, Seville or Gibraltar. Now thirty or so of them are in Somiedo – mostly in the neighbourhood of Arbeyales – and although protected by law they are relentlessly hunted by international sportsmen who are happy to pay the equivalent of £3,000 for the pleasure of killing one.

No one can even guess at the number of wolves harbouring in these mountains. They are on the increase, and co-exist with a wide variety of game including deer and wild boars that conduct nightly raids upon village potato patches. Here they survive under protection of the mountains, the ancient forests of chestnut and oak, landscape virtually without roads and an appalling winter that keeps man, the adversary, out of the way for up to six months of the year.

These are the conditions which have also preserved the Celto-Iberian customs of pre-history, the circular stone houses providing shelter both for man and his animals, and the tribal language *bable* – so called by the Spanish from the outside world in an allusion to the biblical Tower of Babel and the linguistic confusion its building produced.

Don Juan Fernandez Serra is not only the ministering priest of Arbeyales but, in the absence of any other established authority, unofficial mayor and even honorary village police-man. He is also, according to Ricardo Magadán, the inspector of the Department of Natural Resources who took me to see him, the only priest in the country who is also a cowherd.

Don Juan turned out to be a man in his fifties, lean, bony and muscular, dressed in a boiler suit and wearing the standard clogs of the area with two-inch wooden spikes projecting from the soles. Far below, a meadow with beautiful cows charging through the grass took shape like a surfacing whale in the mist, before sliding from view again. Rain fell in icy splashes, and seed pearls of moisture had formed on eyebrows and beards. 'There is no more intelligent animal than the wolf,' said Don Juan, 'but our Asturian cows are a match for them. They form a circle to defend themselves and they're terribly fast with the horns. Once in a while a wolf gets skewered and the word soon gets around. The only time we lose a cow, it's one that's slowed down by being in calf. We can't keep sheep and goats because there's no pasture in the village itself, and there's no way of protecting them.'

This was at the heart of the priest's problem. It was 3 June, with the animals not long released from the byres under the living rooms of the houses ('We need them in winter to keep warm') and taken to the summer pastures, and the villagers were still cleaning out the muck and carrying it down to the ledges on which they grow spinach of giant proportions. By tradition each family cultivates only enough vegetables for its own use, its principal occupation being the cutting and storing of hay for winter fodder. The village income depends entirely on the milk, cheese and meat its animals provide.

A deep cleft in the mountain leads to the best meadows where the cattle graze. The path up to this is so steep that steps have had to be cut in the rock, and the cattle are hauled over them by middle-aged and elderly villagers to the grassy heights, and there left much to their own devices until the first snows of October. The physical effort involved in these tiny migrations is very great, and now, with the population down to 23, with not a single inhabitant under 50, and half the houses empty, they were reaching the end of their tether.

'Last year,' the priest said, 'they built the road up to us.' (He mentioned that so far as he knew I was the first foreigner to visit the village.) Now the government promised the construction of three ski-lifts to carry the villagers and their animals to and from the upper pastures. The scheme had met with opposition. In this fiercely democratic and egalitarian community people laid claim to more than their tiny vegetable patches, and a man was entitled to pasture his animals or cut wood anywhere in the mountains. But some conservationists who came here were inclined to see Arbeyales as a surviving corner of a vanished paradise. 'Let the place alone,' they said. 'Ski-lifts would bring in the tourists. It would be the end.'

'Of course it will help us if it ever happens,' Don Juan said, 'but it's almost too late. In summer here we work a 13 or

14-hour day. And what do we do in the winter? We breathe in the air from our animals' lungs, and we make clogs. There's no demand for them anywhere else, so we give them to each other. There's no inducement for a young lad or a girl to stay in a place like this. Naturally they've taken off. And even if they build the ski-lifts, does anyone really believe that after a taste of life in the city they'll want to pack up and come back here? Frankly they'd be mad to do so.'

Like all such subsistence-economy communities, the people of Arbeyales were born into a social climate in which every man, woman and child filled an indispensable place in the life of the village. Here, as Don Juan said, there was freedom. Here no one worked for a boss. People joined forces to build one another's houses, to manhandle the animals up and down the steep slopes, to bring in the hay. It was hard to believe that unemployment could exist anywhere. Now the young have gone, and with their escape to the town the underpinning of village society has collapsed. And there is no such thing here as hired labour with which they could be replaced.

In Arbeyales, come what might, they stuck the winter through. In other villages, such as La Perál and Santa María del Puerto, they gave in with the first snows, moving down to temporary shelter, sometimes no further off than the nearest deep valley, sometimes as far away as the coast. The custom was to leave a *vecineiro* – a sort of professional village-minder – to look after their houses during the five months or so of their absence. This man, having stocked up with firewood, cheese, chestnuts, chorizo sausage, dried beans and bundles of tapers to provide the occasional solace of artificial light, would settle with practised resignation to his clog-making, his thoughts, and the great white silence of the snow. In some extraordinary emergency he could be awakened from his semi-hibernation by anyone able to struggle as far as the church and ring the bell. On the day in April when the bell eventually rang to announce the villagers' return, the *vecineiro* would throw open the door of his hut and drag himself out into the weak sunshine to greet the new arrivals in proper style with a Roman salute and as broad a smile as he could manage.

All these people, who are not quite nomads but who chop and change habitation according to the season, are known as *vaqueiros*. Their origin, although subject to endless discussion, remains a mystery. An incomprehensible language and strikingly different customs have set them apart from their neighbours, resulting in the past in their subjection to social discrimination. Until a century ago *vaqueiros* living in mixed villages were seated separately in the churches, and even in death were buried apart in the cemeteries.

The account published by the Spanish Council for Tourism suggests that they may be descended from tribes entering Spain from Italy in the first century BC. It goes on to list other possibilities – that their ancestors were released Roman slaves, or converted Muslims driven in 1517 from their last stronghold in southern Spain, or Christian renegades banished from lands recaptured from the Moors some centuries earlier: a mixed bag, in fact, of second-class citizens exiled to the Spanish Siberia of their day. The *vaqueiros* still keep their own company, and marry among themselves. The area is one where bull-sacrifices in one form or another are frequently included in local fiestas, but of this the *vaqueiros* will have nothing, preferring to concentrate on domestic themes. They are particularly strong on weddings, a principal feature of which, as in the *vaqueiro* village of Aristébano, is a procession formed to display the marriage bed, followed by musicians with *peyetchas* – an instrument from the dawn of history resembling a long-handled pan, on which a lively if monotonous accompaniment is beaten out with a heavy key.

In their dealings with outsiders the *vaqueiros* are most at ease in the company of the true nomadic shepherds who drive their flocks all the way in summer from the sun-scorched prairies of Central Spain, taking a month over a transhumance which is now accomplished, largely by train, in a matter of days. In early June the southern nomads were pouring into Asturias where they were welcomed as ever, for under these permanently weeping skies there was grass for all. It was a swing of the human tides that had been going on, whoever the rulers and despite all the wars, for thousands of years.

Pola de Somiedo is the capital of this, the most sparsely inhabited area of an under-populated province. It crouches under the craggy mist-draped silhouette of the peak of La Palumbera, a matter of some hundred houses, a small square, a town hall like a provincial football-club headquarters, a grey little church and a bar. The bar has the only fruit machine within 50 miles and sells wine to which a sprig of vine foliage has been added during fermentation. This imparts the slightly acidulous flavour appreciated by those who earn their bread by the sweat of their brow. There are jelly-babies, too, in a jar for the children that remain. But they are few, for in common with all the villages of the zone there is here a slow wastage of people.

The gossip in the bar, understandably in cattle country, was the price of cows. The beautiful and agile Asturian mountain breed, rarely seen elsewhere and probably closer than others to the original wild cattle depicted in mesolithic cave-paintings all over the country, is in great demand. Asturian cows produce a relatively small amount of exceptionally rich milk, incomparable meat, can be left to look after themselves, and flourish in the rain. The price in Oviedo for a top-grade cow had reached 500,000 pesetas, about £2,500, and the breeders of Somiedo were naturally jubilant.

For Ricardo Magadán the news was a mixture of good and bad. A villager claimed to have seen a bear with four cubs. Normally a litter is limited to a maximum of three – tiny, blind, toothless creatures hardly bigger than a rat at birth, and weighing no more than a pound. His excitement was coloured with scepticism. It seemed too good to be true. On the debit side was the strong rumour that a clandestine hunter had shot an adult bear in the vicinity. This, said the inspector sorrowfully, he found more believable.

After Somiedo the search for the old Europe narrowed into a pilgrimage to Balouta which, although only 35 miles away as the crow – or in this case the eagle – flies, calls for a long, roundabout journey down into the province of León, then northwards up the Ancares Valley and once again into the Cantabrians. Until quite recently it would have been fair to describe Balouta as the most remote village in Spain. Even now the village itself, and the road leading to it, are marked only on large-scale maps. It lies at the bottom of a deep valley on the north-western slope of the mountains across the Mira-valles Pass, cut off during seven months of the year. This extreme isolation has preserved a way of life hardly to be found elsewhere in the country. A year or so ago the telephone reached Balouta so that now in an emergency a doctor can be called from San Román, some 30 kilometres away, although in winter part of the journey will have to be made on a horse. Five children attend the school. The population, estimated at 200 five years ago, is down to 88.

A third of the 40 or so dwellings in Balouta are *pallozas*. The remains of prehistoric structures of a similar kind are to be found in Cornwall and the north of Scotland, but here they have survived in their purest Celtic form, offering no concession to architectural developments in the succeeding 3,000 years. These normally circular or oval buildings are constructed with great skill and art, with drystone walls up to 18 inch thick and about 4½ foot in height, supporting a steeply conical thatched roof, devoid of a chimney. The *palloza* is divided into a main living-room and partitioned-off cooking and sleeping areas, plus stabling for the animals. A family possessing a substantial number of these will generally add a pen to the side of the house. Light and air are admitted by small window-slits or the open door and, although some of the *pallozas* now have electricity, their inhabitants seem to have accustomed themselves to the gloom, managing as ever in semi-darkness (and when meals are in preparation a fair amount of smoke). Visitors recommended to a view of the village from the mountain road high above will find them-selves looking down on what appears to be an African village. Nevertheless, everything in sight here belongs to a far remoter past than that reflected in the African equivalent.

Last spring in Balouta was cold and wet. It had snowed in May, thereafter raining for 30 consecutive days before my arrival in June, and the children were going about like little Andean Indians in knitted caps with side flaps pulled down well over the ears. This was the time the maximum possible effort was required from the whole population to set the year on course, with every day filled with urgent tasks, in this instance to be carried out in the rain and mud. Despite this there were smiles everywhere. Balouta appeared a cheerful place.

Reference to the village was made a number of years ago in the journal of the *Consejo Superior de Investigaciones Científicas* of Madrid. 'Those of us who wish for a greater understanding of the lives of our Celto-Iberian ancestors,' said the writer, 'should spare no effort to visit Balouta. It may convince them that the gap that divides us is narrower than they suspected.' Evidence gathered from burial sites, he said, showed that the villagers of old had possessed good physique and lived on the whole to ripe old age. The very isolation of such villages had spared them in a later epoch from the plagues of the Middle Ages. There had been nothing, either, said the expert, to deflect the course of natural selection; thus Balouta and the other villages of the area had developed their own well-adapted human strain.

Two thousand years had passed in which Balouta, roughly unchanged, had survived the oppressions of the Romans, the Visigoths and the Moors. The Inquisition had sent its agents into all these villages to stamp out local brands of faith, but little or nothing was remembered of them, and the repeated hurricanes of war had been forgotten, too.

I discussed the future with Rafael Campos in the San Pascúal family's bar. Rafael, a bachelor of 40, is the owner of seven cows, making him by local standards a rich man. He admitted smilingly to his wealth, adding pleasantly: 'Not that it matters much one way or another when there's nothing to spend it on. We're busy now, and again in the autumn, but in summer I spend most of the time hunting or fishing. I can count on getting hare every time I go out. We all get together to round up the wild boars. These streams are full of trout. City people pay thousands for what we have for nothing.'

The bar was a table in the low-ceilinged, smoke-cured living room in which the San Pascual family and friends fiddled with the knobs of Balouta's only television set to produce a variety of flickering ghost images with which they seemed well content. We sipped *aguardiente* in which cherries had been steeped, with which came hazelnuts to be broken up with a hammer.

An overladen oxcart passed the door, interrupting us with a tremendous squealing. Balouta carts resolutely follow Bronze Age models, their wheels solid with the axles which turn in unlubricated bushes. 'I love the sound,' Rafael said. 'So do we all. A friend of mine was offered a share of a farm in another village but he only agreed to the deal if he was allowed to take his "screamer" – as we call them – with him. His new neighbour complained of the noise, so he came back.'

'But people are leaving?' I said.

'Yes. There are fewer of us with every year. By the time you're 40, you're a fixture of the place. But the young are on their way out. What can you expect?'

Our world has pushed forward its frontier here to La Vega de Espinareda, 30 kilometres across the mountains from Balouta. This once almost equally isolated village was reached by a hard-surfaced road back in the fifties, being by this unrecognisably changed almost overnight. Before that it had been distinguished by its gracious wooden houses, with their enormous Alpine-style balconies, but now the angular breeze-block constructions have taken over. La Vega of our days is part of the new Spain, a country with a crime-rate slightly lower than ours, but unemployment much higher, and the incidence of AIDS in heterosexuals higher still. La Vega has a supermarket with Bulgarian tinned stew currently on offer in this land overflowing with milk and honey, three *discotecas* and two English-style 'pubs'. The first graffiti have appeared on the walls, the first degutted car lies abandoned in the street and the first mugging has been reported in the press. This is the Mecca to which local youth flocks.

'What is to happen to Balouta?' I asked.

It would disappear, Rafael thought. The government had done something for Pioredo, the other *palloza* village just over the pass, by designating it an historical and artistic complex. Their idea was to attract tourists, and there had been a hand-out of money to tidy the place up, but for all that the population was down once again to 67, and falling as fast as ever.

The Balouta smile, almost invulnerable to adversity in its many guises, had faded. Rafael seemed to be listening. Rain struck like a fistful of tiny pebbles at the window, and a second oxcart turning into the street began its comforting screech. He appeared encouraged, and the smile fought its way back.

'The only hope would be to open a *discoteca* here,' he said. 'Then everybody would be happy.'

A HARVEST
OF SOULS

O N 27 DECEMBER 1986 a party of thirty-four 'tame'
Indians, armed by the New Tribes Missionaries, set out
from the sect's headquarters at Campo Loro in the Gran
Chaco, Paraguay, to capture a small group of Ayoreo Indians
spotted in the jungle from the mission's plane. These, the
survivors of a number of previous attacks, had established
themselves in a village some 50 miles from Campo Loro. The
attacking party, too, were Ayoreos, although of a different
clan, and traditionally the enemies of their quarry – a fact of
which the missionaries were well aware. The mission Indians
were carried in trucks as far as these could be driven into the
jungle and, after that, left to continue on foot. It took them
three days to hack their way through dense undergrowth and
reach the village of the Pig People, as they were called by the
missionaries.

There have been many and varying accounts – all from
missionary sources – of what happened next. Early versions
spoke of the tame Indians advancing to the assault with New
Testaments in their hands, and it was only in an issue of the
missionary journal, *Brown Gold*, that any mention of guns was
made. 'The village had been prepared for war,' said the

213

journal, 'and was always kept that way because of the tremendous fear they [the forest Ayoreos] had of the leader of the mission Indians and his group. A bush fence had been put up round the village and only a couple of small paths led into it . . . where the attacker would trip and fall in this area it was easy to spear or club him . . .'

A verbal description was given of the mechanisms of such a jungle attack by a missionary speaking to a representative of Survival International. He said that 'when the mission Indians entered the village they "grabbed" members of the other group and became their owners. . . . People who are grabbed are in a way slaves of the ones who grabbed them'. In accordance with this system, 'One of our men grabbed Porai [a Pig Person] and had him put his weapons down . . . when he went to grab another man, Porai picked up his spear and speared one of our men. When this happened the killing started.' In the course of the battle that followed, five of the mission Indians were killed and four wounded. After some hours the fighting came to an end and the surviving mission Indians with the twenty-five Pig People they had been able to round up returned to their base at Campo Loro.

There was nothing new about such expeditions. A book entitled *Mision: Etnocidio* has been published investigating practices of the fundamentalist New Tribes Mission sect which have long been obscure. In it a contributor, Volker Von Bremen, an anthropologist who has carried out field studies for the past ten years among the few remaining Ayoreos, said that manhunts had been frequent and had caused great loss of life in the 20 years preceding 1974, after which the attacks had died down as the forest emptied of Indians. Such hunts were conducted in secret, and little or no mention of them appeared in the muzzled press. Astonishingly, the information that had leaked out was usually to be found in missionary publications, which the missionaries might have assumed the public would never bother to read. These could be bewilderingly frank, sometimes hardly bothering to conceal chilling facts behind the façade of biblical quotations and conventional pieties.

Indian women had been chased round the forest for three days, and one was severely injured (a breast had been shot away on a previous hunt). However, 'It was a joyous occasion when we arrived at the mission. There was a lot of hugging and hand-shaking going on, even though the Pig People weren't familiar with these customs.' Missionary reports in further issues of the journal paint a gloomier picture of the scene. Of the eight women captured, four who were pregnant aborted there and then. As a missionary admitted to Survival International: 'The Pig People who were brought in didn't keep many children because it was hard to run away. They killed many children.' Another evangelist was more specific: 'one woman killed four.' Mr Sammons, head of the New Tribes Mission at Campo Loro, told Survival International: 'some of them are looking pretty bad. They want their jungle food, and haven't got used to eating hamburger-type food yet.' Les Pedersen, the NTM Field Co-ordinator for Latin America, said he did not know how many Ayoreos brought in to the mission had survived. 'We don't keep that kind of detailed record,' he said, adding, 'they're all pretty well mixed up with the others down there, and those Indians all look pretty much the same.' Von Bremen was able to conduct a further investigation from which potentially sinister facts emerged. The Indians had told him that the captured chief, with his wife and daughter, had been shut in a room and given strong medicine (remedio fuerte) from which they all died.

Yet, despite the many casualties of the operation, a few captives survived in a somewhat miserable fashion. Sharon Burkhart writing in *Brown Gold* in March 1983 says, 'Life has not been especially full of blessing for them since they left their wandering ways in the woods. They were contacted in 1979. Within several months Orojoi's father, mother and sister had all died. The next year Ijerai's parents passed away. In 1981 Ijarai and Orojoi contracted measles, a killing disease among primitive people.' Even on the evangelical front the thing had been a disaster, for these wretched people clung stubbornly to their old beliefs. 'The greatest prayer request for them', Sharon asks, 'would be that they would see the need of accepting Christ as their personal saviour.'

It was estimated at the end of the thirties that some 4,000 Ayoreos roamed that vast amalgam of forest and swamp, divided between Bolivia and Paraguay, known as the Gran Chaco. They were constantly at risk from the small-scale raids of farmers, who carried a few off as slaves, but they held their own in the labyrinth of the 'Green Hell' in which only they could find the way. Doomsday came with the ending of World War II, in the rush for gold, for 'strategic metals', for oil, for gas, for valuable timber. Latin America was found to possess all of these in abundance. With the advent of new road-building techniques, the bulldozer, and planes that could put down and take off from a couple of hundred yards of airstrip, the jungle ceased to offer refuge. To the loggers and the exploration teams, the Indians were at best a nuisance. To the missionaries, swarming overseas again, they were a rich harvest of souls waiting to be gathered in. Within ten years of the return of peace, 300 missionary sects, nearly all of them American fundamentalist, were in action in South America where the evangelist concentration was by far the greatest in the world. By 1982 *Time* counted 9,250 Protestant missionaries in the sub-continent, noting that in some small communities the missionaries outnumbered those they had come to convert.

Competition for souls was intense and eventually many of the less successful contenders went to the wall leaving the two largest organisations, the Summer Institute of Linguistics and the New Tribes Mission, virtually to divide up South America between them. Of these, the SIL – which despite its name is in no sense a scientific body – is the larger and richer; the New Tribes Mission is, if possible, more fundamental. The NTM rejects the use of Bible translations other than its own – thus opening the way to considerable re-interpretations of the Holy Writ. It is obsessed with its struggle with Satan, seen as eternally locked in a combat with God from which he sometimes emerges as at least a temporary winner. Open letters to Christ sometimes appear in its publications. 'Dear Jesus Christ, we acknowledge receipt of your memo. . . . We appreciate your offer to serve as our resource Person, and should we care to undertake the project sometime later, we will be in contact. Cordially, the Christians.' In its recruitment of missionaries it advertises its indifference to educational standards. The sect fields 2,500 missionaries (about 1,000 less than its rival) in sixty different countries, and it is supported by its own airfleet and by all the computerised panoply of a giant multinational corporation. Its home base is in Sanford, Florida, and its European headquarters are in England, at Matlock, Derbyshire.

It seems natural that in 1956 General Stroessner, the seemingly permanent dictator of Paraguay should have chosen the NTM to receive the contract to 'settle and civilise' the Indians of his country, seen as standing in the way of progress. He would no doubt have been impressed by the text from Romans 3:1, 'There is no government on earth God has not permitted to come to power,' which features so prominently in fundamentalist literature, and which in the English Bible's version appears more simply as: 'The powers that be are ordained by God.' At that time, of all the areas of Paraguay thrown open to international development, the Gran Chaco was seen to offer the greatest prospects of instant wealth, and it was to the Chaco that the General's fundamentalists were assigned. They were to deal with the Ayoreos, and several thousand hectares of land were made over to the mission to facilitate their task. When, some years later, I asked a Paraguayan army officer why it had been decided that missionaries rather than the army should get rid of the Indians, his reply was, 'They're better at it. When we go in we shoot some, and some get away. They get the lot. The missionaries know how to talk to them. When the missionaries clear an area they leave it clean.'

He had seen them at work in a previous clash – the first in which the NTM had been involved – in the Bolivian half of the Gran Chaco. Jean Dye Johnson, a New Tribes missionary who was there, gives an unforgettable account of the scene in a book describing her experiences. The Ayoreos, she tells us, were under attack from the air. At the sound of a plane they would all throw themselves to the ground. Mothers prostrated themselves over their children, keeping perfectly still, the brown of their bodies perfectly camouflaged with the browns and greens of the jungle. Witnessing the terror to which they were subjected, her determination, she assures us, was even stronger to win these souls for Christ.

And here is the account given to me personally by an Ayoreo of a similar encounter with Bolivian troops some twenty years later in the Chaco to the south of Santa Cruz. 'I must have been about nine,' he said. 'The soldiers came and killed my mother and sister. They bayoneted them in the throat to stop them screaming. My brother and I ran away and hid in a swamp. There was a missionary with the soldiers. He found us and took us away.'

By 1987, after a struggle carried out against terrific odds and lasting 40 years, the Ayoreos had come to the end of their history. Father Zanardini, head of the Salesian Mission at Maria Auxliadora in the Chaco, which has consistently opposed forcible conversion, collected what evidence he could find of the continued existence of Indian groups in the jungle. He had heard of a group of seven, made up of the members of two families, of three adult males in isolation and of a man and his wife. There were reported to be about 800 Ayoreos confined in NTM camps, but of them no one could say anything for certain. The NT missionaries, little people from little towns in their own country, but here invested with the power of mad Roman emperors, were a law unto themselves. They surrounded their actions with secrecy, accountable to no one. No records would ever be produced of the flights of their spotter plane and the raids that had followed. They had spoken in their publications of many deaths, but there was no one to count the graves and ask how? and when? The little men had put an end to a remarkable race. The Ayoreos esteemed not only valour and intelligence, but – perhaps above all – a sense of responsibility. Von Bremen says that when a member of a band was bitten by a snake, the chief had to allow himself to be bitten. If a man was burned, or otherwise injured, the chief submitted to the infliction of similar injuries on his own body.

When an investigating commission was sent to Campo Loro, its members were debarred by mission Indians – now guards – from any access to their captives. Only surreptitious visits were possible. The few accounts published in the Paraguayan press were sometimes harrowing, always sad. The Indians, they said, were housed in subhuman conditions, sleeping in the mud in the rainy season. Able-bodied males were transported for labour as peons on farms of the Mennonite sect – being rewarded with vouchers exchangeable only for clothing and food. Pabla Romero, a Chamacoco Indian, took the considerable risk of speaking out at the camp at Puerto Esperanza. Desperate to find a momentary escape from the dreariness, she and her friend had wanted to dress up as *payasos* (clowns). The application was met with a stern refusal. 'Senorita Wanda Jones told us that when we have clowns it starts off an epidemic in which our children suffer. If we don't have clowns she promised to help us and see that we have enough to eat.'

Nevertheless, the sect had been losing ground. It had aroused general disgust following the scandal unleashed in the seventies when its usual zealous collaboration in the elimination of the Aché Indians of Eastern Paraguay was exposed. A description, published in Europe by a German anthropologist who witnessed these events, led to Paraguay being charged with complicity in enslavement and genocide by the League for the Rights of Man. Following this, a US senator took to the Senate floor to add to these charges denunciations of torture, massacre, the withholding from the Indians of food and medicine, and the compulsory prostitution of their women. He also produced the copy of a receipt given by a missionary for money paid for work done by Aché slaves from the mission camp. The US Ambassador was recalled from Asunción to admonish him, thus setting a precedent for the State Department's protection of the sect, and confirming the view generally held throughout Latin America of the NTM as the religious arm of the CIA.

The camp at Cerro Moroti had already had some publicity by the time of my visit in 1975 due to the evidence of casual passers-by in its vicinity who had seen Indians screaming, bleeding and vomiting over each other as they were brought in from the jungle. It was a sinister place in the extreme, but only a description provided by a missionary – in this case the head missionary's wife – can give an idea of what this forest Belsen could have been like at its worst. Whether arising from injuries received in the manhunts, from sickness, or the refusal to take food, there were many bodies to be disposed of, these being commonly thrown into a hole in the ground and cremated. Mrs Stolz, the missionary, describes one young woman, determined not to be separated from her dead grandmother, jumping into the hole after her, saying she would go to the sun where her grandmother was going. It took four men, Mrs Stolz said, to pull her out. She added, 'Will they believe there is a fire, hotter than anything they could make to cremate a body, waiting for anyone who dies without Christ?'

There were signs, even at this stage, that Paraguay's military leadership could be having second thoughts about what had become a damaging association, and be getting ready to call it a day. General Marciál Samaniego, Minister of Defence, defending the action taken against the Achés, had adopted an uncustomarily apologetic tone, admitting that crimes against the Indians had taken place, but arguing that 'as there had been no "intent" to destroy the Achés one cannot speak of genocide'.

The NTM were becoming a little over-confident in their dealings with the government. Latterly, as it turned out, they had not even bothered to keep General Stroessner informed of their intentions and actions. When Luke Holland of Survival International asked Mr Keege, at that time head of the mission at Campo Loro, whether the authorities had sanctioned the 1979 hunt, he received the astonishing reply: 'We refrained from informing the authorities to avoid outside interference with our plans.'

What then had the General and his followers to gain from the continuing presence of the sect in Paraguay? The latest massacre had been no more than a drop in the ocean of Indian misery, but it had given the country a bad name. The fundamentalists had been criticised by the Pope on the occasion of his visit, and now faced the united opposition of the Catholic Church. In terms of mere expediency, their presence no longer served any purpose, for, in fulfilment of their contract, they had 'settled and civilised' the Indians and, although they promised to continue to 'press contacts', it was hardly worthwhile launching expeditions against Father Sanardini's two families and three single men.

It was still said in Paraguay that, with the exception of the NTM's unannounced manhunts, nothing was ever done without the President's knowledge and sanction, and that nothing escaped his eye. The publication of *Mision: Etnocidio*, the most powerful and documented attack ever made on the sect, was a sign of the times, and a sign that the General's patience was wearing thin.

In Venezuela in the same year, the NTM suffered the worst setbacks in its history. The missionaries had been expelled from several countries, but until then had encountered no great difficulty in mustering support back home to arrange for a return. There had been no question of the sect being permitted to conduct manhunts, Paraguay-style, or to set up camps to which Indians could be taken and held against their will prior to conversion to 'non-salaried labour'. Here, the Indians of the area in which they chose to settle were attracted by gifts; in the first instance, these were often iron tools of a useful kind, but later they gave objects of little real value such as electric torches and toys of various kinds, operated by batteries which required renewing and could only be obtained through the mission store.

With this cargo-cult which provides Indian children with T-shirts, and Indian families with an assortment of dehydrated soups and canned foods, an iron dependency is finally established. When this happens, the rule is cash on the nail. The Indian has been enticed away astutely from the self-sufficiency that is his racial custom, based upon hunting, collecting, and the cultivation of his vegetable garden, and must now be prepared to settle himself where he is readily available as a wage-earning labourer. Within a few years 50 per cent of the active males of a tribe broken up in this premeditated fashion become alcoholics, and the provincial towns of Venezuela are full of them.

In 1972 when the first NT missionaries dropped from the sky into the Panare Indians' settlement at Colorado in Venezuela, they found them living on comfortable terms with their white neighbours, with whom they exchanged vegetables grown in their gardens, small game and fresh fish for things like axes and hoes. Impressed by a plane (which they had never seen before), by a kitchen full of purring and blinking gadgetry, and by the radio transmitter with which they believed the evangelists were in direct and daily contact with God, the Indians were inclined to listen to what they had to say.

The first missionary task was to explain to them the meaning of sin and guilt – such concepts being inexpressible in most Indian languages, as well as absent from tribal thought. It took years to do this. Practically every Panare activity carried out before the landing of the first missionary plane turned out to meet with God's disapproval, spoken through a missionary mouth. 'God wants us to wear pants and to use soap. He says we should stop living together in *malocas* and move into one-family houses with proper locks on the doors. When we are sick there is no need for us to go to a healer. The Lord in his faithfulness gives us aspirins. It's OK to pay with money, but we have to quit giving things away.'

In Paraguay, opposition to the sect had been stifled until the last moment by press censorship. In Venezuela, a democracy, the clamour raised by the NTM's virtual takeover of the lives of its Indian minorities was vociferous. A congressional investigation of the sect went on for nearly two years, during which time a whole catalogue of bizarre facts came to light. A naval officer spoke of scientific espionage, noting that the missionaries inevitably installed themselves in areas known to contain strategic minerals. The captain had found missionary baggage, labelled 'combustible materials', to contain military uniforms and 'other articles' – this being taken by the press to mean geiger counters. At this point it became clear that, as in the case of Senator Abouresk in Washington, powerful influences were at work for the NTM behind the scenes. The captain claimed that the US Embassy had intervened in their support. 'I ordered the arrest', he said, 'of two American engineers who were carrying out [illegal] scientific investigations. Later it was proved that James Bou [head of the New Tribes Mission in Venezuela] had organised their journey . . . Mr Bou telephoned the US Embassy, and the Counsellor of the Embassy then called me, asking me to release the two men.' He hastily did so, but lost his job all the same.

Indians were called to describe the experience of compulsory conversion, involving such alarming devices as microphones hidden in trees which shouted threatening messages at them in their own language. One witness said his tribe had been told that the appearance of a comet heralded the end of the world. The head missionary had rounded them up to give them three days to break with their wicked past, on pain of a fiery extinction. To be effective, reform required the abandonment of such sinful pleasures as imbibing juices in which any trace of fermentation can be detected, skin painting, using feather ornaments, singing, dancing, smoking or playing musical instruments, doctoring with herbal remedies, attending funeral ceremonies, and following the tribal custom of arranging marriages within the framework of kinship groups. The weapon of Armageddon and the imminent fiery destruction of the world, from which only the missionaries and their converts would be saved, was constantly brandished. The Indians were warned of a communist plot to drive the missionaries out of the country, and were told that if this were to happen US airforce planes would be sent to bomb their villages.

A Venezuelan anthropologist, scrutinising mission literature, noted that the scriptures had been manipulated to such a degree that in one book entitled *Learning About God*, the Panare tribe had been accused of Christ's crucifixion. 'The Panare killed Jesus Christ' it began, 'because they were wicked.' After a description of Christ's nailing to the cross and his death, the passage ends with the promise of God's vengeance: 'I'm going to hurl the Panare into the fire,' said God.

The Venezuelan congressional investigation into the activities of the NTM fizzled out – as everyone knew it would – leaving the Venezuelans with the unpleasant sensation that the sect might have to be regarded as a state within a state. The missionaries heralded a victory over communism and, in the years that followed, extended and intensified their operations, tightened their grip on Indian groups under their control and moved into new tribes. Venezuelans noted that multinational companies, particularly those involved in mining, were setting up in areas where the missionaries had established themselves – sometimes referred to in company prospectuses as 'pacified zones'. However, in 1987 a coalition of leading churchmen, anthropologists, newspaper editors and the heads of several government departments was formed to carry on the resistance.

This was based upon the familiar complaints of psychological terror, mental and physical cruelty and the instigation of panic among Indian societies, and was treated by the NTM as no more than another communist manoeuvre, and as such destined to certain failure. At this point, to the consternation of the sect, the Army moved in with charges of its own. These included accusations of damage to national sovereignty by the establishment of colonial enclaves, the occupation of strategic territories, unauthorised construction of numerous landing-strips, the unconstitutional use of short-wave radio to transmit messages in a foreign language, and the use of military uniforms for the purpose of intimidation. It called for the closure of the mission school at Tama Tama, and this was done.

Further and more significant news was that missionary visas would not be renewed. As a newspaper put it, 'the Army's action has accelerated the campaign against the New Tribes Mission, and will serve in part to neutralise the pressure of the powerful interests that have supported it.'

Apart from the minor problems of organising a supply of missionised Ayoreos to perform what elsewhere might be described as slave labour, the NTM's long and arduous involvement with the tribes in Paraguay was coming to an end. This was bound to leave 'contact personnel' with time on their hands, and the new generation of young evangelists, straight out of MK (missionary kids) schools with diminished opportunities for the expenditure of energy and zeal. Two prime targets for mass conversion had been under sporadic assault for a number of years and now once again occupied a prominent place in missionary reports. These were the Macu of Colombia and the Yuqui of Bolivia.

It was to the Macu's advantage, after their discovery deep in the jungles in 1971 by a missionary spotter plane, that their tribal homeland should have been regarded as guerrilla territory. This deterred attempted contact for a while, and when an advance party moved in and cut an airstrip this was put out of action by the guerrillas who placed oil drums on it to prevent planes from landing. The Macu were handicapped in their encounters with persistent evangelists by the fact that although this area abounded with rivers they could neither swim nor handle a boat. When, therefore, the Macu made it clear that the missionaries' presence was unwelcome by using their blowguns to shoot darts at them, the newcomers took refuge on an island in a lake, and there established their base.

Years passed. The missionaries sat on their island and the Macu watched them mistrustfully from the other bank. Once, when the missionaries crossed over in their boat, they came under attack and one of them was struck in the neck by what was called a poisoned dart, although without ill effect. Some reference to a missionary shotgun was allowed to slip out at this point; the Macu fled and stayed away for three months. In 1978 another evangelist was slightly wounded. Significantly, *Brown Gold* records that this 'was the first time we had known the Macus to attack with no obvious provocation'.

By 1981 some ground had been gained. Until this time the missionaries had been unable to learn the language. 'Months went by and we could hear the Indians shouting, but never saw them.' Now it was decided to shower them with gifts and, paddling softly across the lake, machetes were left along the trails. This seems to have done the trick. The Macu invited them to their village, providing an opportunity to conceal a microphone in the roof of one of the huts by which the language was recorded. A return occasion was even more successful. The evangelists cooked popcorn in a pan for their visitors; a drawing of this episode shows the Macu warriors encircling the pan, spears raised to defend themselves if necessary, in the face of this new evidence of the white man's magic powers.

This was the instant when their fate hung in the balance. It was the equivalent of the moment in the bull-ring when the torero stands before the weakened but still belligerent bull and slowly draws the sword from the *muleta* in which it has been concealed. The Indians should have thrown their spears and run. Instead they stayed and they and the missionaries shared the popcorn, and the bond of a disastrous friendship was thus sealed. Those who come first to such meetings become almost certainly the first to accept conversion, and next they are skilfully detached from their backward and conservative friends wishing to continue in their old ways. It is the eventual fate of these to suffer isolation, then expulsion from the community, then extinction. This tactic has not changed since the London Missionary Society used it to conquer the Pacific in a single decade.

In 1986 the guerrillas withdrew and the missionaries were at last able to use their airstrip and bring in reinforcements. 'Two previous flights had found the airstrip covered with 55-gallon barrels. . . . With a Vietnam-style landing the helicopter arrives.' The Macu gardens are located nine hour's walk away, and here the Macu are the missionaries' old friends from the popcorn days, now become allies in the fight against their unsaved fellow tribespeople. 'The most savage, naked people in the world are hugging, embracing and dancing for joy. Their friends are back . . .'

A year later, the NTM is well dug in, with total victory in sight. 'Forty other [unconverted] Macu arrived who were from far away . . . This situation was touchy for a while, and still is. The rest of our group is to arrive soon, and there's going to be a big confrontation between the two groups, involving about one hundred Macu.' Remembering the Ayoreos we should all know what comes next.

★

The fate of the last of the Yuqui has been, if possible, more unkind. In 1964 an NTM contact team took a party by surprise in the corner of a jungle in Central Bolivia, carrying off 25 of them to their camp. Thereafter, contact work lapsed. Further advances into Yuqui territory met with stiff resistance as exemplified by the adventures of Bruce Porterfield, a missionary with combat experience in World War II, who wrote a missionary classic, *Commandos For Christ*, saturated with the spirit of military adventure.

To prepare him for such jungle encounters, Porterfield was sent to a mission 'boot camp', where the training by Army NCOs simulated as closely as possible the stresses evangelists might encounter among hostile Indians and 'hence toughen them up as "commandos" for the Christian battlefield'. In the boot camp they taught him to make a strong house 'with two rows of flattened gasoline drums . . . nailed against the outside, making a crude wall of armour plate about seven feet high'.

This is what Porterfield built in Yuqui country and into it he and the other members of the team withdrew with their Bibles, their shotgun and a .22 pistol to withstand a long and unproductive siege.

The Indians, hidden in the jungle, whistled at them and they whistled back, and this was the only form of communication. In the short interludes of peace they stole out to lay gifts, as instructed, along the Indian trails. The stratagem in this environment was ill-advised. White farmers of the poorest and most degenerate type, whose habit it was to shoot Yuquis on sight and carry off their children to be sold as slaves, scratched a living in the vicinity. These added their own contributions of sugar mixed with arsenic to the missionaries' gifts. One of the evangelists, straying too far from the strong house, was shot to death with arrows.

There was nothing to be done here except cower behind armour-plated walls and wait. In between evangelising bursts it was normal for missionaries elsewhere to augment mission funds by engaging in the trade of such things as jaguar skins and Indian artefacts, but here inactivity was absolute. Quietly, the curtain came down, and the contact that never was came to an end.

Then in the early eighties, valuable stands of timber were discovered in Yuqui territory and the logging companies moved in. Most of these were there illegally. They employed clandestine *espontáneos* to fell the trees, providing the finances and the equipment for their operations, and even building the roads. When – as they were bound to do – the loggers ran into trouble with the Yuqui whose livelihood they were destroying, they turned to the NTM for help. By 1984 the missionaries were back in full force, cutting an airstrip in the heart of Indian country.

The new missionary team took with them several of the now tame Yuqui from the original contact in 1964, from whom they had picked up a few words of the language. Even so, the expedition was a failure. 'We called out friendly phrases and prayed as those we sought fled into the jungle.' Although twenty-eight Yuqui had been seen, it was not possible to 'bring them in'. A further three years passed before partial success could be announced with the arrival of twenty-two Indians at the NTM camp at Chimoré. 'In the quest to bring these wild Yuqui under the sound of the Gospel, three missionaries and three of their Indian helpers have been wounded, shot with eight-foot arrows by those they thought to befriend,' said *Brown Gold*. The fate of the Yuqui bowmen who engaged them can only be guessed.

Nevertheless, the number of free Yuquis dwindled constantly, and by the summer of 1988, the end was very close. Now only one major group, the Arroyote Yuqui, remained at liberty. In response to an appeal by a logging company, 'Larry got his team together and headed for the woods.' Once again the outcome was unsatisfactory. The Yuquis' 'treacherous behaviour was in full display', arrows flew in all directions, two of the team were wounded and the retreat was sounded.

Twice again the loggers called in the missionaries by which time it was clear that the treacherous Yuquis were close to the end of their tether. However, the shadow of the future falls across Larry Depue as he writes: 'Since that time (the last encounter) Satan has done all he can to see the New Tribes Mission expelled from the country. Accusations were rampant and rumours spread like wildfire.'

In February 1988 the Bolivian newspaper *Presencia* reported that an 'evangelical sect' had used a clandestine plane to remove 200 Yuquis to its camp. Half this group, it said, had disappeared. It published the statement of the Pro-Vida Committee organised by the Bishop of Santa Cruz in which the bishop expressed alarm at the operations of the North American organisation in the zone. The statement deplored the unexplained deaths of nine Yuqui Indians and continued: 'The New Tribes Mission has given assurances to the Attorney-General of the State of Santa Cruz to cease the transfer of Yuquis to its camp at Chamoré.'

This it might well have done. The most recent estimate put the number of those remaining at large as 75, divided into three small bands, about half of them being women and children. *Presencia* informed that Yuqui bows and arrows, from which the owners traditionally refuse to be parted in their lifetime, were on sale in the market of Santa Cruz, being, on account of their rarity and the beauty of the feathering, in great demand by connoisseurs of such things.

On 8 December 1988, in his message for the World Day of Peace the Pope stressed the right of all religious minorities to worship according to their own rites. This freedom has been violently opposed by the NTM, with irreversible damage to the tribal peoples with which it has come in contact. Now that the tide has turned against it in Latin America, with expulsions to be expected, it is surely unacceptable that the sect's principal training-ground outside the US should continue to exist on British soil.